"The renewal of rural communities is happening all around us today as organized creative leaders are building economic models that can rebuild our gathering places, re-energize the local foods marketplace, and bring the community together as participants in new forms of community enterprise. This important study by Norman Walzer and colleagues around the world is a great starting point in evaluating the importance of Community Supported Enterprises, and it can help leaders across the nation learn from successful projects and advance dynamic new enterprises for their communities."

— **Paul Costello**, *Executive Director, Vermont Council on Rural Development, USA*

"As smaller more rural communities struggle to maintain a vibrant local economy, many are seeking new and innovative ways to support local businesses. The strategic approaches detailed by Walzer and his colleagues in this volume reflect that spirit of innovative thinking. Both scholars and practitioners of community economic development should seriously consider the ideas developed in this volume."

— **Steven C. Deller**, *Professor and Community Development Specialist, University of Wisconsin, USA*

COMMUNITY OWNED BUSINESSES

This book analyses community-owned businesses in countries around the world to show successful approaches and important strategies to improve access to essential services in vastly different economic contexts.

Through eleven chapters, authors from various countries use case studies and analyse findings in ways which can be applied to new development initiatives, including rural grocery store retention in Kansas, socially responsible community cooperatives in Italy, preserving pubs and shops in England and Wales, serving residents with special needs in Canada, and financing basic goods and services for aging populations in Taiwan, plus other examples. The chapters explore practices and approaches used in various locations to address concerns about loss of access to essential services, making clear that this approach to financing is useful in different scenarios.

The chapters provide key insights suggesting that these approaches will be even more prevalent in the future and will be of interest to students, scholars, and community-development practitioners around the world.

Norman Walzer, Ph.D., is a Professor Emeritus in the Illinois Institute for Rural Affairs located at Western Illinois University, USA. He was a Senior Research Scholar in the Center for Governmental Affairs at Northern Illinois University when the materials for this book were compiled. He has written extensively on local public finance and development issues with more than 25 books plus numerous scholarly and professional articles.

The Community Development Research and Practice Series Volume 16

As the series continues to grow, it is our intent to continue to serve scholars, community developers, planners, public administrators, and others involved in research, practice, and policymaking in the realm of community development. The series strives to provide both timely and applied information for researchers, students, and practitioners. Building on a long history since 1970 of publishing the Community Development Society's journal, *Community Development* (www.comm-dev.org), the book series contributes to a growing and rapidly changing knowledge base as a resource for practitioners and researchers alike. For additional information, please see the series page at http://www.routledge.com/books/series/CDRP/.

The evolution of the field of community development continues. As reflected in both theory and practice, community development is at the forefront of change, which comes as no surprise to our communities and regions that constantly face challenges and opportunities. As a practice-focused discipline, change often seems to be the only constant in the community-development realm. The need to integrate theory, practice, research, teaching, and training is even more pressing now than ever, given rapidly transforming economic, social, environmental, political, and cultural climates locally and globally. Current and applicable information and insights about effective research and practice are needed.

The Community Development Society, a nonprofit association of those interested in pushing the discipline forward, is delighted to offer this book series in partnership with Routledge. The series is designed to integrate innovative thinking on tools, strategies, and experiences as a resource especially well-suited for bridging the gaps between theory, research, and practice. The Community Development Society actively promotes continued advancement of the discipline and practice. Fundamental to this mission is adherence to the following core Principles of Good Practice. This book series is a reflection of many of these principles:

Promote active and representative participation towards enabling all community members to meaningfully influence the decisions that affect their lives.

Engage community members in learning about and understanding community issues, and the economic, social, environmental, political, psychological, and other impacts associated with alternative courses of action.

Incorporate the diverse interest and cultures of the community in the community development process; and disengage from support of any effort that is likely to adversely affect the disadvantaged members of a community.

Work actively to enhance the leadership capacity of community members, leaders, and groups within the community.

Be open to using the full range of action strategies to work towards the long-term sustainability and well-being of the community.

We invite you to explore the series and continue to do so as new volumes are added. We hope you will find it a valuable resource for supporting community development research and practice.

Other books in the series:

Community Visioning Programs
Processes and Outcomes
Norman Walzer, Gisele F. Hamm

Catalysts for Change
21st Century Philanthropy and Community Development
Maria Martinez-Cosio, Mirle Rabinowitz Bussell

Theory, Practice, and Community Development
Mark Brennan, Jeffrey Birdger, Theodore R. Alter

Schools and Urban Revitalization
Rethinking Institutions and Community Development
Kelly L. Patterson and Robert Mark Silverman

Knowledge Partnering for Community Development
Robyn Eversole

Social Capital at the Community Level
An Applied Interdisciplinary Perspective
John M. Halstead and Steven C. Deller

Arts and Community Change
Exploring Cultural Development Policies, Practices and Dilemmas
Max O. Stephenson Jr. and Scott Tate

Community-Built
Art, Construction, Preservation, and Place
Katherine Melcher, Barry Stiefel, Kristin Faurest

Using Collective Impact to Bring Community Change
Norman Walzer and Liz Weaver

Addressing Climate Change at the Community Level in the United States
Paul R. Lachapelle and Don E. Albrecht

The Heart of Community Engagement
Practitioner Stories from Across the Globe
Patricia A. Wilson

Culture, Community, and Development
Rhonda Phillips, Mark A. Brennan, Tingxuan Li

Community Capacity and Resilience in Latin America
Paul Lachapelle, Isabel Gutierrez-Montes, Cornelia Butler Flora

50 Years of Community Development Vol I
Norman Walzer, Rhonda Phillips and Robert Blair

50 Years of Community Development Vol II
Norman Walzer, Rhonda Phillips and Robert Blair

Community Owned Businesses
International Entrepreneurship, Finance, and Economic Development
Norman Walzer

COMMUNITY OWNED BUSINESSES

International Entrepreneurship, Finance, and Economic Development

Edited by Norman Walzer

Routledge
Taylor & Francis Group
NEW YORK AND LONDON

First published 2021
by Routledge
605 Third Avenue, New York, NY 10158

and by Routledge
2 Park Square, Milton Park, Abingdon, Oxon, OX14 4RN

Routledge is an imprint of the Taylor & Francis Group, an informa business

Library of Congress Cataloging-in-Publication Data
A catalog record for this title has been requested

ISBN: 978-0-367-48546-7 (hbk)
ISBN: 978-0-367-48545-0 (pbk)
ISBN: 978-1-003-04159-7 (ebk)

Typeset in Bembo
by codeMantra

To Emma, Brennen, and Nicholas Walzer

to help them support local business activities in their community.

CONTENTS

FIGURES AND TABLES

Figures

Tables

CONTRIBUTORS

Michele Bianchi, Ph.D., is a Researcher at the Yunus Centre for Social Business and Health, Glasgow Caledonian University, UK. He is now engaged in research on global challenges and sustainability with a particular focus on how hybrid organizations deal with the tensions deriving from the multiple logics inherent in their structures; this examination is related to the strategies for implementing Sustainable Development Goals efficiently at micro level. Michele obtained his Ph.D. in Sociology of Governance, Social Participation, and Citizenship at the University Carlo Bo (Urbino, Italy) examining the phenomenon of community co-operatives. His main research areas are social enterprises, non-profit, and community development; he has contributed to the scientific debate with two working papers published by Euricse, a conference paper published by the United Nations, and four papers in international scientific journals.

Jessica Brauer, B.A., is a Communications Consultant and Freelance Writer based in Laramie, Wyoming, USA. She received a Bachelor of Arts in Communication and Journalism with a focus in Advanced New Media and a minor in Cultural Anthropology from the University of Wyoming in 2013 and an Associate of Arts from the Art Institute of Charleston in 2011. She is passionate about capturing the authentic stories of people and their places. Her work has allowed her to champion for local neighborhoods with economic development agencies, non-profits, and small businesses since starting her first business in 2011. She ardently believes in the power of play, a shared narrative, and a heart-centered approach. She has been storytelling with The Local Crowd since 2015.

Klaus Hegemann, Ph.D., is a Professor at the Rhine-Waal University of Applied Sciences in Kamp-Lintfort, Germany, where he teaches in the degree program "International Business Administration" with a focus on ethics and sustainability.

He has worked in several applied international projects with both rural and urban communities to further their livability and to study collective action. The societal systems of economics, politics, and ethics are the content of the research and teaching activities of the financial planner and political scientist Klaus Hegemann: How economics, politics, and ethics come together.

Chaimei Hsia, Ph.D., is a Senior Research Associate at the Center of Partnership for Community Development at Arizona State University, USA. She is also the co-founder of nonprofit organization Global Community Development Partnership and in charge of programming international community practice exchange project. This special project aims to make a social and economic change through local engagement and international collaboration. Hsia's research focuses on community capacity building through a variety of community engagement activities. She also explores the social identity theory by conceptualizing the community identity formation through art practices and place-making. Prior to her doctoral study, Hsia had more than seven years of work experience as a community development practitioner and specializes in community partnership facilitating and conflict management.

Stephen McCusker, RIBA RIAS FHEA, is both a practitioner and academic. As well as being on the UK regulatory board for Architects (Architects Registration Board), he is appointed part-time as a Senior Lecturer at the Manchester School of Architecture (UK) where he combines his research interests with his ongoing practice as an Architect-Director at Loop Systems Co-operative; an award-winning, Manchester-based practice. He delivers value-led projects, largely focusing on co-operation and the re-appropriation of existing buildings for the social solidarity economy. Through this, he has been involved in many community-led ventures about which he has written in professional outlets.

Sean Park, M.S., is the Program Manager for the Value-Added Sustainable Development Center at Western Illinois University, USA. He works with rural entrepreneurs, cooperatives, and communities to develop business plans, find financing, and operate needed services successfully. He currently teaches in the WIU Community and Economic Development Master's Program. He was the Economic Development Director for the City of Rushville Illinois from 2015 until 2019. He owned Park Foods, Inc. operating as a small grocery store in Rushville Illinois. He is a Certified Exit Planning Advisor with the Exit Planning Institute, a Certified Business Advisor with the State of Illinois Small Business Development Centers, and is a doctoral candidate in Public Administration at University of Illinois – Springfield.

Rhonda Phillips, Ph.D., FAICP, is a Community and Economic Development Specialist with a particular interest in locally focused approaches to revitalization and community well-being. She is founding co-editor of the journal *Local*

Development & Society with Taylor & Francis and the Community Development Society. As Dean and Professor at Purdue University, she leads the Honors College and the new Happiness Learning Collaborative.

David E. Procter, Ph.D., is a Professor of Communication Studies at Kansas State University, USA, and directs the Rural Grocery Initiative. He is also the former director of K-State's Center for Engagement and Community Development. He has studied the economic, nutrition, and civic value rural grocery business operations provide their local communities. He has presented and published research primarily on innovative models of rural grocery business operation and the access to healthy foods rural grocery retail provides.

Bruce F. Seifer, B.S., is a private Economic Development Consultant based in the city of Burlington, Vermont, USA, where his efforts are focused on local entrepreneurs, non-profits, and community revitalization. He led the city of Burlington's Economic Development Division for three decades under the progressive administrations of Bernie Sanders and Peter Clavelle. During his tenure with the city, he co-founded numerous organizations to support the field of sustainable economic development including the statewide Sustainable Jobs Fund and Burlington's South End Arts + Business District. He also helped private companies, government officials, nonprofit government agencies, and the Federal Reserve Bank of Boston. He coauthored *Sustainable Communities: Creating a Durable Local Economy* (Routledge, 2013).

Ushnish Sengupta, MBA, is a Ph.D. candidate at the Ontario Institute for Studies in Education, at the University of Toronto, Canada. He is researching the impact of government policy on nonprofit organizations serving equity-deserving communities in the province of Ontario, including organizations employing people with intellectual and developmental disabilities. His other teaching, community development, and research activities include work in Open Data, Blockchain, Artificial Intelligence, the Digital Divide, and how they intersect with equity-deserving communities in Canada.

Michael H. Shuman is an economist, attorney, author, and entrepreneur, and a leading visionary on community economics. He's Director of Local Economy Programs for Neighborhood Associates Corporation, and an Adjunct Professor at Bard Business School in New York City. He is also a Senior Researcher for Council Fire, where he performs economic-development analyses for states, local governments, and businesses around North America. He is credited with being one of the architects of the 2012 JOBS Act and dozens of state laws overhauling securities regulation of crowdfunding. He has authored, coauthored, or edited ten books. His two most recent books are *Put Your Money Where Your Life Is: How to Invest Locally Using Solo 401ks and Self-Directed IRAs* and *The Local Economy Solution: How Innovative, Self-Financing Pollinator Enterprises Can Grow Jobs and*

Prosperity and *Local Dollars, Local Sense: How to Shift Your Money from Wall Street to Main Street*. A previous book, *The Small Mart Revolution: How Local Businesses Are Beating the Global Competition* (Berrett-Koehler, 2006), received as bronze prize from the Independent Publishers Association for best business book of 2006.

Felix Sohnrey, M.A., is a Scientific Assistant at Rhine-Waal University of Applied Sciences in Kamp-Lintfort, Germany. There, he started his career working with rural communities to further their quality of life and accompanied several initiatives who founded a community-supported enterprise. He gained in-depth experience working with engaged volunteer citizens and investigated, both theoretically and practically, the interconnectedness of community capitals. In the study program "International Business Administration," he teaches method-related subjects such as research methods and statistics.

Norman Walzer, Ph.D., is a Professor Emeritus in Illinois Institute for Rural Affairs and the Department of Economics at Western Illinois University. He was a Senior Research Scholar (Retired) at the Northern Illinois University Center for Governmental Studies when this book was compiled and now engages in special projects researching state and national policy issues. In 2019, he prepared a *Guidebook with Resources for Starting a Community Supported Enterprise* to help local leaders organize these types of efforts. He actively contributes to the professional community and economic development literature with numerous scholarly books on development or public finance-related topics and presentations to scholarly and practitioner conferences around the world.

ACKNOWLEDGEMENTS

Demographic trends with expected population declines, especially in rural areas, plus economic setbacks from recent recessions threatened essential services in many communities. Shrinking markets plus relatively low profits have limited access to traditional sources of private capital. Consequently, attention has been focused on finding alternate local investment sources that can help these business ventures continue.

Community-supported enterprises (CSEs) involve an approach in which residents engage directly in supporting a local venture. They have various names in different locations but are similar in pursuing a common purpose, namely the betterment of the community. In addition, they are designed to be economically sustainable by marketing a product or service rather than relying on regular donations of funds. In most cases, they engage a group of residents who do not always expect a direct financial return on their investment. Rather, their primary motive is to assure that an essential good or service will be available locally in the future.

Perhaps, the most important aspect of using the CSE approach is that it builds support within the community. The increase in local social capital may result from participating in a worthwhile community project or from volunteering time and effort in the venture. These activities engage residents in directly promoting community interests and give them a broader stake in the future of the community.

This book is designed to acquaint readers with various ways that CSE financing methods are used around the world. In some instances, they are intended to retain an essential private business such as a grocery store. Other uses include public services that, otherwise, would not be provided with strictly tax dollars. While specific approaches differ, they all involve residents actively investing time and/or money in the process.

In looking ahead with the COVID-19 recession and demographic projections, use of CSE methods of finance is likely to increase as local leaders struggle with finding financing alternatives to maintain services to keep communities viable and attractive places to live. Assembling the chapters in this volume has been an exciting process. They can contribute to future discussions about CSEs and hopefully will help local leaders find successful solutions.

Thanks go to Paul Costello, Vermont Council on Rural Development and the late Paul Bruin, former director of the Preservation Trust of Vermont, who provided early opportunities to learn about CSE efforts. That information was part of the motivation for this book.

Norman Walzer

1

CHANGING USES OF COMMUNITY SUPPORTED ENTERPRISES

Norman Walzer

Introduction

Demographic trends during the next decade will reshape the economic future especially of those nonmetro areas projected to face significant population declines as the Baby Boom Generation reaches retirement age. Almost important are changes in purchasing patterns as internet shopping with rapid delivery methods increases competition for brick and mortar stores that have been the mainstay of local economies.

The projected population aging will raise special issues as owners of small businesses reach retirement age and close their businesses. While the ventures may still be profitable, they cannot compete effectively with investment opportunities elsewhere. In the past, heirs were sometimes ready and willing to continue a family business. However, smaller family sizes and more graduates pursuing higher education mean fewer heirs in the community available or interested in continuing the businesses. The outcome will mean that some traditional services will no longer be available locally.

Evidence of these trends already exists in vacant buildings on main streets in some small towns as more residents now commute longer distances to work and shop in larger regional employment centers. While these trends have been underway for many years, residents in smaller towns now must act to preserve these communities as viable and attractive places to live. These decisions are especially important because living preferences expressed by both elderly and young adults include high quality of life, local experiences, and a walkable living environment, among other factors. Nonmetro areas often offer these attributes but will have to retain basic services to compete successfully.

Another movement underway that can help nonmetro areas is a shifting focus toward local investing and buying local. Shuman (2012; 2015) discusses the opportunities and advantages to both investors and communities when residents divert their investments from large corporations to local businesses. This growing interest in investing locally opens opportunities for community leaders to work with retiring business owners.

When faced with a potential business closing because of pending retirement, three options usually are considered. First, the owner can sell the business through a realtor or other traditional approach. Given a lower expected rate of return due to shrinking markets and competition from stores in surrounding areas, selling the business in this way may be more difficult than in the past.

A second strategy is to work with an intermediary group that helps transition businesses to new owners. Redefining Retirement (RedTire), managed by the University of Kansas School of Business, provides an electronic business-matching program where owners interested in selling a business provide basic information electronically with potential buyers. The intent is to transition these businesses to new owners and keep them in the community (University of Kansas). The university provides technical assistance to both buyers and sellers during the transition process.

In a more direct approach, Goodworks Evergreen LLC in Montana, as part of several initiatives, buys businesses and improves their profitability. It then resells them to interested parties (Goodworks Evergreen, 2020). The overall intent is to keep the businesses operating in Montana rather than have them close or relocate elsewhere. The focus is beyond small main street stores but also includes manufacturing, distribution, and service businesses with the aim to retain high-quality jobs in Montana.

A third option for local leaders facing a potential business closing involves organizing residents and creating a pool of investment funds to purchase, or reopen, the business. This approach has been used effectively around the world with several local advantages. It retains local access to essential goods and services that otherwise might be lost. Local investors also gain stronger affiliations with the community where many have grown up or lived for long periods with substantial investment in housing or other properties. Likewise, investing in the business gives them a stake in the success of the venture with an incentive to patronize it.

A related advantage is that investors and other residents have opportunities to volunteer time and efforts in a worthwhile community project. These opportunities help build social capital and strengthen quality of life in the community, which can be important in its ability to retain and attract new residents. These community-supported businesses (CSBs) have involved many types of activities with one of the most common being to maintain a local grocery store. Later discussions will show other purposes and approaches involving residents investing in local enterprises and ventures.

Social gathering places are important to the viability of small places, which generated interest in the dwindling number of community-owned pubs and shops in England (Plunkett Foundation). These ventures have now expanded to other social and health-related services which help residents overcome social isolation and loneliness that have been linked to health issues (National Institute on Aging, 2019). Continued projected population declines and growth in numbers of elderly with limited mobility will make retaining small businesses or ventures especially important not only in rural areas but also in urban neighborhoods facing losses of local establishments and institutions.

This book describes how community-supported enterprises (CSEs) and community-owned businesses (COBs) are often used as approaches to financing local efforts to retain businesses or provide services. These two terms are used interchangeably in later discussions. Common elements are that residents invest in a local venture or business with a supportive social purpose. The activity is designed to be financially sustainable without continued financial contributions from donors as in the case of a social enterprise. However, these distinctions become somewhat blurred in practice.

Community-owned or -supported businesses can operate under different legal forms including Limited Liability Corporations (LLCs), cooperatives, or nonprofits such as Social Benefit Corporations. The specific legal form usually reflects the purpose of the venture. For instance, the Hinesburgh Public House in Vermont is a Social Benefit Corporation with the goal of providing nutritious meals and quality jobs for residents in a designated area of Vermont (USA) (Hinnesburg, 2020). It also helps local nonprofit organizations with fundraising efforts by collaboratively providing meals for area residents.

In another case, a municipal government, such as St. Paul, Kansas, owns and operates a grocery store as a profit-making activity. While ownership by a municipality is less common, it may become more prevalent in the future in response to the COVID-19 economic downturn with business cutbacks and shutdowns without replacements. The CSE financing approach is sufficiently flexible to address many of these types of issues.

The importance of broad-based local support for both community and economic development practices has long been recognized in the professional literature (Macke, Markley, & Fulwider 2014; Markley, Lyons, & Macke 2015; Perodo & Chrisman, 2006). Financial investments in businesses are a natural extension of these efforts. Thus, in this book, the broad term "community-based enterprises" is used to include diverse projects that actively engage residents. This local support can vary from buying local to directly investing in the businesses as is the case with CSEs in the current discussions. Lack of commitment by residents can seriously disadvantage new business start-ups as well as negatively affect the longevity of established businesses relying on these markets. For this reason, places with active community development efforts underway are strategically positioned to launch CSEs.

Given the need for innovative financing arrangements in areas facing population declines and business closings, community-owned or -supported enterprises are becoming an important local development strategy around the world. In England, they include community-owned shops or pubs. In Canada and Italy, this financing approach is used to support social and health services. These activities are not typically owned by a public agency such as a municipality like in St. Paul. Rather, they involve direct participation by resident-investors in some way. The basic approaches vary but with several similar characteristics.

First and foremost, most such businesses are owned by local investors who, in many instances, expect no direct financial return on their investment. Instead, they use a pooled investment strategy to retain or reopen a business activity considered important to the community. The ventures are organized to be financially sustainable. The businesses must meet the requirements of any private business activity but often are advantaged by investors or residents donating time and efforts to the operations. In these cases, the venture can operate on a lower profit margin and compete more effectively than a strictly privately owned business.

Second, the ventures have a visible social purpose or mission other than simply engaging customers in marketing decisions or product development as in the case of membership clubs. Instead, organizers want to build social capital in the community and improve the quality of life by providing access to important goods and services plus engage residents in a community-wide project that enhances the future of the area. While making a profit is essential to sustainability, it is not the primary motive for the business. COBs should be differentiated from social enterprises where a not-for-profit organization pursuing a specific social cause operates a retail unit. These businesses may sell goods or services, but they can still rely on continued donations from the sponsoring organization and are not driven as much by local market conditions.

Third, COBs have a focused approach with a local champion who spearheads the endeavor. Residents who invest in the business activity usually do not engage in daily decision-making activities except in cooperative organizations where each investor has one vote. Even then, the average investor does not participate regularly in management.

Fourth, CSEs must have widespread community commitment to the project. Residents must not only be willing to invest funds and effort, but they must also be willing to patronize the business venture. This may be less true for social services, but in those cases, residents must be willing to contribute through taxes and other fees.

Purposes of Book

While CSE models are becoming more common around the world, relatively few comparisons of approaches used, outcomes achieved, or processes used are available. Walzer and Sandoval (2016) documented examples of CSEs in the US. Later, Walzer (2019) produced a guidebook to help local leaders start community-supported ventures with synopses or mini-case studies of 40 or more CSEs within the US. The Plunkett Foundation provides discussions of community-owned pubs and shops in England (Plunkett, 2019). Additional information about how CSEs start and are operated is needed to help interested community leaders evaluate whether this financing approach is well-suited for local needs.

Growth of community-owned organizations and lack of systematic comparisons or information led to the compilation of materials in this book. A call for abstracts was sent to Community Development Society and International Association of Community Development members inviting submissions of materials about experiences with CSEs and how they function. The intent is to go beyond sharing examples of successes to share what has been learned in designing and implementing these ventures. The materials illustrate a wide diversity in programs and services. The examples go beyond business ventures and include community financing for local public services.

The chapters in this book will also benefit both scholars and policymakers looking for new and innovative methods of financing ventures whether business-oriented or to provide social services during periods of declining populations and tight resources. Legal institutions and policies differ by country so a review of successes in various settings can suggest policy changes needed to promote this community financing approach.

The approaches used and described in this book have not been judged as the most effective or best by any absolute criteria. Each has a unique purpose and intended outcome(s). Their value is to illustrate activities that have worked and are effective for different purposes under various settings. In some cases, the approaches are not directly transferable, but potential users can learn from the processes and can adjust them to new locations. Perhaps, most important is to see the diversity of applications where they have succeeded.

Subsequent discussions are presented in two major sections. The first set of chapters focus on the importance of local investments in business ventures and the supportive environment needed. Authors discuss examples where local groups launched an initiative to organize an investment pool to start or continue ventures and activities they see as essential to the social and economic viability of the community. The strategies range from social benefit corporations to social cooperatives, depending on legal institutions and requirements.

Later chapters address ways in which community-supported financing approaches have been extended or broadened to include social or public types of services with examples from Italy, Canada, and Taiwan following the 2008 recession. These approaches will probably become even more prevalent as ways to rebuild lost social infrastructure in the post-COVID-19 recession period that is adversely affecting the financing of local services.

At the center of the community-owned approach is the interest and willingness of residents to divert investments from larger corporations to on-going local business activities. Shuman (Chapter 2) argues that the perceived risks involved with small business discourage residents from investing in small local businesses, and instead, they invest in large corporations. On closer examination, the reputation of high risk with small businesses relates more to business starts than size. Local stores or outlets about to close due to retirements may have operated profitably for decades, but the operations will discontinue due to lack of financial support. Some would continue if local investment funds were available.

Crowdfunding approaches to financing projects helped to finance COBs in at least two ways. They made residents more comfortable in contributing to local ventures. In addition, the crowdfunding platforms simplified the process of organizing and financing local efforts. These efforts were bolstered by a growth in third-party organizations such as The Local Crowd in Wyoming that helps community groups raise revenues for local businesses or community projects along with technical assistance to help them succeed. More detail regarding these programs and how they work is available in Brauer (Chapter 9).

Key to the interest in using a COB financing approach is a realization that, without local investment, residents could lose needed access to services and face traveling long distances for essential items such as groceries. In rural England, community pubs had long been social gathering places for residents but were closing rapidly increasing rural isolation and loneliness that led to health-related issues. It was in this type of setting that the Plunkett Foundation took the lead in working with local groups to revive the pubs not only as social gathering places in the community but also to provide other services in small towns. The purposes and venue of the pubs adjusted to community needs resulting in a high survival rate (Plunkett, 2020).

Overview of Chapters

Discussions in subsequent chapters begin with an analysis by Shuman (Chapter 2) regarding the need for vehicles that encourage residents to reallocate investments from national or international companies to local businesses. He makes a strong case for local investments based on several issues. First, a large majority of local investors fund global corporations that have little direct impact on the communities where they live. These investments are encouraged by a perception that investments in large corporations are both more secure and more profitable despite evidence to the contrary based on analyses of Canadian businesses.

Second, successes with community-owned ventures require an environment in which residents are comfortable investing in them and have relatively easy access to obtaining funds from local investors rather than borrowing from financial institutions. This local access is currently not readily available in many locations and encouraged other approaches such as crowdfunding and efforts by organizations such as The Local Crowd to promote these efforts.

Third, key local businesses become "pollinators" that stimulate other local investment opportunities and change attitudes about investing locally. As interest grows and local businesses succeed, residents are more willing to consider them suitable for investment when opportunities become available. Later, authors, e.g., Brauer, describe cases including crowdfunding or other approaches where residents can support local businesses. Changing the attitude about investing in local businesses is key to building the social capital that will make communities viable in the long term.

The role of securities regulations is especially important in these discussions because they have created a system that is costly for small local businesses to access. Extensive legal requirements and regulations, in the name of providing added security to investors, limit access by small businesses to investment funds. Shuman makes the case that extensive legal reporting and documentation requirements may benefit groups preparing the required financial documents as much or more than they increase the safety of the investments. At the very least, the requirements differentially increase access to large global corporations while ignoring financing needs of small businesses. Consequently, there are limited alternatives where small businesses have direct or easy access to small investors even when the businesses have succeeded for many years.

Shuman also makes a strong case that small businesses have been substantially more profitable (three times) than large businesses (Chapter 2). The apprehension about investing in small companies is driven more by start-ups with higher failure rates than size of businesses especially those with a long track record. Diverting even a fraction of funds currently invested in large corporations would greatly expand financing in communities of all sizes and would stimulate employment and economic activity. COBs and crowdfunding are examples of how this tide may be changing in a positive way.

A need for more access to local investment funds led several nonprofits to take innovative approaches to address this financing concern. Shuman discusses efforts by Goodworks Evergreen in Montana. Other efforts such as The Local Crowd and Milk Money in Vermont (Milk Money, 2020) also help local civic and development groups launch activities that directly benefit the community.

Not only is the regulatory system important in promoting and/or stimulating investment in local businesses, the legal environment and institutions within a community are crucial in financing local enterprises. Marketing, zoning, and other factors all blend into local decisions about types of businesses or ventures in which to invest. Many such policies have been years in the making, and some states or localities are more open to promoting a positive business investment environment than others.

The state of Vermont (USA) has led in promoting development and expansion of COBs for several reasons. Vermont, a small rural state, experienced a sluggish economy in the post-recession period. Population outmigration and setbacks in agriculture, a significant industry in the state, forced state and local leaders to consider new opportunities to stimulate the economy. A progressive political philosophy led state agencies to take a more supportive approach with policies and regulations that encourage business formation including CSEs.

Phillips, Seifer, and Walzer (Chapter 3) describe innovative efforts in Vermont to build a local environment that is not only conducive to investing locally but also aggressively encourages residents to take active ownership in business ventures including through employee ownership approaches. These programs, with adaptations to local conditions, can be used elsewhere to accomplish similar results. While Vermont is unique in its setting and needs, many basic concepts are readily adaptable in other scenarios with relatively low-cost adjustments.

For example, Vermont was an early state to implement a Low-Profit Limited Liability Company (L3C in Vermont) with a hybrid for profit and nonprofit business structures. The intent is to encourage and support organizations with low-profit charitable or educational goals. While the main purpose is not income-generation, it opens opportunities to support a wide range of other local efforts. The state legislation is such that organizations located in other states, meeting certain requirements, can register in Vermont offering opportunities to use this structure that addresses similar opportunities elsewhere.

A benefit corporation is a second approach to address community or social interests. In this case, entrepreneurs must have a social purpose, complete a work plan with intended outcomes in the application, and then file an annual report showing how they have met the goals. The Hinesburgh Public House, mentioned previously, is an example (Hinesburgh Public House).

Another common way to retain businesses is for employees to buy the venture when the owner decides to sell. This approach continues the business operations locally and supports buy-in from the community plus it offers an exit strategy for retiring owners. To stimulate and promote this process, Vermont started a Vermont Employee Ownership Center (VEOC, 2020) in 2001 to help employee-owned businesses during the transition process and continued support in the management process.

The state government also plays a strong supportive role through its Preservation Trust of Vermont (PTV). In addition to promoting historic preservation, PTV provides grants and helps local groups identify businesses possibly facing closures and helps them reorganize these ventures into sustainable businesses. These and efforts in other states are described in more detail in Walzer (2019). Like many other states, Vermont also offers a variety of statewide programs to stimulate downtown businesses, investment in new technology, and otherwise promote businesses in rural areas. While some programs exist elsewhere, it is the combination and focus of these programs that has made Vermont succeed with COBs and other local investments.

McCusker (Chapter 4) describes experiences in England, Scotland, and Wales with preserving local pubs that had been declining in substantial numbers. Central government agencies and philanthropic organizations including the Plunkett Foundation and Power to Change provided grants, technical assistance, and success-sharing educational materials to support local efforts. He analyzes examples of pubs and local shops that engaged in these types of processes to help understand how a local initiative to save a pub or other establishment can become a community-wide initiative. Not all community-owned enterprises began with a local pub, but one was involved in each community analyzed by McCusker. Based on analyses of ventures especially in England and Wales, he identifies several key ingredients in successful local initiatives.

England has long recognized the value of retaining jobs and businesses in small rural areas with programs that provide grants and other technical assistance to areas interested in promoting collective ownership approaches. Properties considered valuable or essential to the community's future can have a special designation that governs how they are sold and managed. These programs caused private philanthropic organizations to help local groups work with local businesses considered especially important to community quality of life and viability.

While grants and other funding opportunities are provided along with technical assistance, in many instances, the grants or external funding seem less important than the support generated by residents in maintaining the momentum of the ventures. Many transfers of ownership and financing were arranged through informal relationships and associations rather than more formal programs. Cooperatives or other community-based ownership approaches enabled local groups to raise sufficient funds to purchase and operate the ventures successfully. This does not lessen the importance of the national programs or the external financial support because, in some instances, the external interest and opportunities motivated the local processes initially.

Of special note are the early findings showing that the community-owned shops and pubs expanded during the COVID-19 period. The fact that they are locally owned and managed seemed to motivate more local purchases. In response, the shops diversified the range of offerings and services offered to help stabilize the community. Discussions with participants in the process revealed that they value the local establishments and wanted to help them succeed in making the community more self-reliant. Once again, the local population and attitudes determine the success of CSEs rather than the financing, physical capital, and other aspects. An important issue is how to extend the initial support and investment beyond the business start-up into similar support for a broader range of community initiatives.

Using a somewhat similar research approach but under different scenarios, Sohney and Hegemann (Chapter 5) examine local factors contributing to successes with CSEs in German villages. Community support and community capital are cited as essential ingredients to be built for implementing many community business financing approaches. Keeping communities alive and vibrant as places to live is vital to their success with strong motivations for residents to invest in these ventures so these motivational factors are important to understand.

Approaches used by several small villages in Germany to retain or reopen local stores offer insights into underlying decision-making processes and importance of the Community Capitals (Emery & Flora, 2016) in achieving successful outcomes. Sohney and Hegemann analyze experiences in the Village of Grieth (pop. 830) in reopening a local supply (grocery) to illustrate the interactions between Social Capital and the Political, Finance, Natural, Built, Human, and Cultural Capitals.

Based on interviews and discussions with local leaders and residents involved in the processes plus an analysis of the Capitals in the communities, the authors estimate their importance and relationships in successfully revitalizing a closed local grocery store. The community revitalization effort succeeded bringing a substantial subsequent decline in vacant buildings and other vestiges of past economic difficulties. The authors then contrast these experiences with those in other villages in the area that had taken different approaches, some of which were less successful.

Several findings from this study are especially insightful for those interested in pursuing similar efforts. Natural Capital did not seem to be important in this case. The availability of community-owned buildings (Built Capital) as places to congregate was important in revitalization efforts in several communities. Access to Financial Capital and Political Capital were not strong motivators, and Human Capital was a necessary condition but was not strongly related to development. While Social Capital receives considerable attention in the literature for its importance in stimulating local development, this relationship was not confirmed in the analysis of German villages. Rather, it is the connectedness and interactions among multiple capitals that seem to make the main difference.

While COBs, by definition, are typically not often owned by a city or governmental agency in the US, there are examples where after several attempts to follow the community-owned model, a municipal government such as St. Paul, Kansas (USA) bought a grocery store and operates it. Procter (Chapter 6) describes the process and how it worked.

Grocery stores are key to the continued viability of small communities for several reasons. First, and most obvious, is the access to healthy foods without which some sparsely populated rural areas could become food deserts due to the distance from other locations and relative immobility of older residents. This concern will likely become even more important with projected demographic trends.

A local grocery store also serves other functions in the community. Often, it is one of a few economic engines in the downtown and, while small, can be a relatively large local employer. The daily traffic to the commercial district attracted by the grocery store stimulates purchases in other businesses creating substantial multiplier effects. Furthermore, grocery stores purchase fresh produce or other locally grown products that provide stable markets for these producers. The overall economic impact is especially important in small communities.

But the impacts of a grocery store go well beyond economics when the store provides a neutral meeting place that encourages social interaction and networking. In fact, as later discussions show, broadening the lines of merchandise sold and hosting social activities are trademarks of COBs. These opportunities are especially important in small towns with declining networking opportunities due to growing numbers of relatively immobile elderly populations.

St. Paul, Kansas (USA), with an estimated 595 residents in 2020, experienced a steadily declining population and faced loss of its only grocery store. The responses by the community illustrate a successful collaborative strategy involving residents and the municipal government to reopen a store and make it succeed. Procter describes the process used during several years when the municipal government purchased the building and finally operated the store. This relatively uncommon example shows the possibilities with collaboration among local groups to finance an essential local business.

The CSEs or enterprises discussed thus far involve spontaneous actions by local groups interested in retaining and/or preserving a business. However, similar financing approaches have also been used to provide social and public services in the face of cutbacks in traditional public funding sources as was the case with Italian community cooperatives described by Bianchi (Chapter 7).

The 2008 recession in Italy substantially reduced or eliminated financial support by public agencies for local services and infrastructure, especially in sparsely populated and remote rural areas. The local economies were devastated in some cases and were unable to respond especially during a period of long-term population declines. Community leaders responded by launching a cooperatives movement to replace lost businesses using a CSE approach.

The success of these efforts led to a national movement of community cooperatives in Italy to address a wide range of local issues. The result is that they helped revitalize economies and communities in remote areas. Two national organizations, namely, Legacoop and Confcooperative, joined forces to shift the focus of cooperatives more toward community issues such as managing public assets and enhancing local community development. The efforts led to programs and funding opportunities that enabled local groups to use cooperative financing arrangements with community projects.

Bianchi further shows, based on a survey of 29 responding cooperatives, that a majority (24) were organized by an informal group of citizens. The main interest was to pursue local economic development issues for 19 respondents with 14 reporting a need to revitalize and maintain rural areas, followed by nine respondents reporting that the intent was to manage local services.

The broad range of activities in which the cooperatives engaged illustrates how this financing approach can be applied to other issues. While a substantial number (11) of the cooperatives reported funding from member shares only, others are funded with more than member contributions, which suggests opportunities to also engage in profit-making ventures. Likewise, a relatively small percentage of coop members live in the immediate area showing support for the cooperative from a broader region. Respondents reported collaborations with local public authorities, private businesses, and third-sector agencies reinforcing the value of support from other local groups.

The experiences in Italy illustrate the broad applications for CSE financing approaches. They go well beyond transitioning essential local businesses threatened by owner retirements. Instead, the techniques can be used to provide social and health services and other community needs as shown in more detail later.

Blending Private and Community Interests

Key to successes with community-supported financing is integrating a social purpose or dimension with a business enterprise as in the case with Italian cooperatives. This process can take many approaches, and the experiences with community pubs in England offer rich insights into successful ways to help communities make this transition

Sforzi and Bianchi (2020), based on in-depth surveys in a sample of three community pubs in London, examine specific roles that Social Capital played in creating these enterprises. Specifically, they find that entrepreneurs used Bonding Capital to organize the need for the enterprise and then used Bridging Capital to finance the endeavor. They also show that the specific organizational framework used in launching an endeavor is important in successfully building the two types of capitals. In addition, the COB approach helped maintain the connections required for the business to succeed.

CSEs have been effective in diverse environments and organizational structures. Arrangements and procedures used differ, but the basic elements regarding community support and a social purpose remain the same. Chaimei Hsia (Chapter 8) uses a community-based enterprise framework to describe efforts in two regions of Taiwan that were seriously affected by the 2008 recession. One project involved preserving the cultural heritage in a remote region by using eco-tourism to market the area to a wide audience. High-quality mushrooms are one of the key commodities grown in the area and were exported to external markets. An alternative development strategy was to bring tourists to the region to buy the mushrooms and participate in local events building on the heritage of the region, rather than focusing on exporting the mushrooms as a commodity.

The rationale is that attracting tourists supports a wide range of local customs and events with a multiplier effect much greater than focusing only on exports. This approach also supports local institutions and preserves customs for future generations. More importantly, this approach recognized that local activities, which sometimes go unpaid or are undervalued in traditional economic analyses, are more highly valued in supporting local community development. The CSE efforts used highlight the importance of these indigenous activities and integrate them into successful economic development efforts. Taking a more comprehensive view of community and economic development issues laid the groundwork for an active tourism plan that incorporated native agricultural practices into marketing efforts.

A second example is a Shia-An Community Coop in a small rural village losing population while experiencing growth in elderly population that required geriatric care which was not available in the village. A donated van helped provide access to the geriatric care, but community leaders needed ways to finance supplies, fuels, and other items to transport residents to a neighboring center offering this care. So, they explored local fundraising opportunities and settled on a CSE approach.

Rice is a major crop grown locally, and farmers had become accustomed to using chemicals to boost the yield, even though it adversely affected the environment and broke with traditions. A coop was formed to promote the use of natural growing processes by covering the production differences between the chemical-based approach and more natural growing methods.

The purpose of the coop was to support various community needs, and it generated large numbers of volunteers throughout the community helping the effort succeed. It expanded into other business endeavors including those that engaged younger generations in growing and processing the rice. This initiative will attract and retain future populations as well as stabilize the economic base. These efforts succeeded in improving conditions and engaging residents in many different age groups.

The growth in COB approaches, along with the introduction of crowdfunding platforms, stimulated interest by local groups in investing in business enterprises with a social purpose. Small communities that could benefit from these approaches often do not have sufficient local expertise to successfully manage such an endeavor. The need for expertise and technical assistance caused several agencies to work as intermediaries either in financing local businesses or in raising funds for social projects. In some instances, these investments involve raising funds to provide no-interest loans to local businesses (Community Sourced Capital, 2020).

Other agencies work with civic or development groups to provide crowdfunding platforms that finance community improvements to build social capital. Brauer (Chapter 9) describes a successful effort based in the state of Wyoming (USA), The Local Crowd (TLC), that provides technical assistance and education efforts to local agencies on both community development and business enhancement projects. The initial attempt was piloted in 11 states to provide proof of concept. Then, it was operationalized and expanded to communities in other states.

The program helped communities with a sense of localism and community-wide interest in projects ranging from starting businesses to community infrastructure facilities such as improving educational facilities. Specific projects are determined by community interests and those that residents are willing to support. The focus is not exclusively on creating jobs; rather, it involves community well-being and improvements as well.

In 2018, TLC created the 4th sector program (TLC 4SE) to build or strengthen an entrepreneurial ecosystem in communities where residents will commit time and money to local betterment. This program includes a crowdfunding platform along with educational materials followed by technical assistance. The concept of the 4th sector includes focusing the business, government, and nonprofit sectors on community betterment efforts. Results of the pilot activities demonstrated that communities can succeed in local fundraising efforts to launch enterprises with residents showing a positive interest in patronizing the ventures. Residents and others invest in projects in which they have specific interest, and they reported a willingness to pay higher prices from local vendors rather than purchase elsewhere in the future. Given these initial findings, the TLC 4SE program was launched in other areas. The program has been used extensively to help communities finance local projects.

A somewhat similar effort to help residents invest in local business ventures is the Community Sourced Capital program that offers short-term no-interest loans to businesses that meet specific conditions including a viable business plan.

Rather than financing start-ups, this program enables local investors to work with on-going local businesses in which they are interested. Investors are compensated as the businesses repay their loans. The investments are in designated businesses rather than being pooled with multiple business ventures, so investors can select specific businesses rather than assume the risks of multiple businesses. Unfortunately, due to financial difficulties that small businesses are experiencing during the COVID-19 economic downturn, this platform was shut down in July 2020, even though it had had successful past experiences (Community Sourced Capital, 2020).

TLC or other agencies can help communities select potential projects, create funding platforms, and implement local initiatives. This assistance can make the difference for small communities without extensive local expertise in working with these types of local development issues. An important consideration is that these investments can directly support current or new businesses. The driving factor in most instances, however, is a socially motivated purpose such as an essential business that otherwise would close or another project that adds significantly to local quality of life.

The versatility of CSE financing approaches for public services is further highlighted by Sengupta (Chapter 10) in describing work in Ontario, Canada to provide funds to employ persons with intellectual and learning disabilities. Although a different approach from those discussed previously, this example illustrates ways that CSE-financed ventures can be used to help with services that, in many other places, are provided by local governments with solely public funds that may be shrinking. It also offers opportunities to engage residents in financing these services with people served contributing directly to the economy while gaining valuable work experience.

Another dimension of a CSE approach in Canada is that employing persons with learning disabilities in the workplace reduces the perception of the public agency as relying as heavily on public dollars. Instead, the work performed is more generally accepted as valued in the private economy, which generates additional support for agencies delivering the service. This perception may be even more important in the future as budgets tighten.

Several common themes run through the previous chapters even when the scenarios and services provided differ. These themes are especially important to highlight as local officials try to replicate some of the examples. Walzer and Park (Chapter 11) identify key concepts identified by previous authors and show where a community supported or owned business financing approach could help communities respond to difficulties, especially in the post-COVID-19 period. Even beyond the immediate needs created by the recession, however, long-term declining populations and growth in elderly will create even higher demands for elder-friendly services. Without a local investment approach, these services will be difficult to maintain in an era of shrinking public finances.

Previous discussions have several common themes. First, residents must be convinced about the importance of the venture proposed. That perception must include a willingness to commit both time and/or financial resources to make it happen. In some instances, such as a grocery store in St. Paul, Kansas, the importance of the project was almost immediately recognized. In other instances, such as providing work opportunities for people with learning disabilities, opportunities to use a CSE method of finance may be less obvious and take more directed action(s) by community leaders.

Second, the proposed venture to be financed with a CSE must be viable and scalable in the community where proposed. In some instances, the project must become economically self-sufficient. In others, there may be continued injections of funding such as with member shares in a cooperative or support by a governmental agency.

Third, once launched, the progress toward the intended outcomes must be regularly communicated with investors and residents to build and maintain continued interest, patronage, and community support. This continued communication can sometimes become lost in the daily activities of managing the operations.

The chapters in this volume illustrate the variety of ways in which the CSE type of financing has been used in various environments. There is no preferred approach, and adaptations of CSEs may be needed to accomplish local objectives. The collection of experiences in the following discussions illustrates these opportunities and offers insights into local adaptations to a financing approach that is almost sure to grow in importance in the future.

References

Community Sourced Capital. 2020. Olympia, WA. Available at: https://www.communitysourcedcapital.com

Emery, M. & Flora, C. 2006. Spiraling-up: Mapping Community Transformation with Community Capitals Framework. *Community Development*. 37(1) 19–35.

Goodworks Evergreen. 2020. Continuing the Montana Tradition. Available at: https://gwevergreen.com

Hinesburgh Public House. 2020. Available at: https://hinesburghpublichouse.com

Macke, D., Markley, D., & Fulwider, J. 2014. *Energizing Entrepreneurial Communities: A Pathway to Prosperity*. Lincoln, NE: Center for Rural Entrepreneurship.

Markley, D. M., Lyons, T. S., & Macke, D. W. 2015. Creating Entrepreneurial Communities: Building Community Capacity for Ecosystem Development. *Community Development*. 46(5) 580–598.

Milk Money. 2020. Bringing Entrepreneurs and Investors Together. Available at: https://milkmoneyvt.com/

National Institute on Aging. 2019. *Social Isolation, Loneliness in Older People Pose Health Risks*. Available at: https://www.nia.nih.gov/news/social-isolation-loneliness-older-people-pose-health-risks#:~:text=Health%20effects%20of%20social%20isolation%2C%20loneliness%20Research%20has,depression%2C%20cognitive%20decline%2C%20Alzheimer%E2%80%99s%20disease%2C%20and%20even%20death.

Perodo, A. M. & Chrisman, J. J. 2006. Toward a Theory of Community-Based Enterprise. *Academy of Management Review*. 31(2) 309–328.

Plunkett Foundation. 2019. Available at: https://plunkett.co.uk/about-us
Plunkett Foundation. 2020. *Community Pubs: A Better Form of Business.* Available at: https://plunkett.co.uk/wp-content/uploads/PLUNKETT_BB_PUBS19_download2.pdf
Sforzi, J. & Bianchi, M. 2020. Fostering Social Capital: The Case of Community-Owned Pubs. *Social Enterprise Journal.* Available at: https://www.emerald.com/insight/1750-8614.htm.
Shuman, M. H. 2012. *Local Dollars, Local Sense.* White River Junction, VT: Chelsea Green Publishing.
Shuman, M. H. 2015. *The Local Economic Solution.* White River Junction, VT: Chelsea Green Publishing.University of Kansas, School of Business.2020. *RedTire.* Available at: http://redtire.dept.ku.edu/retired-business-listings/business/index.shtml
Vermont Employee Ownership Center. 2020. Available at: www.VEOC.org.
Walzer, N. 2019. *Guidebook and Resources for Starting a Community Supported Enterprise.* East Lansing, MI: North Central Regional Center for Rural Development.
Walzer, N. & Sandoval, J. 2016. *Emergence and Growth of Community Supported Enterprises.* East Lansing, MI: North Central Regional Center for Rural Development.

2

FINANCIAL CSEs

Lessons from North America

Michael H. Shuman

Introduction

Among the most critically important community-supported enterprises (CSEs) are those providing finance to locally owned businesses.[1] Financial CSEs provide communities with the ability to underwrite all kinds of businesses for local prosperity. In a community without strong financial CSEs, almost all business expansion – including the expansion of CSEs themselves – is difficult at best and impossible at worst. As Aladdin would appreciate, financial CSEs give a community stuck with three wishes permission to have more wishes. This chapter explores the evolution of financial CSEs in North America, mainly in the United States but also some noteworthy innovations in Canada.

According to periodic reports published by the Federal Reserve, just prior to the COVID-19 crisis, Americans had approximately $13.8 trillion in banks and $56.5 trillion invested in securities.[2] A security is basically any financial instrument, usually some kind of agreement on paper, that pays a return to the holder. It can be a loan paying interest, a stock appreciating, or a royalty payment (usually a percentage of profits or revenues, up to some ceiling).

Most securities are regulated by a national agency, and sometimes, by state and local agencies as well. In the United States, the supervisory agencies are the Securities Exchanges Commission (SEC) and its equivalents in every one of the 50 states. The $56.5 trillion Americans hold in securities are in stocks, bonds, mutual funds, pension funds, and insurance funds. These investments are the focus of this chapter, along with the following question: How can more of these savings be put to work on behalf of community economic development?

Technically, the relationships people and businesses have with banks, credit unions, and thrifts also involve securities. A bank deposit that pays interest is a security, as is a bank loan that requires periodic payments. But most countries have special laws governing banks and credit unions that effectively constitute exemptions from securities laws. For brevity, this chapter focuses only on securities outside banking.

A common misperception of the capital universe is that most financial activity goes through banks.[3] In fact, as the data in the United States cited above show, securities outside banking are far more important in determining the direction of economic development. One helpful generalization, however imperfect, is to think about banking as mediating short-term financial transactions serving consumers and businesses, while securities mediate their long-term investments. The average American uses securities primarily to save for retirement, education, or unexpected emergencies.

This chapter focuses on US securities law and makes four arguments: First, securities laws historically have kept finance away from CSEs. Second, recent reforms of securities laws, especially in crowdfunding, offer a glimpse of how those flows of capital can be altered and redirected toward local businesses and CSEs. Third, further reforms under consideration could substantially shift the flow of capital from Wall Street to Main Street. Finally, as CSE advocates in the United States contemplate possible reforms, they might study and replicate emerging models in Canada.

While the discussion focuses mainly on American and Canadian securities laws, the author has spent time reviewing similar laws in Australia, Brazil, France, Germany, Japan, Mauritius, and the United Kingdom. Their security regimes mirror many of the same features found in North America. Given that, this chapter not only can inform CSE strategies in North Americans but may also help readers from outside the United States contemplate the reforms reviewed.

How US Securities Law Has Failed Communities

Were securities laws operating effectively, capital would gravitate effectively to every business sector, every type of business, and every size of business relative to its role in the economy. Today, the capital overseen by US securities law goes almost exclusively to the small portion of the US economy occupied by global corporations.

The Local Majority of the Economy

Contrary to conventional thinking, the US economy is mainly made up of small, locally owned businesses.[4] One in ten working Americans is a sole proprietor, many running home-based businesses. One in five works in small businesses with 1–99 employees. Approximately three in ten are in medium-scale businesses having 99–500 employees. Nearly, all these businesses are locally owned. The only real category with non-local businesses is where businesses have more than 500 employees, and those businesses represent approximately 40% of the economy in terms of jobs and output. Also worth pointing out is that many very large companies, such as hospitals or universities, are locally owned. Thus, while almost all small businesses are locally owned, not all of these businesses are small.

Dun & Bradstreet, which maintains an updated inventory of business establishments in the country, has a slightly different definition of "local." It calls an establishment – an office, a factory, a store – local if its headquarters is in the same state. By that definition, approximately 80% of the economy in the United States, again by jobs and output, are locally owned.[5]

So, depending on definition of "local," locally owned businesses account for 60%–80% of the US economy. And in a well-functioning investment marketplace, 60%–80% of securities capital would support 60%–80% of the economy. In fact, almost all securities capital in the United States goes exclusively into the stocks and bonds of global companies.[6] Even so-called "impact investing" and "socially responsible investing" are largely about investing in more environmentally friendly or labor-friendly publicly traded companies. This means that local businesses and the CSEs supporting them cannot obtain the capital necessary to succeed. It also explains why so many CSEs resort to the tiny and unstable streams of funding from public agencies, foundations, and philanthropists.

The Misallocation of Capital

What if the US capital market operated efficiently? What would be the impact of Americans shifting just 60% of their investment capital into local businesses? A shift of this magnitude would mean that every community in the United States would have at least $100,000 more capital to invest in local businesses for every local resident. A small town of 10,000 people thus would have a billion dollars more of capital to regenerate the economy. Or a city with 100,000 people would have $10 billion more. It is hard to imagine any policy or governmental program that could deliver even a small fraction of the potential impact of residents changing their investment choices. This underscores the critical importance of understanding and reforming securities laws.

If locally owned businesses provided smaller returns to investors than globally traded companies, this misallocation of capital might be justified. In fact, however, the available evidence suggests that smaller companies are *more* profitable than large firms. The most recent data from the US Internal Revenue Service (IRS), from the year 2013, show that sole proprietorships, which most small businesses are or start out as, are three times more profitable than C corporations, with the profitability of partnerships falling in between.[7]

In Canada, the latest data show that the most profitable companies have 10–20 employees, while the least profitable have more than 500 employees (Lafrance, 2012). Because businesses with higher profit rates generally pay investors better returns than those with lower profit rates, rational return-minded investors should be focusing on local businesses.

The Riskiness of Local Investments

Another possible explanation for investors shunning locally owned businesses is that they may be perceived as riskier. Many investment advisors tell their clients not to invest locally because "most small businesses fail." This is untrue. All start-ups, big and small, nonlocal and local, have high failure rates. Most do not survive past five years or so. *But more than 90% of all small businesses are not start-ups.* Risk-averse investors then should stay away from startups and not necessarily local businesses.

This is not to say that investing in an existing local business is without risk. It's worth remembering that *all investments carry risk.* And there are some special risks posed by local investment worth paying attention to:

- *Limited Investors* – Businesses looking exclusively for local investors will have more difficulty locating them. Compared to the universe of Wall Street investors, the universe of local investors is small.
- *Limited Businesses* – Investors looking exclusively for local companies have fewer options, and the chance of choosing wrong is greater. This could change in time, but right now, the marketplace for local securities is immature.
- *Geographic Risk* – Every regional economy naturally goes through ups and downs. If an investment portfolio includes exclusively local businesses, losses will be greater if the region declines. (For this reason, a risk-averse local investor might try to have locally owned businesses from different places.)
- *Information Is Limited* – For Wall Street investors, many easily accessible data sources can provide key facts about companies prior to investment decisions. Professional investors can purchase analytical reports from companies such as Moody's. Currently, there are no such uniform reports about local companies.

But there are also several ways that local investments can *reduce* investors' risks:

- *Better Information* – Even though no formal information sources about local businesses exist, most of the needed information is readily available to local investors. They can visit a business, pose questions to the manager, talk with the workforce, and evaluate the company's products or services. Direct conversations are often the best way to evaluate companies anyway. We know, for example, that community banks with long relationships with borrowers have lower default rates than global banks relying strictly on computer-generated credit scores.
- *Social Returns* – Many local businesses deliver both a private return and a community (or social) return. Unlike a nonlocal investment, there are multiple ways a local investment can benefit a community. Even if the company does not deliver much of a profit, investors can benefit from a stronger local economy, cleaner streets, better schools, and so forth. Different investors will value the social return differently, but it is definitely positive.

- *Local Synergies* – A third way local investment can reduce risk is by enabling new investment strategies. While the risk of geographic concentration is real, there is another side. A well-constructed portfolio of interconnected local companies can enjoy potential risk-reducing synergies. An investment in an established restaurant that puts its second eatery in an otherwise dead downtown will increase pedestrian traffic and help every other new business in that area succeed. A smart local investor might invest in the restaurant, *and* the movie theater next door, *and* the coffee house across the street. Being mindful of the risks of geographic concentration, investors might create a portfolio like this with multiple downtowns across the country.
- *Increased Diversification* – The idea behind having a diversified portfolio of investments is that if one fails, the others will be untouched. The investments should be different enough so they cannot fail in the same way, at the same time, or because of some common cause. The essential problem with a typical portfolio right now is that almost everything in it – stocks, bonds, commercial paper, mutual funds, even currencies – is tied to the performance of global companies. A trade war, a global capital crisis, or the collapse of major currencies will adversely affect everything in the typical portfolio. Truly local investments, in contrast, are somewhat more insulated from the global economy.

Origins of the Capital Market Failure

The main reason for the misallocation of capital in the United States, therefore, has nothing to do with the returns or risks concerning local securities. It has more to do with the reality that securities laws were created to serve a different audience: large companies on the one side, and wealthy investors and financial institutions on the other. To clarify, this does not mean that the wealthy conspired to rig the market on their own behalf, but rather that the law was shaped by those actors who were using it most frequently.

Economies of scale are relevant too. All things being equal, an investment institution prefers connecting big investors to large companies because it means less work and bigger fees. No matter the size of the company or its long-term profitability, the law requires the same level of due diligence before money changes hands. Assume that this due diligence costs \$100,000 per company. Since fees are a percentage of the deal, investment dealmakers naturally prefer to do the \$100,000 of work for a corporate giant like Home Depot than a neighborhood hardware store.

High finance outside of banking used to be exclusively undertaken by a small number of tycoons. Very few Americans, for example, could afford a seat at the New York Stock Exchange. The democratization of investment in the 1920s meant that the grassroots investors could more easily purchase shares of large companies, not local ones. The unhappy ending in 1929, with the stock market collapsing and the subsequent Great Depression, ushered in legislation that still defines securities law today: the Securities Act of 1933; the Exchanges Act of 1934; the Investment Advisors Act of 1940; and the Investment Company Act of 1940.

The foundational law is the Securities Act, which basically says that every company that wants to sell securities first must register them with the SEC. The burdens imposed depend on who is buying the securities. If the buyers are wealthy, the paperwork is light. The law presumes that wealthy people understand their investments, and even if they do not, they can afford the loss. Selling securities to average investors, in contrast, requires considerable legal paperwork and often prior permission from the government.

In one way, the logic is unassailable. The Securities Act protects Americans from being misled. But the law has had another consequence as well, probably unintended. The burden of complying with the legislation, often $25,000–$100,000 per securities offering, was reasonable for large companies but not small businesses. Local entrepreneurs concluded that the legal expenses associated with soliciting small amounts from grassroots investors were not worth the small benefits. This explains why, even today, local businesses seeking outside money tend to go to angel investors, venture funds, or other avenues involving mainly wealthy investors.

The entire investment market has evolved primarily to serve wealthy individuals investing in large companies. Even the first retirement now used by grassroots investors – the Investment Retirement Account and the 401k – were designed primarily to give wealthy individuals another way to save. It was only later that these were repackaged and marketed to grassroots investors.

Securities law calls wealthy investors who are free to do what they want "accredited investors." Depending on the math, accredited investors represent between 1% and 5.5% of the US population.[8] The rest are "unaccredited." They are allowed to invest in businesses only after the companies have done the proper paperwork.

All the above impediments apply to just the *issuance* of a security. Once a security has been purchased, the Exchange Act of 1934 has other rules controlling when and how sales can occur. If you want to invest in a pool of securities, you must comport with the rules of the Investment Company Act of 1940. And if you want to invest pension funds, you need to follow, among other things, the Employee Retirement Income Security Act of 1974. All these laws make it expensive and difficult to create financial CSEs serving small businesses and grassroots investors.

The consequence of these laws, in the end, is a misallocation of capital away from local businesses and the CSEs that might support them. In a mature marketplace, such as has developed during the last century around big businesses, professionals would help grassroots investors find promising local investments, evaluate them, trade them, put them into funds, and connect them with retirement accounts. In the real world of today's local investing and CSEs, however, these professionals barely exist today. The burden is on grassroots investors and local businesses to spend disproportionately more time, energy, and money on establishing even the most basic relationships. Clearly, this must change if local businesses and CSEs are ever to receive the capital they deserve.

Crowdfunding: A Case Study of Reform

The advent of investment crowdfunding in recent years has made it cheaper and easier for the average American to invest in local business. A review of how reforms in crowdfunding came about in the United States suggests strategies that could be used to reform other aspects of securities law.

Types of Crowdfunding

The term "crowdfunding" refers to at least four different types of local investments, all of which allow many people to invest small amounts of money in business ventures. The first type, *donation crowdfunding*, is arguably not an investment at all, since investors receive only a social rate of return, not a private one. Sites such as Kickstarter and IndieGogo allow contributions of $1, $25, or $1,000 – whatever amount is preferred – to an exciting idea, project, or business. While investors do not receive a financial return, they may receive a perk such as a tee-shirt or a product sample. Some beer companies have even promised to name new beers after their top donors. Because donations are not regarded as "securities," these sites are largely unregulated. There are now literally thousands of these donation sites on the internet, and they attract billions of dollars of largely local donations every year.[9]

The second type of crowdfunding is *interest-free lending* to businesses. One example is Kiva, which allows investors to find microentrepreneurs around the world, learn about their businesses, and help them start and grow. This kind of lending has proliferated as well because loans without interest also are not regarded as securities. Again, perks might be provided from the investment, in addition to receiving a return of the principal, but the main satisfaction is personal. Investors also enjoy a social return from the business's success if it involves a local entrepreneur.

Peer-to-peer lending is the third type of crowdfunding. Prosper and the Lending Club are examples that provide individuals and businesses with the opportunity to borrow as much as $35,000–$40,000 from small investors. These sites currently pay interest rates of approximately 10%, but the loans are risky. One problem for local investors, however, is that they can see only the state in which the borrowers live. The community location is hidden.

The fourth type is what Title III of the JOBS Act of 2012 legalized and is often called *equity crowdfunding*. Small businesses can put an offering up on a federally licensed portal, such as WeFunder, and investors can provide as much as $2,200 per year (more if their income is over $107,000). The term "equity" crowdfunding is a misnomer because the offerings can be for stock, debt, royalty, pre-sale of products, or a combination of all the above. As of this writing, 34 states and the District of Columbia also have laws allowing local businesses to raise investment within their states using crowdfunding.[10] Many states allow larger offerings by small business and larger investments by grassroots investors than the federal law does. But because the states never reformed their laws governing web-based portals (for example, they only allow licensed broker-dealers to run them, while the feds allow anyone), these laws have not been used as much.

The JOBS Act Debate

Several features about the crowdfunding reforms are worth noting.[11] First, they were passed with supermajorities of both US parties in Congress. The JOBS Act was introduced by Tea Party Republicans rebelling against the regulatory hurdles faced by investors. But the reforms also had the enthusiastic support of young techies and local economy advocates, who argued that a key to economic revitalization was getting more capital to small and local businesses.

The most stalwart opponents of reform, securities attorneys, mustered remarkably unpersuasive arguments for maintaining the status quo. The main argument was that current securities laws were necessary to prevent fraud. Requiring every small business to produce extensive "disclosures" statements, they insisted, provides notice to small investors about the risks. While the argument had superficial appeal, securities attorneys could not prove the effectiveness of the disclosure statements. To be clear, under the traditional law, if a small business wanted to borrow even a small amount from a single unaccredited investor, the proprietor had to incur legal costs of $10,000, $25,000, or sometimes even more. Typically, the document produced was 100–200 pages of legalistic fine print that very few people ever read. Put another way, these legal requirements probably benefitted securities lawyers more than they did grassroots investors.

Another argument by securities regulators was that unaccredited investors, being naïve and susceptible to misleading pitches, needed special protections. But the massive scandal involving Bernie Madoff in 2008 involved the deception of hundreds of *accredited* investors, none of whom recognized that they were the victims of a multi-billion-dollar pyramid scheme. While fraud prevention is a worthy objective, trusting people's judgment based on their wealth was clearly no longer a reliable approach.

Still, another argument was to prevent the risk of unaccredited investors losing everything. But a comparison of the law governing another risky endeavor – gambling – made this argument look absurd. Today, Americans can enter a casino in nearly every state, risk, and lose everything over time. Casinos are not restricted to accredited gamblers nor are they required to read disclosure statements on the risk. In fact, gamblers can lose everything, *independent of income.* And yet, when it comes to investing in local businesses and saving communities, grassroots risk-taking must be heavily limited. The logic was indefensible, especially after the recession of 2008.

The JOBS Act, passed in 2012, reduced but did not eliminate the legal paperwork required of businesses. It created a simplified set of disclosures every business had to produce before they could be listed on federally licensed portals, and more importantly, it gave small businesses an affordable pathway to raise $1 million in investment capital per year from any American. (This ceiling was raised to $5 million in March 2021.) Unlike donation crowdfunding, investment crowdfunding enables businesses to borrow money from interested parties or fans and pay them interest, sell stock and pay dividends, provide royalty payments on revenues or profits, or enter into many other kinds of investment arrangements. Virtually everyone can participate. Small businesses can seek grassroots investors, and these groups can put their money into small businesses.

What's Next?

According to a recent assessment of investment crowdfunding, since 2016 more than 700,000 grassroots investors have placed more than half a billion dollars into several thousand businesses (Crowdfund Capital Advisers, 2020). The average raise is now $342,000. These numbers will grow, but in the larger scheme of things, this revolution is still in its early stages. Of the 330 million people living in the United States, fewer than one in a thousand have participated in crowdfunding.

Many ideas are now being explored to expand crowdfunding options. They include the following:

- Increase the amount of money a business can raise from $5 to $10 million.
- Increase the amount a grassroots investor can put into a company each year from $2,200 to $10,000.
- Set up education campaigns for businesses and investors to learn about grassroots opportunities.
- Make it cheaper and easier for grassroots investors to move tax-deferred pension savings into local securities through self-directed Individual Retirement Accounts (IRAs) and Solo 401Ks.
- Allow local, state portal operators to earn a success fee for successful crowdfunded offerings, which would give them a more viable business model (currently only federal portal operators can do so).

In the end, however, crowdfunding faces one potentially insurmountable challenge. Expecting grassroots investors to evaluate companies, one by one, without the kind of third-party reports available on global companies is unrealistic. Groups of local investors and investment clubs can help lessen the homework for participants. But it is clear from the mainstream investment universe that most people prefer to have investment professionals evaluate companies and create diversified portfolios within funds. People without significant wealth are more at ease investing in a diversified pool of capital.

The Importance of Community Investment Funds

Investment funds are financial institutions where investors pool their money and where fund managers make prudent investment decisions on their behalf. Even though the United States has nearly 10,000 funds, only about a dozen specialize in assembling portfolios of local securities and are open to unaccredited investors (Beckon et al. 2020). While the JOBS Act made it easier for small businesses to issue securities to grassroots investors, no comparable legal reforms have yet been initiated for funds serving small businesses.

The Investment Company Act of 1940 makes it exceedingly expensive to create and operate investment funds, especially if they accept any money from unaccredited investors. Just the set-up cost for a mutual fund, for example, can involve hundreds of thousands of dollars. Many fund managers prefer to take advantage of one of the many exemptions in the Act to lower the cost of legal compliance. For example, the "hedge fund" exemption provides that any fund with fewer than 100 accredited investors can operate largely unregulated.

Starting in the 1970s, despite the legal impediments, a few investment funds tried to be more community-friendly through "socially responsible investment" (SRI) strategies (Shuman, 2020). The idea was to screen out companies selling goods and services harmful to communities such as tobacco or nuclear weapons. Firms such as Pax World, Parnassus, and Calvert convinced millions of Americans to shift billions in retirement savings this way. As the SRI industry matured, it shifted from negative screens to positive ones, enabling grassroots investors to place money into funds with companies focusing on, say, renewable energy or sustainable farming. The nexus between socially responsible and community-focused, however, has been imperfect at best because all the companies in these SRI funds are large and publicly traded. Local businesses have been and remain largely excluded.

During the past decade, some funds, such as Calvert Impact Capital, have enabled grassroots investors to support community-friendly banks, CDCs, CDFIs, and related pools of small businesses across the country.[12] The Clinton administration introduced New Markets Tax Credits for wealthy investors who wished to support distressed communities, and new funds emerged to serve as intermediaries.[13] The tax reforms enacted by Congress in December 2017 encouraged wealthy investors with capital gains to place them in new Opportunity Zone funds to revitalize distressed communities (Tankersley, 2020). While it is premature to know-how exactly this law will unfold – the biggest beneficiaries thus far appear to be luxury condos, chain stores, and large redevelopment projects – in theory, some of the beneficiaries could be local businesses. But because only richer investors worry about sheltering their capital gains, these funds remained largely unavailable to unaccredited investors.

Table 2.1 lists the small number of funds investing in local businesses that *are* open to unaccredited investors. Early pioneers were the Vermont Community Loan Fund, the New Hampshire Community Loan Fund, and the Mountain

TABLE 2.1 U.S. community investment funds allowing grassroots participation

Fund Name	*Location*	*Focus*
Boston Impact Fund	Boston, MA	Businesses with economic-justice mission
Boston Ujima Fund	Boston, MA	Entrepreneurs of color
Community Vision Lending	San Francisco, CA	Community enterprises in California
East Bay permanent real estate cooperative	Oakland, CA	Affordable housing
Economic Community Development Institute	Columbus, OH	Local businesses
Iroquois Valley Farmland REIT	Evanston, IL	Farms in 14 states
Mountain BizWorks	Asheville, NC	Local businesses
New Hampshire Community Loan Fund	Concord, NH	Small businesses in New Hampshire
New York City Real Estate Investment Cooperative	New York, NY	Affordable housing
Northeast Kingdom Prosperity Fund	St. Johnsbury, VT	Small Businesses in northeast Vermont
Northeast Real Estate Investment Cooperative	St. Paul, MN	Affordable housing
PV Grows Investment Fund	North Deerfield, MA	Food businesses in the Pioneer Valley
Runway Project	Oakland, CA	Loans to entrepreneurs of color
Vermont Community Loan Fund	Burlington, VT	Small businesses in Vermont

Source: Compiled by the author.

BizWorks Fund of North Carolina. Most took advantage of an exemption in the Investment Company Act for nonprofits. Under the law, a nonprofit can create a fund, relatively easily and inexpensively, and provide modest loans in the service of its mission.

A few *national* nonprofits, committed broadly to community development, used a similar approach.[14] The Rudolf Steiner Foundation created a funding vehicle called RSF Social Investment Fund to allow grassroots investors to invest in its Waldorf schools and gradually expanded the fund to focus on cutting-edge food and arts programs. The Calvert Foundation issued "community investment notes" that pooled and then reinvested grassroots capital in community-development financial institutions and community development corporations in low-income communities. Neither of these pools are local, per se, but both attempt to allocate investment to states and regions more or less proportionally to the residence of their investors.

The small number of community investment funds is due to several factors. Because small business securities have been rare, small-business funds pooling them have been even rarer. Another problem is the valuation of local securities. A fund knows the value of a small business loan in its portfolio but can only guess the probability of that loan failing. And how can potential investors know the value of local stock without local stock exchanges, which do not exist?

That said, in just the past few years, the number of new funds opening with a community focus has accelerated, many with striking and promising new features. This reflects the growth of public interest in local investing, a growing distrust of Wall Street, and the emergence of crowdfunding alternatives. Consider four striking examples.[15]

Example #1: Boston Impact Initiative

The Boston Impact Initiative (BII), in the words of cofounder Deborah Frieze, is "a place-based, integrated capital approach to closing the racial wealth divide." From 2013 to 2017, the Frieze family put $3 million of their own wealth into 30 different investments in eastern Massachusetts. Satisfied with the results, they created a charitable loan fund. It took two years and 30 lawyers, but the resulting document, says Frieze, now can serve as a model for others. By November 2019, it had raised $6.5 million of a $10 million target.

The fund has deployed $3.3 million so far in 30 ventures, including Maven Construction, a female- and minority-owned general contracting firm in Dorchester; Mobile Cuts, a mobile barber shop; and Democracy Brewing, a worker-owned brewery and pub in Boston. The portfolio also includes ventures that BII supported in its pilot phase, such as Cooperative Energy Recycling and Organics (CERO), a worker- and people-of-color-owned recycling cooperative. BII has supported CERO through grant funding, a zero-interest loan in 2013, a direct investment in the coop's direct public offering in 2014, and a working capital loan in 2017.

BII offers three types of notes: *Community Notes* that target unaccredited investors in the state are three-year notes that pay 3% interest. Fifty percent of the principal is protected via a loan loss reserve, so community members investing the minimum $2,000 could lose only $1,000 in a worst-case scenario. The bulk of the fund is from *Solidarity Notes*, aimed at accredited and institutional investors anywhere in selected states. They come in two types: a three-year, 3% note; and a seven-year, 4% note. Both have reserve protection of 10%. A third tier is a *Philanthropic Note*, a five-year, 1% note, similar to a recoverable grant, that funds half of the $2 million loan loss reserve (the remaining reserve is funded by grants).

At the core of BII's work is a conviction that it is not enough to reallocate capital to the underserved; *power* must also be reallocated to those who historically have not had it. The investment committee members represent a mix of financial and grassroots backgrounds. Investment decisions are ratified by the board, which is majority controlled by three-partner organizations with deep roots in social justice: the Center for Economic Democracy, which is also home to the Ujima Project; City Life/Vida Urbana, a housing justice organization; and RSF Social Finance.

Example #2: East Bay Permanent Real Estate Cooperative

Another example of a new type of community investment fund is the East Bay Permanent Real Estate Cooperative (EBPREC), which is a multi-stakeholder housing cooperative that buys real estate to keep it affordable. More than a dozen real estate projects are currently in the works. The goal, the group says, is to build community sovereignty and collective wealth among underserved and historically disenfranchised communities of color. For example, in California's East Bay, long-time residents, primarily people of color, are being displaced by rapid development that is exacerbating inequality, homelessness, and economic instability.

The EBPREC crowd-finances its projects by selling membership shares to community members and investors. It became a cooperative to take advantage of a recently passed California law, the California Cooperative Corporation Statute, that allows coops to raise as much as $1,000 per individual through the sale of memberships without requiring securities registration.[16] Investment is open to California residents only. Investors receive shares that pay a 1.5% annual dividend (they may also choose to forgo dividends to support the cause). The group has cultivated philanthropic funders to support staff and operations so that those costs are not passed along to individual projects or their resident owners.

Potential real estate acquisitions are identified by residents and tenants, and each project typically has a resident lead. "We select for people of color or people of color-allied democratic and justice-based goals," says EBPREC director Noni Session. Ideally, they are mixed-use projects combining residential and commercial space to diversify the revenue stream.

Once purchased, the buildings are placed in a community land trust, permanently removing them from the speculative market and creating permanent affordability. The residents, often at risk of displacement, can then secure long-term affordable housing and build equity ownership over time. They also participate in a training program to learn how to democratically run the property. Other projects in the works include the development of a cluster of tiny houses on an abandoned plot, an accessory dwelling unit, and the creation of a cultural corridor.

Example #3: Goodworks Evergreen Fund

A third example of a community investment fund is Goodworks Evergreen Fund in Montana. When the founders of the fund began researching the state's legacy businesses, they discovered that approximately $1 billion of assets are at risk of being lost as their owners contemplate retirement. The acquisition price to keep most of these businesses alive is too large for a few local investors and too small for most institutional buyers, says Dawn McGee, CEO of the Missoula-based impact fund.

Since 2007, Mary Stranahan had used her personal inheritance from Champion spark plugs to fund Goodworks Ventures, LLC (2020), a

Montana-focused impact fund that aims to "support, nurture, and empower visionary people and organizations that are creating the world we want to live in," as the website states. The fund has provided loans, equity capital, or hybrid investments to 35 diverse, largely Montana-based companies with strong leadership and innovative business concepts in the technology, sustainability, sciences, and food sectors.

With Goodworks Ventures working well, Stranahan launched Goodworks Evergreen to preserve Montana's legacy businesses. Phase one involves acquiring, managing, and improving up to five companies with an emphasis on keeping and retaining jobs, paying a living wage, and reinvesting in rural economies.

Goodworks Evergreen's first acquisition was Don's Home Center in early 2019. "We bought a hardware store and learned how to run it," McGee says. "Every one of Goodworks' employees has spent time behind the counter, because the people who work for us have to see our commitment."

Goodworks Evergreen also was able to do a complete makeover of Don's. The Evergreen staff bought new equipment to deliver lumber more efficiently. They cleaned and reset shelves, got rid of dead inventory, started tracking SKUs, bought a billboard, started a social media campaign, and distributed value pack flyers. They also hired and replaced several managers. Since taking over Don's Home Center, Goodworks Evergreen has raised the prevailing wage to $15 per hour, provided health insurance to full-time employees, increased staff by 50%, and enacted a retirement plan for employees.

Example #4: Pioneer Valley Grows Investment Fund

A fourth example of a cutting-edge community investment fund is the Pioneer Valley Grows Investment Fund (PVGIF), which is unlocking the social and community potential of the local food system in Western Massachusetts. Seventy investors, including individuals, a church, a private school, and nonprofits, have so far invested $2 million. Investors are motivated by improving local access to healthy food, protecting the environment, and generating jobs for the region.

PVGrows began as a collaborative network in 2009 to connect people and organizations involved in the Pioneer Valley food sector. The network's nine-member Finance Working Group, including community lenders, foundations, and agricultural technical assistance providers, identified an urgent need for gap financing, particularly to help viable farms and food businesses that were not fully "bankable." A five-year pilot offered a small number of loans; thanks to grants from two local foundations.

In 2015, the Working Group launched PVGIF, a registered nonprofit administered by the Franklin County Community Development Corporation. The offering memorandum states that the objective is "to provide financing and technical assistance at the right time and right terms to mission-driven and finance-ready farm and food entrepreneurs and businesses."

The Working Group now serves as PVGIF's Advisory Committee and assesses PVGIF applicants for mission fit and technical assistance needs. The committee recommends needed support for the business in addition to funds, such as strengthening the business plan, applying for subsidiary grants, and training staff. The final package combines the loan with financial and technical assistance. This is a way that PVGIF can take on greater risk than traditional lenders. So far, the default rate on the 35 packages given in the past four years has been zero.

One success story is Mycoterra Farm, a producer of gourmet and medicinal specialty mushrooms. The loan allowed the founder, Julia Coffey, to convert a horse stable in South Deerfield into a new and larger mushroom facility to meet growing market demand. PVGIF held an open house at the farm so that investors could see their dollars at work. Its program manager likened the experience to entering the City of Oz: "The huge indoor horse arena is just overflowing with mushrooms, and Julia impresses you with mycelium facts."

These four examples barely touch the universe of possible community structures within the Investment Company Act. In an extensive review of the law, attorney Brian Beckon identified 15 different "compliance" models, only a handful of which have been tested.[17] But Beckon also argues that some simple federal reforms could greatly expand these community fund experiments. One possibility is to create an exemption for small funds serving businesses in nearby communities and to limit (as is the case with the JOBs Act) the dollar amount invested by a grassroots investor. Another possibility is that the federal government could give states the option to create and regulate funds involving only intrastate businesses and investors.

As Americans consider other financial CSE models, they also might look to other countries for inspiration and ideas. And they might begin with Canada.

Canadian Models of Securities Reform

The Canadian system of securities law is very similar to that of the United States. The universe of investors is split into a small number of wealthy accredited investors with few limitations on their investment options versus unaccredited investors who cannot touch businesses without expensive disclosure statements. Crowdfunding has helped increase the opportunities for local investment, but few Canadians have taken advantage of it. In one important respect, however, Canadian law differs significantly from US law: The provinces have significant more latitude than the US states in forming the rules for grassroots investment funds.

For example, the provinces of Alberta and British Columbia allow cooperatives to be formed explicitly to facilitate local investment. American cooperatives, in contrast, typically must be organized on behalf of consumers, producers, or workers – not investors. The exception is real estate and that explains the legal structures of the East Bay Permanent Real Estate Coop in Oakland, discussed earlier, and the Northeast Housing Coop in Minneapolis. In Alberta and

British Columbia, all types of local businesses can be acquired, started, run, and financed through a low-cost cooperative structure.

Even more impressive is the latitude provided by the province of Nova Scotia. In 1998, legislators enacted the Community Economic Development Investment Funds (CEDIF) Act, which laid out a simple process by which unaccredited investors can pool money and provide loans to local businesses. The funds must be for-profit and must have at least six directors elected from the community. Residents of Nova Scotia can place their tax-deferred retirement savings in these funds, provided they keep them there for at least five years, and they then qualify for a substantial tax credit.

Since the start, Nova Scotia, a province with a million people, has witnessed the birth of nearly 60 funds that have raised more than $63 million from 6,000 investors. All the funds support some form of local economic development, and several focus on helping farmers and local food businesses. If the United States had as many funds per capita, it would have more than 20,000 such community funds operating nationwide.

One reason why Nova Scotia passed the CEDIF law was an awareness that conventional investing was taking money out of the province. For example, Nova Scotians invest more than $600 million every year in RRSPs, the Canadian equivalent of IRAs, and only about 2% of that money was being invested in Nova Scotia.[18]

One of the more sophisticated grassroots funds in Nova Scotia is named FarmWorks, run by Linda Best.[19] Growing up on a farm in the Annapolis Valley and spending much of her childhood in 4H programs, Best's roots in agriculture run deep. "Back in the 1960s," she recalls,

> we had 12 thousand farms in Nova Scotia, and 60–70 percent of our food was being produced here. Now we have fewer than 4,000 thousand farms, and apart from supply managed dairy, chickens, and eggs, we probably only produce 10 percent of our food – maybe 20 percent if you count the milk, chicken, and eggs. We need to start rebuilding that food-producing infrastructure. A huge amount of our produce comes from Mexico, South America, and California, and how long can we rely on them?

As of late 2020, Farm Works just closed its ninth offering. It has invested nearly $4.5 million in 110 local farms and food businesses. Interest income covers the expenses of its mostly volunteer staff.

Next door to Nova Scotia is the small province of New Brunswick. Leaders there recently became so convinced of the value of local investing that they enacted a 50% provincial tax credit.[20] Every dollar over $1,000 invested in a qualified local business removes 50 cents from an investor's provincial tax bill. This law recently inspired a Michigan state legislator to introduce a similar bill in the name of post-COVID relief.

Conclusion

Despite impressive innovations around crowdfunding and community investment funds, the US capital marketplace is still effectively broken. Until at least 60% Americans' investment dollars go into the local businesses responsible for at least 60% of the economy, the market will continue to underfund local businesses and CSEs. Current levels of US local investment do not yet account for even 1% of long-term total investment. More significant legal reforms and CSE innovations such as those pioneered in Canada are needed. The CSEs prototyped there – investment cooperatives of Alberta and British Columbia and the community pension funds of Nova Scotia – could be enormously useful to their American neighbors in the south. It is worth noting, however, that these innovations have not fundamentally changed the capital marketplace in Canada either. Too many mainstream financial institutions have successfully convinced their customers – contrary to the available evidence – that the best investments are conventional stocks and bonds.

Ultimately fixing today's broken securities markets will require at least four stages of work:

- Stage I: Make it easier and cheaper for small businesses to issue securities to unaccredited local investors.
- Stage II: Make it easier and cheaper for those unaccredited investors to trade their shares on local stock exchanges.
- Stage III: Make it easier and cheaper for unaccredited investors to invest in local investment funds, where financial specialists can perform the hard work of choosing and trading local securities.
- Stage IV: Make it easier and cheaper for the fiduciaries running pensions, trusts, and other funds to place unaccredited clients' money into local investment pools.

These four changes must proceed in the above order. That is, few fiduciaries will begin to invest pension funds locally if there are few local investment funds with a track record of profitability. Likewise, few such funds will be established until there are local exchanges that allow the funds to buy and sell securities (illiquid securities are potentially worthless). And no local exchanges in a region will be set up until there are enough local securities to trade.

This logical sequencing underscores why it is inadvisable to begin with a Stage IV question like "How can my workplace localize my pension fund?" College organizers are now pushing for their campuses to divest from fossil fuel companies responsible for greenhouse-gas emissions and reinvest in community businesses, with little awareness that the infrastructure needed for redirecting those investments barely exists. They must be patient because we are barely at Stage I. That sounds like bad news, but a decade ago, we were not even at Stage 0.

Canada shows that jumping ahead to Stage III innovations, while inspiring and helpful for some communities, cannot provide much of a short cut. The entirety of North America is missing local stock exchanges that can help funds value their assets and provide liquidity to their investors. Only when larger pension funds in British Columbia, Alberta, and Nova Scotia begin moving capital into the investment coops and CEDIFs – measured, not in the billions of dollars, but in the trillions – could it be said that a significant shift is occurring.

In the United States, and to a lesser extent in Canada, a small number of grassroots investors are reinventing Stage IV with do-it-yourself (DIY) pension funds. Americans can use self-directed IRAs and Solo 401Ks to move their tax-deferred pension funds into local investment, and Canadians can use self-directed RRSPs. The CSEs providing these services are expensive and labor-intensive, but prices could come down as more providers enter the marketplace.

The bottom line is that until financial CSEs mature, the entire universe of local economic development will remain hobbled and tiny. Or perhaps that's the pessimist's conclusion. The optimist might observe supplementing existing CSEs (crowdfunding facilitators and community investment funds) with missing CSEs (local stock exchanges and local pension vehicles) could just begin to tip a critical mass of North Americans to invest in the local businesses with the lowest risks and highest returns. Time will tell who is right.

Notes

1 In Michael H. Shuman, *The Local Economy Solution: How Innovative, Self-Financing Pollinator Enterprises Can Grow Jobs and Prosperity* (White River Junction, VT: Chelsea Green, 2015), I offer an extensive discussion of CSEs under the descriptor of "pollinator businesses." The term "CSE" in this chapter is used here to adopt the language of this volume.

2 The Federal Reserve of the United States, "Financial Accounts of the United States, First Quarter 2019," June 2019, 3. All the financial assets of the U.S. households and nonprofits now total about $85 trillion, and all their liabilities total $16 trillion. Banking assets include checking ($1.6 trillion), savings ($9.7 trillion), and money market funds ($1.8 trillion). Long-term assets include stocks ($15.6 trillion), bonds ($5.6 trillion), mutual funds ($7.9 trillion), pension funds ($25.7 trillion), and insurance funds ($1.7 trillion).

3 Many "community finance" advocates, schooled in the Saul Alinsky tactics to pressure big banks to give community organizers money through the Community Reinvestment Act, have largely overlooked the larger role of securities.

4 The total number of business establishments with employees in 2015 was 6,872,350, of which 1,251,702 had more than 500 employees and were not considered small businesses. The total number of nonemployee businesses that year was 24,331,403. The 96% figure assumes that every business with more than 500 employees is not locally owned. These data were calculated by combining the U.S. Census Bureau's County Business Patterns (https://www.census.gov/programs-surveys/cbp.html) with its Nonemployer Statistics (https://www.census.gov/programs-surveys/nonemployer-statistics.html).

5 The most accessible free site providing access to the Dun & Bradstreet data, which also integrates several other national databases, is www.youreconomy.org.

6 By definition, publicly traded stocks and bonds cannot be considered local investments. Mutual funds, pension funds, and insurance funds are incentivized under the law to invest in publicly traded securities. For example, public markets provide legally required liquidity (many local investments, in contrast, cannot be easily resold). See Michael H. Shuman, *Local Dollars, Local Sense: How to Shift Your Money from Wall Street to Main Street and Achieve Real Prosperity* (White River Junction, VT: Chelsea Green, 2012).

7 IRS Integrated Business Data, https://www.irs.gov/statistics/soi-tax-stats-integrated-business-data (accessed August 24, 2019). The IRS does not provide profits per se, but a rough estimate is possible in all three business categories by dividing "Net Income (less deficit)" by "Total Business Receipts."

8 The SEC offers three different ways an investor can be deemed accredited. An investor must earn $200,000 per year individually, $300,000 per year as a couple, or have a household with $1 million of wealth (excluding the value of the house). A business is deemed accredited if it has assets over $5 million. How many Americans are actually accredited?

On the first two criteria, data from the Internal Revenue Service are helpful. In 2016, the most recent year for which data are available, the total number of tax filings above $200,000 (adjusted gross income) is 6,900,372. According to the U.S. Census, the population in 2016 was about 323 million. Even assuming that every tax filer above $200,000 was single, accredited investors would constitute 2.1% of the population. In fact, however, the number of taxpayers filing as a couple was 5,893,163 – about 85% of the total – and these taxpayers would be subjected to the higher threshold of $300,000. Because the IRS data are presented in a large bracket of $200,000–$500,000, we can only guess what the reduction would be. But a fair assessment would say that, by income, 1%–2% of the population is accredited.

On the third criterion of wealth, the web site DQYJA.com, which specializes in providing financial data, suggests that $1 million in wealth, excluding your home, puts you in the 91st percentile of American households. Since there are about 125 million American households, the site argues that 12,417,040 are "accredited investor households." The number of accredited investors would include the head of the household plus spouses. According to the 2010 Census, 48% of the households have a spouse. This would suggest about 18 million accredited investors or about 5.5% of the population.

The percentage of the population that is accredited has gone up over time with inflation, rising incomes, and rising stock portfolios. Many at the SEC, however, would like to raise these thresholds and make the accredited investor club more exclusive.

9 Fundera, a New York-based financial institution specializing in small business loans, claims that $17.2 billion is raised annually through crowdfunding sites in North America. See https://www.fundera.com/resources/crowdfunding-statistics (accessed October 4, 2019).

10 The North American Securities Administrators Association publishes an updated inventory. See https://www.nasaa.org/industry-resources/securities-issuers/intrastate-crowdfunding-directory/.

11 For a history of the JOBS Act, see Thaya Brook Knight, "A Walk Through the JOBS Act of 2012: Deregulation in the Wake of Financial Crisis," Cato Institute Policy Analysis 790, May 3, 2016, Retrieved from https://www.cato.org/publications/policy-analysis/walk-through-jobs-act-2012-deregulation-wake-financial-crisis (accessed July 12, 2020).

12 https://www.calvertimpactcapital.org/invest (accessed July 12, 2020).

13 https://www.cdfifund.gov/programs-training/Programs/new-markets-tax-credit/Pages/default.aspx (accessed July 12, 2020).

14 Shuman, supra note 6, pp. 184–191.

15 These examples are drawn from original case studies prepared from *Community Investment Funds*, Beckon et al., 2020. The case studies on the Boston Impact

Initiatives and the East Bay Permanent Real Estate Cooperative were done primarily by Amy Cortese. Those on Goodworks Evergreen and the Pioneer Valley Grows Investment Fund were done by the author. The details and quotes were drawn from interviews with fund managers and developers.
16 "AB-816 Cooperative Corporations: Worker Cooperatives (2015–2016)," California Legislative Information, August 12, 2015, https://leginfo.legislature.ca.gov/faces/billTextClient.xhtml?bill_id=201520160AB816
17 Beckon et al. (2020), pp. 61–72.
18 *Local Economy Solution*, supra note 1, p. 183.
19 This case study is elaborated in ibid., pp. 182–186.
20 https://www2.gnb.ca/content/gnb/en/departments/finance/taxes/credit.html

References

Beckon, B., Cortese, A., Shade, J., & Shuman, M. H. (2020). *Community Investment Funds: A How-to Guide for Building Local Wealth, Equity, and Justice* (monograph). Pioneer Valley, MA: Solidago Foundation.

Crowdfund Capital Advisors. (2020). "Small Business SOS: It's Time to Supercharge Local Crowdfunding to Unlock Needed Capital," September 16, 2020.

GoodWorks Ventures. (2020). https://goodworksventures.com

Lafrance, A. (2012). "Firm Dynamics: Variations in Profitability across Canadian Firms of Different Sizes, 2000–2009." *Research Paper for Statistics Canada*, 2012, Tables 5 & 7.

Shuman, M. H. (2012). *Local Dollars, Local Sense: How to Shift Your Money from Wall Street to Main Street and Achieve Real Prosperity.* White River Junction, VT: Chelsea Green.

Shuman, M. H. (2015). *The Local Economy Solution: How Innovative, Self-Financing Pollinator Enterprises Can Grow Jobs and Prosperity.* White River Junction, VT: Chelsea Green.

Shuman, M. H. (2020). *Put Your Money Where Your Life Is: How to Invest Locally Using Self-Directed IRAs and Solo 401ks.* San Francisco, CA: Berrett-Koehler.

Tankersley, J. (2020). A Trump Tax Break Is Not Spurring Tax Creation, Study Finds, *New York Times*, 17 June.

3

CREATING A SUPPORTIVE ENVIRONMENT FOR COMMUNITY ENTERPRISES

Bruce F. Seifer, Rhonda Phillips, and Norman Walzer

Introduction

Successfully launching and maintaining effective community-supported enterprises (CSEs) involves crucial activities. First, a recognized need for a local service threatened or that has been discontinued must be identified and accepted to the extent that local investors are motivated to act. Second, depending on the legal business structure used, the enterprise, per se, must be economically viable and sustainable in the long run. Third, the business opportunity must be communicated sufficiently to potentially interested residents that they rally others to invest time and/or funds in such a project. Equally important is for residents to patronize the business after it starts operations. Finally, the legal and environmental setting in the community must be conducive to this type of enterprise.

In some ways, the local legal and environment structure may be the most difficult element to overcome in launching a CSE. Financing practices, zoning or ordinances, and decisions by public leaders must foster, or at least be conducive, to investments by residents in a collective business. Investors must be able to leverage their capital and may need financial incentives similar to other privately owned businesses. Most important, conducive attitudes toward public investment, tax concessions, and other local characteristics must exist in the community, and these attitudes may have been built up over many years. For instance, Vermont (USA) was an early state in adopting Social Benefit Corporations that incentivizes various enterprises addressing community needs.

Vermont is relatively unique in that it is a small rural state faced with long-term economic changes forcing it to consider innovative approaches and adjustments. It has a progressive political philosophy that encourages innovative strategies by both the state and local governments. Its willingness to use new approaches has been key in being an early adopter of CSEs as an approach to retaining essential businesses threatened by closures, which would seriously limit the potential of small communities. The result is that communities in Vermont have succeeded in restarting essential local businesses such as grocery stores or restaurants, among other businesses, and has made them viable (Hewitt, 2010). Residents are willing to invest, and public policies are conducive to stimulating investment in these ventures.

This chapter discusses local and institutional arrangements needed to help CSEs prosper. It provides examples of CSEs in Vermont, starting with a discussion of building or enhancing a locally focused culture to foster them. The next section reviews the types of policies and programs in Burlington, Vermont with many also used throughout the state to foster CSE efforts. Several strategies and approaches designed to encourage the start-up of a range of locally owned and controlled, for-profit business enterprises, and nonprofit and civic organizations – the "social enterprises" – needed to foster well-being and build resiliency are discussed in detail.

Vermont and especially its largest city Burlington (2018 pop. 42,889) have led in community-supported and community-owned enterprises, since at least the early 1980s, and, prior to that time, promoted a supportive community environment. It is recognized for some of the most well-developed examples of how CSEs have been implemented successfully. Even though Vermont is one of the most rural states, with significant demographic changes including outmigration, it has created a highly supportive environment for community-owned and community-supported businesses and enterprises.

The situation in Vermont emphasizes the importance of authorizing statutes and a legislative environment that permits and fosters CSEs. Such supporting environments are found in other contexts, especially in rural areas and are key to successes as shown later. Strategies and approaches used in Burlington may guide other places struggling with similar issues; likewise, some of these strategies can be modified for a variety of contexts, especially in creating a supporting culture.

Overview

Community-owned businesses are growing in use especially in rural areas faced with possible losses of long-term locally owned businesses considered essential to their future viability. The need for innovative strategies to both sustain these businesses and transition them to new owners will be even more important in the future with demographic trends that predict population declines and growth in the elderly especially in rural areas. There is growing recognition that creating age-friendly communities can obtain substantial economic and social advantages from working with older residents (Neal & DeLa Torre, 2016). One potential advantage is access to local investment funds to support businesses.

As noted in Chapter 1, community-owned businesses are financed in many ways. The efforts with community pubs and community shops in England differ from approaches used in Vermont but lessons or insights can be gained from the diverse approaches and motivations. Detailed examples of community-owned shops and pubs are available in Plunkett (2019). Important in all these efforts is the institutional support available from both private and public sources. In Vermont, the Preservation Trust of Vermont (PTV) actively engaged community groups in organizing groups willing to invest and participate in local ventures ranging from reviving general stores such as Pierce's Store or the Hinesburgh Public House restaurant or reviving the historic Latchis Theater. These and many other examples of successful community-owned enterprises are described in more detail in Walzer and Sandoval (2016) and Walzer (2019).

The intended purpose of this chapter is to look behind the scenes to determine the types of support that both local and state governments can provide to foster community investments in local businesses. These insights can help understand how to build a community entrepreneurship eco-system that allows and encourages community leaders to recognize and seize opportunities to cause this investment. While many ventures closely resemble small businesses, they have an overriding common purpose which is to build social capital and make the community more viable for the future.

Locally focused businesses can aid a community in gaining benefits for all involved and help define a place. Community businesses and social enterprises help create a definitive sense of place with connections and relationships strengthened and thereby can help an area prosper with positive community development and community economic development approaches. Helping create this environment goes well beyond considering the quantitative aspects of an economy. Approaches of this type touch on myriad aspects central to community development and well-being such as social capital, sense of place, participatory and inclusive governance, innovation, and willingness to invest socially, financially, and emotionally in the host community.

As noted, locally focused businesses are also often socially minded and can play integral roles in communities. Tolbert (2005) describes these roles of locally oriented businesses and civic establishments as critical entities that

> are posited to benefit communities through an enhanced quality of life, more civic engagement by the citizenry, and a strong capacity for local problem solving. Locally oriented businesses have stakes in the local labor market, the local economy, the local infrastructure, and – usually – the local product market.
>
> *(p. 1311)*

These aspects of more civic engagement and building capacity are vital benefits of community-owned or locally focused enterprises. Tolbert reported that civic context can condition individual-level processes. For example, the presence of locally focused enterprises promotes civic behavior in young people. The Plunkett Foundation demonstrated the benefits to older residents actively engaged in volunteering or otherwise participating in community shops and pub activities (Plunkett, 2019). Further, Tolbert reports that better-educated residents are likely to exhibit civic behaviors. These analyses indicate a strong relationship between the presence of high levels of locally focused enterprises and more civic behaviors in communities. In the rural context, he suggests that one constant remains in communities – the presence of locally oriented enterprises and organizations – and that this basis be used for community and economic development.

Community Support and Co-Creation as Important Elements

Insights can also be gained from community-supported agriculture (CSAs), organizations that have a longer period of implementation and research. Although started by farmers in the mid-1980s as a way to sell directly to consumers, the model has spawned other CSEs such as community-supported fisheries, bakeries, yoga, and art enterprises (White, 2013). Restaurants such as the Bobcat Café in Bristol, Vermont use a modified CSA model (Preservation Trust of Vermont, 2020) as well "embracing the community-supported approach, but instead of receiving boxes of produce, those members are entitled to meals worth a specific dollar amount" (Kelley & Eller, 2018, p. 46). A somewhat similar arrangement is used in the Hinesburgh Public House (Walzer & Sandoval, 2016).

While specific CSAs may differ in operations, there are commonalities such as building connections between producers and consumers with resulting increases in satisfaction and loyalty (Kelley & Eller, 2018, p. 46). White describes the tenets on which CSAs have been founded as including those that "emphasize a symbiosis of sustainable livelihoods for farmers and consumers, interdependent local communities, and ecologically nurtured landscapes (while) CSA also privileges meeting local needs over expanding markets geographically" (White, 2013, p. 6). This model provides an excellent example for considering the "potential of diverse community-based economics in a larger context beyond agriculture" (p. 7) that can help support and grow enterprises at the community level.

This new way of thinking about creating and supporting CSEs is gaining ground, especially given a paucity of choices for other economic activity in some communities especially those in rural areas. A member of the Vermont Agency of Agriculture, Food, and Markets explains:

> Community Supported Agriculture has become a familiar part of Vermont's economic landscape. Today, there are similar models emerging in other business fields – 'Community Supported Enterprises.' This concept responds to the idea that many businesses, especially in Vermont's most rural areas, play an irreplaceable part in community life that isn't captured in the daily sales transactions. Customers and community members are willing to honor that role through creative financial support that can take many forms.
>
> *(Jordan, 2020)*

There seem to be strong connections between locally focused businesses and social entrepreneurship characteristics by owners. In other words, positioning one's business in a way that embeds and connects it to the host community for purposes beyond the immediate need for financial profitability benefits all involved. A case of a community-supported baker in Arizona provides insights into this approach. Seeking to help develop the community's local food system and create a business, a baker developed a model of consumer co-creation. This model "positions customers not only as the purchasers of his product, but also as marketers of his breads, promoters of local grains, and champions of the Southern Arizona food movement" (Mars, 2015, p. 63). The case explores entrepreneurial leadership as a pivotal element in the consumer co-creation model, including ways to build community with not only individual consumers but also organizations (such as schools). This arrangement effectively creates a "community co-creation" effect via experiential learning and engagement while promoting the value of local food production and consumption. Arizona has supportive policies for business development, including for cooperatives (with multiple members or owners) and for-benefit corporations (enabling a business to serve a social as well as a profit purpose).

This co-creation strategy and approach can be very beneficial in the community development context and can be applied in a variety of community capacity building efforts to increase assets. For example, the PTV provides information and resources for CSEs, including an innovative initiative by 28 local investors in Vergennes, Vermont who formed a limited liability corporation (LLC) to renovate a significant downtown historic building for mixed use (Preservation Trust of Vermont, 2020). Vermont has traditionally embraced innovative approaches that support business and enterprise development, including passing a variety of state legislation discussed later in this chapter.

Another CSE success story is the Latchis Theater and Hotel complex in downtown Brattleboro, Vermont. Spanning over a three-year period, this project combined historic preservation with placemaking and enterprise. Box 3.1 provides a synopsis of the story, written by Paul Bruhn, previous PTV director, who enabled much success for CSEs in the state.

BOX 3.1 THE LATCHIS THEATER AND HOTEL COMPLEX BY PAUL BRUHN

The acquisition phase of the Latchis Complex in downtown Brattleboro is now complete. It was a complex three-year process including many adjustments in the original plan, and even Planet Mercury played a role in the final steps.

(Continued)

How it Happened, the First Steps

Fifteen years ago, the Latchis complex in downtown Brattleboro was in derelict condition. That was when Spero Latchis returned to rescue the property that had been built in the 1930s as a tribute to his grandfather. Ever since, Spero and his wife Elizabeth have spent their lives rehabilitating the Art Deco site room by room and piece of furniture by piece of furniture; they have been great stewards. The day-in and day-out work of improving the property and operating it had taken a toll, and in 2000, they decided to sell the property that included:

- a 30-room hotel plus 10 additional rooms that needed rehabilitation,
- three retail spaces that are fully occupied,
- a full-service restaurant and brew pub, and
- three operating movie theaters, the largest of which seats 779.

The Latchis is one of Vermont's great architectural treasures. It was completed in 1938 as a tribute to Demetrius P. Latchis, a Greek immigrant who started selling fruit from a cart and built a business that included 3 hotels and 15 movie theaters. The Latchis was the gem – Greek murals, statues of Greek gods and goddesses adorn the theater and public spaces, complete with exquisite terrazzo floors throughout.

After learning of Spero and Elizabeth's plan, the Preservation Trust began the process of looking for a local organization interested in preserving this irreplaceable part of Brattleboro. The Brattleboro Arts Initiative, with a mission to develop and promote high-quality venues for the presentation and education of the visual and performing arts, saw this as a once-in-a-lifetime opportunity for an arts facility in southeastern Vermont. It is also an opportunity to play a key role in the effort to revitalize downtown Brattleboro – a community that has had some major challenges over the most recent past. The Book Press with its 300 manufacturing jobs closed last year, Vermont National Bank was taken over by the Chittenden, and many top management jobs were lost, a Walmart located across the Connecticut River has had a negative impact on downtown retailing, and a mortgage processing center was moved to Maine. Despite these and other challenges, the community understood that the Latchis could be the key to a better future, and the Brattleboro Arts Initiative leaped at the opportunity.

Fundraising And Acquisition

In partnership, BAI and the Preservation Trust then began the process of raising $1.4 million for the acquisition plus the funds necessary for project management, interest costs, fundraising, and an operating reserve. In the best of economic times, it would have been a near Herculean task, but the good economic times disappeared, making the task even more challenging.

BAI concentrated their efforts on local sources including individuals, businesses, and foundations interested in the Brattleboro area. Together, BAI and the Preservation Trust worked on developing state support. And, finally, the Preservation Trust sought support from foundations and lenders.

Ultimately, more than $1.3 million was raised as a result of great generosity on the part of many. An additional $550,000 was provided by a variety of lenders committed to downtown Brattleboro and the arts. Because of the complex nature of the acquisition and multiple lenders, closing was complicated. The fact that Mercury was in retrograde (a concern of the owners) at the time of the original closing date meant that the acquisition wasn't completed until mid-March!

Next Steps, Operations, and Rehabilitation

With the acquisition complete, BAI (and its subsidiary the Latchis Corporation) tackled the challenges of day-to-day operations. A general manager was hired to oversee the hotel operations, movie business, and property rentals as well as coordinate the BAI's arts programming needs.

Of special importance, BAI established a Building Committee to advise them on developing a plan to rehabilitate the Complex. The Committee includes representation from the community as well as from the Preservation Trust. The first step involves a plan for $300,000 of federal funding obtained for the project by Senator Patrick Leahy.

Over time, BAI plans to develop the complex to provide expanded live performance as well as space for the visual arts and arts education activity. As "the Latchis" metamorphoses into "the Latchis Center for the Visual and Performing Arts," the history, identity, and heritage of this cultural cornerstone will remain intact, while a new artistic energy will emerge. Just as the original Latchis reflected the arts and culture of its times, so the new Center will stand; in Shakespeare's words, as a "mirror held up to nature," reflecting back to us a contemporary vision of our modern times.

Source: Preservation Trust of Vermont, May 15, 2003

Local Focus

Pending demographic trends with potential aging of residents and population declines in rural areas means that more attention is being paid to encouraging local economy development and ways that state governments can promote these efforts. These efforts include buying local campaigns and promoting more locally connected businesses. The issues, however, go far beyond buying locally approaches as noted by Shuman (2015). Increasing awareness of locally focused businesses has been described as a way to create community enterprises or a business culture that becomes more sustainable and helps foster desirable community development outcomes over time. Socially responsible and vested enterprises (both public and nonprofit) along with culturally competent businesses and organizations can create more sustainable economies (Phillips, Seifer & Antzcak, 2013).

Socially responsible business is an important element to consider with locally focused businesses or community-owned and supported enterprises since businesses with a higher level of social responsibility will possibly help the local or regional economy be more sustainable. Co-founder of the Business Alliance for Local Living Economies (BALLE), an organization that promotes locally focused and socially responsible businesses, Michael Schuman elaborates on this issue in *The Small-Mart Revolution* (Shuman, 2007). He proposes that local ownership is a critical aspect within communities when fostering more sustainable economies for several reasons, including that locally focused businesses generate long-term wealth, and entrepreneurs are less likely to leave the community.

Also, there are typically fewer destructive exits and upheavals in a community's economy due to a variety of locally focused businesses adding diversification, higher labor and environmental standards with often a commitment to sustainability (such as buying local for sources), and higher economic multipliers with local spending two to four times that of other types.

Another reason is that local or community-owned enterprises can strengthen an area's prosperity. Some of these businesses can help an area transition to a more sustainable economy. Likewise, when local government policies support efforts to produce more goods and services that would otherwise be imported at higher total costs (including energy, affordable housing, and food), the economy becomes more sustainable.

Support for CSEs

Local and regional governments that design policies and regulations to strengthen community-owned and supported enterprises help ensure that area residents can choose from locally provided goods and services rather than importing a majority of people's needs. This situation, in turn, leads to more desirable community development outcomes especially around trust, reciprocity, and support as basic elements of community development. Because CSEs are often more deeply invested in their locality, other dimensions of community such as social, environmental, and educational aspects may be enhanced. This type of orientation or culture can lead to more long-term and sustainable relationships between enterprise and local/regional governments.

In addition, strong local economic ownership of enterprises helps promote a community's prosperity because these enterprises can serve both local and global markets in many cases. Reasons for these local benefits include that when local government policy support a focus on producing more needed goods and services otherwise imported, the economy often strengthens and builds resiliency (Phillips, Seifer & Antczak, 2013). Those governments able to respond to these opportunities emerge as leaders with policies and programs providing things people need locally rather than importing a majority of products and services. This situation, in turn, enhances community development and well-being processes and outcomes. Many community-supported businesses start small, are generated from within a local economy, or attracted there because of similarly focused enterprises already in the area. These vested organizations tend to be tied more closely with and committed to their host community.

This situation, in turn, can build more social capacity; and the more social capacity a community has, the more likely it can adapt to and work around deficiencies in other types of community capitals (Phillips & Pittman, 2015). Having strong social capital networks in a community is often what makes the difference in resilient responses when facing challenges. Community capitals are essentially the assets of an area; the community capitals framework was created by Cornelia and Jan Flora to map impacts of these capitals on communities. If these capitals can be leveraged, then communities more often succeed with their economy, environment, and social systems. The seven community capitals are financial, built, social, human, cultural, natural, and political (Flora & Flora, 2008). Local and regional policies and regulations can help foster an environment that strengthens community capital, such as community business financing programs and participatory decision-making including plan development and setting priorities.

Burlington, Vermont Context

Burlington is located on the shores of Lake Champlain separating Vermont from upstate New York and Canada. It is relatively small in a metropolitan area of approximately one-third of the entire population of Vermont (2018 pop. 623,000). A state of widely renowned beauty, Vermont has often led the nation with innovative, transformative legislation and approaches in economic, social, and environmental domains. It is predominately rural and depends mainly on agriculture and tourism sectors. There are, however, many enterprises in the state that produce technology or products (such as Seventh Generation or Burton Snowboards).

Burlington has a long history as a leader in innovative economic and community development programs, policies, and overall environment supportive especially of both sustainability and locally focused enterprise. A review of Burlington's journey toward creating a durable, sustainable economy and socially inclusive system shows that it is "one of those unique places that can't be ignored; it is different and in that difference is something special – a palpable, indomitable community spirit that has helped shape an award-winning city" (Phillips, Seifer & Antczak, 2–13: xvi).

Culture has been a defining aspect of communities, and in the case of CSEs, it may play an even more important role than realized at first glance. Why? Because locally focused businesses and CSEs reflect their place, and this is one of the aspects that can make them a special attraction for residents and visitors alike. Burlington has a unique and definitive culture, one that has been supported in its development through the years by residents, businesses and civic sector, and local governance organizations. The idea of building businesses with strong ties to the local culture and the uniqueness of a place is an underlying foundation for this city's efforts in promoting CSEs.

Strategies

Burlington was in the situation that many other cities faced during a time of rapid suburban growth surrounding city limits: how to generate tax revenues to balance economic demands with social and environmental needs when physical boundary growth is not an option? A creative, new way of thinking emerged that continues to support existing businesses while improving worker skills and community capacity for future opportunities. Fueled by the City of Burlington, the Community and Economic Development Office (CEDO) helped foster partnerships across the public, nonprofit, and private sectors to serve as an idea incubator for enterprise. CEDO spawned more than two dozen nonprofit organizations and helped hundreds of businesses start or expand in Burlington.

The choice of a locally focused enterprise development strategy, from a community economic development perspective, is based on several assumptions. These include a recognition that locally focused businesses provide more stable employment opportunities since decisions tend to be made by owners who are residents and are vested in the long-term health of the Burlington economy and community. Also, locally focused businesses tend to retain and invest more wages and profits in the area by local employees and owners and are more likely to hire, train, and promote residents with quality job opportunities.

The overarching economic development approach centers on the concept of locally focused and owned businesses – fusing local business opportunity with employee development. Now, nearly 40 years later, Burlington still follows this community economic development framework, due to an unwavering belief in supporting and fostering a strong local economy. Recent experiences show that this approach has succeeded in helping to revive and sustain the local economy.

The next sections provide examples of strategies, programs, and supporting legislation or policies regarding several key elements in Burlington's efforts to build a local economy supportive of community-focused businesses, enterprises, and organizations. The first provides information about a supportive environment for CSEs; the second is about employee ownership; and the third presents a section on financing. All three elements are important – creating a supportive environment, developing interest in and fostering more local ownership, and providing capital and financing pathways for CSEs.

Building a Supportive Environment

Much is written about culture but less so about how culture influences business development such as CSEs. It is a crucial element since intangibles like culture (which could be defined most simply as what any specific group of people do and say), influence ability to thrive. Things like acceptance, tolerance, openness to new ideas and new things, fairness in access to capital, and other dimensions greatly impact enterprises. Vermont, not surprisingly, has an open feel in its culture and especially regarding small businesses. Some say that support for local enterprise is baked into the cultural DNA of Burlington and Vermont. Box 3.2 presents a conversation with the founder of Vermont's Front Porch Forum (FPF) and provides a feel of the culture there.

BOX 3.2 INTERVIEW WITH MICHAEL WOODS LEWIS, FOUNDER FRONT PORCH FORUM BY BRUCE F. SEIFER AUGUST 1, 2020

What is Front Porch Forum (FPF)? FPF is a place to get together online. You can talk to your neighbors about whatever you want. It is a flexible channel for conversations. You can work on neighborhood projects, so when hard times come, social capital is built up with neighbors who have worked together over time. They then have had a starting point, not just flame wars, bullying, and mocking. Bonds are shored up among neighbors. It is a catalyst – without FPF thousands of micro-businesses would not have launched. There are 185,000 FPF Vermont members, representing about 160,000 household members. Vermont has in total 260,000 households.

> This network of 185 forums covers each town in Vermont as well as a handful in neighboring New York and New Hampshire. 50% of users post on the forum, while 79% take 'off-line actions' due to their membership on their local forum.
>
> (The Verge Feature article, 2019)

There are 10,000 businesses in the FPF directory, with profiles created by the businesses themselves. FPF started in 2000 in the Five Sister's neighborhood of Burlington, incorporated 2006, and went statewide in 2013 and mobile launch in 2019. FPF became a For Benefit Corporation in 2019 and has 20 staff members, many part-time with three in-house engineers. It is a full-time business and staff work in five teams headed by managers.

What is the FPF Business model? FPF provides access to and for small businesses, governments, and elected and appointed officials. Elected and appointed officials are charged a fee to post to their constituents. FPF

(*Continued*)

conducts fundraising every October and members chip in generously. They also sell ads. In 2020, FPF is on schedule with earnings, revenues, and expenses for a robust year because of the model.

Why did FPF choose the Public Benefit Corporation structure? Initially, the FPF was incorporated in 2006 and then switched to a Public Benefit Corporation in 2019. It was a great move since they had always behaved like one, but now, it is formalized. It is helpful so members will donate money more easily; it's easier to get grants from foundations. The mission is aligned with future employees' perspectives, and it is easier to find new employees. The business model allows people with different lifestyles to work there and is willing to work on their social mission.

How does community support help your business? Members contribute money voluntarily, and FPF is cash flow positive. Last October's annual appeal raised their goal. In March 2020, due to the pandemic, FPF asked for donations over a two-day period and raised more funds for support during these unusual times. People take ownership of FPF due to nature of the design of the business.

How does the FPF help CSEs? FPF connects people with local businesses, government, and other community members. People can reach out to their constituencies (i.e., neighbors, customers, and electorate). FPF boosts businesses via postings on the forum.

Examples of success stories:

1. A roofer in the Northeast Kingdom region of Vermont needed more clients. With a $300–$400 advertisement, he was able to promote his business and now reports that he is so busy responding to jobs that he does not have time to do office work.
2. Timely Tire has a similar story. Their at-home tire changeover business needed more clients and, with an ad, have become much more successful.
3. Twincraft soap maker ran ads to hire employees. They stopped ads sooner because they found plenty of qualified workers. They got a different caliber of employees then running ads through the regular channels to find workers.

Has an evaluation been done on the FPF? The Robert Wood Johnson Foundation conducted an evaluation in 2017, surveying 10,000 people. Conclusion of its evaluation was: Most powerful aspect of FPF is, for example, a forum of 500 people witnessing small acts of neighborliness every few days; people are isolated otherwise. It is a taste of neighborliness which packs the biggest punch. See the report at: Robert Wood Johnson Foundation survey report.

What is the scale and ecosystem for FPF? Michael wonders if he could do this in a large urban environment; he thinks that it would take too much money to reach everyone. In Vermont, he could start small and grow at a human scale. It is easier to start in a small community, but it is much easier to start and be successful in a small *vibrant* community. This is important because vibrant communities have more vibrant FPFs; there is an innate organic momentum in these types of communities, supporting FPF to grow. The culture in Burlington and Vermont supports the ecosystem – not necessary to educate people about buying local – it's baked in – "Buy local, click local, invest local, volunteer local."

A state of small towns, Vermont has long been committed to helping "Main Street" thrive. In 1994, the Vermont Downtown Program (VDP) was established to provide technical assistance and training to communities and help them develop skills and strategies for downtown revitalization efforts. It is part of the Vermont Department of Historic Preservation. Burlington had a role in this – the City of Burlington had been playing defense fighting the development of a mall outside its city limits in nearby Williston. A large sprawling retail development seven miles from downtown Burlington was proposed in a green field. The City of Burlington spent 17 years fighting the project including going to court to stop it sometimes working with a citizen group, Citizens for Responsible Growth (CRG) from Williston. Several CRG members had experience working at the iconic ice cream company, Ben and Jerry's, so were well aware of how a socially minded organization can work. The PTV, Chittenden County Regional Planning Commission, and Vermont Natural Resources Council all played a role in fighting the project.

After 17 years of the resistance, the developer of the mall negotiated with the City of Burlington out of court to stop the legal battle. They agreed to redesign the mall with a village green, a two-story retail and office complex surrounding the green. It also included community amenities including a pond, walking path, village green, outdoor community entertainment, and outdoor seating. A second floor was built for office space above the retail space of which some were configured around the village green. None of the larger retail development could be bigger than 50,000 square feet.

The economics of strip malls are that large department stores, at least 100,000 square feet in size, pay lower costs per square foot. Smaller retailers pay significantly more money per square feet. The compromise is that the department stores are the anchors that spend significant amounts of money (hundreds of thousands of dollars) in advertising to attract shoppers to the mall. Small retailers cannot usually pay for this type and level of advertising and rely on foot traffic from the department store customers.

Recognizing the needs of small retailers, the City of Burlington worked to accomplish the following: (1) attract the department store to locate a 150,000-square-foot two-story department store in its downtown shopping mall, (2) expand the downtown mall to attract additional smaller retailers, and (3) build a 600-space parking garage. Using different media to fight sprawl was effective, especially "the Wal," a freestanding structure on Church Street (the main street of the historic downtown area). It engaged people in the effort, made for a great visual for television news coverage, and shoppers strolling by were intrigued enough to stop and chat or sign the Wal in protest against locating a Walmart in Burlington. The Wal was so successful that other towns in Vermont started using it in their own towns in fighting against Walmart locations. Hundreds of news articles were written about the City's struggle against sprawl.

The department store required the City of Burlington to raise $8 million to upgrade the downtown mall, build a parking garage, and provide two hours of free parking in all city parking garages. To raise the $8 million, the City pieced together funding from several sources. One involved designing and creating the VDP as part of the State's Commerce and Community Development agency; the program was approved by the Vermont Legislature. Later, the City of Burlington secured $2 million from the VDP to pay for a portion of the department store's development and the new parking garage.

In addition to literally fighting on behalf of small business, the CEDO and the state took other actions to build and support a culture for CSEs. One major action to note was creating legislation to enable a "for benefit" designation for private businesses. In essence, it allows private businesses to have a social mission in addition to a profit mission. The benefit corporation law allows creation of new and voluntary corporate entities that can consider profit as well as society and the environment (Benefitcorp.net, 2020). Vermont was the first state to pass benefit corporation legislation; this was in 2009 and implemented in 2011. Now, 36 states have legislation with others considering it.

A form of public benefit corporation, B Lab, a nonprofit dedicated to advancing social progress with business, describes for a benefit corporation status as follows:

> This form of incorporation allows a business to balance fiduciary duty between its shareholders and stakeholders. States have passed benefit corporation laws to encourage business growth, provide options for entrepreneurs and to attract the sizable social impact investment community to create new opportunities for economic growth.
>
> *(Benefitcorp, 2020, p. 1)*

The attorney who helped advance the initial legislation had served for years on the Vermont Businesses for Social Responsibility (VBSR) Board of Directors. This nonprofit group takes an advocacy role to influence Vermont legislation to support for benefit and other businesses to promote better economic, community, environmental, and social development outcomes in the state. It is notable that VBSR is one of the first organizations of its type in the US and has helped create the supportive regulatory and policy culture in Vermont.

Comparable legislation had passed previously in 2008 to allow a low-profit limited liability (L3C) designation that provided tax and regulatory benefits of LLCs while also permitting pursuit of social mission. Vermont was the first state in the US to provide this type of legislation for low-profit LLCs. Under the state law, an LLC may elect to become an L3C if it meets the following requirements:

- The company significantly furthers the accomplishment of one or more charitable or educational purposes within the meaning of legislation pertaining to these purposes.
- Would not have been formed but for the company's relationship to the accomplishment of charitable or educational purposes.
- No significant purpose of the company is the production of income or the appreciation of property.
- No purpose of the company is to accomplish one or more political or legislative purposes within the meaning of legislation regarding charitable contributions and gifts (Vermont Secretary of State, 2020).

Other actions to help foster a supportive environment for CSEs include the City issuing a $11.3 million Municipal City bond for energy efficiency through the Burlington Electric Department. These customers include businesses, both large and small, and have helped by saving energy costs as well as keeping $11 million in Burlington's economy each year that would have left the region to purchase energy.

Employee Ownership

Employee ownership can also strengthen ties between business and community since it blurs the ways businesses operate, making them more similar to a social enterprise in many aspects. Empowering employees as owners builds a capacity that spills over to the community where employee-owned enterprises are located. There are several types of employee ownership structures including worker-owned cooperatives that can serve a variety of purposes (National Center for Employee Ownership, 2020).

Burlington has long geared its policies, support, and orientation toward employee ownership and community-supported enterprises and businesses. CEDO started a group to design and initiate policies for employee ownership; this group later evolved into a state-wide organization, the Vermont Employee Ownership Center (VEOC). This is one of the nonprofits that CEDO helped launch by providing $5,000 in seed funding when started in 2001. VEOC has since become a valuable resource by providing counseling, access to various funds, and promoting employee ownership to business owners throughout Vermont.

The success of the VEOC is shown by more than 40 employee-owned businesses in the state, employing more than 3,000 people (VEOC, 2020). They provide support services, counseling and help with identifying funding to businesses interested in converting to an employee-owned structure. In 2005, the VEOC established a revolving loan fund to support the development of and retention of employee-owned businesses in Vermont. The Vermont Employee Ownership Loan Fund provides capital to businesses that are already employee-owned or are becoming so through the purchase of stock or business assets as well as start-ups to be owned by most of the employees. Proceeds may be used for fixed assets, working capital, financing worker shares in cooperatives, or the funding of Employee Stock Ownership Plans.

Cooperatives are enjoying a resurgence of interest and can serve rural areas as well as urban areas with producer, distribution, and other types of functions (Gonzales & Phillips, 2013). One such example is The Adamant Coop in Adamant, Vermont that is a community hub, post office, art studio, grocery store, and a "third space" for residents of a town of 276. It even hosts the annual Black Fly Festival described as a "cult classic" in the state (Preservation Trust of Vermont, 2020).

CEDO started working with nonprofit and cooperative organizations in the 1980s and has since helped establish more than 20 new organizations, many of which now serve not only Burlington but also the entire state of Vermont. They succeeded by supporting start-up and expansion needs, just as private for-profit entrepreneurs receive but calibrated for the unique needs of nonprofits. In other words, they support social entrepreneurs and their efforts to grow these organizations in the community. An example of an organization that CEDO helped expand includes City Market, a coop located in downtown Burlington that has subsequently become one of the most successful in the US.[1]

There are several benefits to a community of employee ownership including retention of local jobs. An owner can sell to the employees, helping keep the legacy of the enterprise alive. Because businesses can be very vested and rooted in a community, it allows more people to join in wealth creation and community enhancements via enterprises committed to the area.

An additional benefit is that employee ownership can "improve business performance, when employee ownership is combined with participation in decision-making, businesses often see significant increases in performance" (Phillips, Seifer & Antczak, 2013). One of the most successful examples of employee ownership is Gardener's Supply in Burlington, now a 100% employee-owned company with sales nationally and beyond. Founded in 1984, it was always about the community with the owner spearheading an effort to restore the floodplain by the river's edge in Burlington. Now, an agricultural showcase model studied nationally, and beyond, the Intervale is a 350-acre farm nonprofit incubator breadbasket, serving as an educational and production center for the city and region producing over one million pounds of food annually. It exemplifies how community-focused enterprise can co-create much benefit with their host community. Gardener's Supply worked with the CEDO to formulate plans soon after it started to establish an employee ownership program (ESOP) for employees to earn stock and share in company profits. By 2009, the company had grown ten-fold and sold 100% ownership to employees (Seifer, Antzcak & Phillips, 2020). Burlington had an employee ownership policy and program already developed, and it helped Gardener's Supply transition to a full employee ownership model for retaining and growing the business.

Another innovative strategy is the Burlington Local Ownership Project, designed by CEDO to encourage the start-up of several locally owned and controlled, for-profit business enterprises, and nonprofit and civic organizations – the "social enterprises" needed to foster well-being and build resiliency. This program serves individually owned start-ups, family-owned start-ups, and employee-owned businesses. It uses several strategies in developing locally focused and owned businesses including:

1. Improving substitution start-ups where a new, locally owned business is started to produce a product or a service that large local employers must now import from out of state. Large employers stand to benefit from these enterprises by a ready, convenient source of supply that reduces their need to carry excess inventory. New, locally owned enterprises receive a temporary, sheltered, local market that can assist a company in early start-up stages.
2. Conventional, entrepreneurial start-ups where local entrepreneurs proceed to organize a locally owned business on the strength of a new product or service idea designed for multiple markets – local, national, and international. Likely sources of new business ideas can include university research and development centers, oriented toward encouraging local ownership.
3. Conversions of retiring owner businesses where current financially healthy, local businesses find no likely or desirable conventional outside buyer and where local, internal management, or management/employee groups move to purchase the firm themselves (CEDO, 2000).

Financing

Access to capital is essential for small businesses and often contributes to success or failure (Matthew, Thomas, Lumina & Fitza, 2017). Many communities have community-based financing funds, such as revolving loan funds or peer-to-peer lending by successful entrepreneurs lending to those starting up or expanding. Others may have grant programs to encourage start-ups or expansions. Burlington and Vermont have been innovative in creative financing for small businesses, and several programs and initiatives have subsequently been developed, funded, and adopted at the state level to scale up access.

Successful and innovative programs include the VDP providing capital to projects as mentioned in a prior section. The City of Burlington conceived of and helped establish this program which works throughout the state to bring resources (tax credits and grants) along with training and technical services to help affiliated or designated downtown organizations preserve and revitalize historic downtowns. This program, in turn, fosters strong communities and supports CSEs since downtown businesses often are locally focused, locally owned, and vested in helping communities thrive. Many more organizations exist because CEDO was motivated to establish a system to expand finance for small businesses and to support start-ups. Here is a summary of similar initiatives:

- *Vermont Development Credit Union* (now called Opportunity Credit Union). Takes deposits for members of the community, municipalities, religious orders, and foundations.
- *Vermont Community Loan Fund* (VCLF) expanded into business lending (from only housing lending) throughout Vermont. Takes deposits and is a community development financial institution (CDFI). In 1994, the VCLF created the Small Business Loan Program to support small businesses in Vermont which provide a majority of Vermont jobs. CEDO suggested expanding from solely affordable housing lending into business lending. CEDO provided $10,000 to develop a market feasibility study to show the need for VCLF to expand into business lending after previously resisting. From 1994 to May 2020, it loaned $28,294,093 to businesses that leveraged into $43,486,617 with 3,587 jobs created or retained. In 1996, it became a CDFI, recognized, and funded by the Federal government.
- *Burlington Revolving Loan Fund* uses stimulus money and ongoing support from Community Development Block Grants (CBDG) and USDA funds to provide $10 million to 140 clients over three decades. Seifer, an author of this chapter, was hired in 1983 to establish and run this program for three decades. The purpose is to serve businesses without enough collateral or equity, and the establishment of funding mechanisms to support small businesses to create jobs for low- and moderate-income people has been important in Burlington. The default rate has been less than 1%. There was a realization of a shortage of a variety of funds needed by businesses. Banks were not making loans under $25,000, and this fund could not meet all the needs but helped address shortages. The criteria for the Loan Fund were to create livable wage jobs and revitalize low- and moderate-income neighborhoods.
- *Vermont Economic Development Authority* (VEDA) was a partner to establish and support the development of business incubator buildings in Burlington. Part of a warehouse district became a node of business incubation through this program and later became a recognized arts and industrial district, hosting the largest annual art festival in Vermont, the Art Hop (Phillips, Seifer & Brennan, 2020). There is a long history since the 1990s with business incubation when CEDO helped create a low-interest loan program from VEDA to establish and support development of incubator buildings. CEDO conceptualized a project to renovate a former bakery, creating 25,000 square

feet of incubator space for businesses. CEDO helped obtain VEDA affordable financing to redevelop this property and spurred revitalization in that area of the city.

- *Vermont Sustainable Jobs Fund* (VSJF) was created by CEDO after the 1994 *Jobs and People Report* and championed by the VBSR with state legislation passed in 1995 with funding provided. The mission is to nurture sustainable development in the Vermont economy, providing business assistance, strategic planning, network development, and value chain facilitation in selected industries. The VSJF provides creative financing in the form of near equity capital (subordinated debt and royalty financing) to growth-stage companies in sustainable agriculture and food systems, forest products, and clean technology. Named the Flexible Capital Fund or Flex Fund, it is the only licensed lender offering royalty financing and invests in companies to help strengthen or fill gaps in their supply chain.
- *Phase 0 Grant Program.* CEDO worked with the Vermont Experimental Program to Stimulate Competitive Research (EPSCoR) using a Phase 0 Grant program that has been replicated in all EPSCoR programs around the US. This program identifies promising proposals in Federal Small Business Innovation Research competitions, a US Small Business Administration program, that benefit start-ups with financial support and reviewer comments.
- *Working Lands Grant Program.* Initiated by the Public Policy Committee of the VBSR, the Vermont Department of Agriculture provides several hundred thousand dollars a year to stimulate the supply chain in agriculture in Vermont. Just recently, the legislature allocated them $5 million from the COVID-19 funds to help the agricultural sector in Vermont. This is mentioned because many growers and processors in Vermont's food supply chain are small businesses.

In 1995, CEDO collaborated with the National Community Development Association to (1) codify Micro-Businesses in the US Housing and Urban Development's CBDG regulations. A definition of micro-businesses was created along with eligibility authorized to receive CDBG support; (2) 1% of CDBG funds at the grantee level must be reserved for micro-business development. Approximately $60 million per year is provided for technical assistance, grants, loans, and other financial assistance to establish, stabilize, and expand micro-enterprises. Micro-enterprises are the smallest, least visible portion of the business world, but can be one of the major job generators in the economy.

Summary

Burlington and the State of Vermont successfully developed and use a locally focused business and community-owned enterprise approach to community economic development that promote CSEs through local focus, policy aspects, and building a supportive culture as summarized in this chapter. The process of developing these ventures continues.

Much remains to be learned about CSEs. As mentioned, research and practice in this area needs more attention as a relatively newer field of application. The model also builds on and is similar in context to that of CSAs, which has a longer history starting in the early 1980s. Commonalities across the models include more civic participation and connection with the local host community. Ideas around co-creation of enterprises and communities help to see the embeddedness that can exist between CSEs and their communities.

Burlington is a case study of how a local government, in partnership with the private, public, and nonprofit sectors, can develop and implement creative strategies and supporting legislative and regulatory environments for CSEs. Fostering local ownership and employee-owned models and providing support for their development have made a difference in Burlington and indeed, the state of Vermont. Many innovations were piloted in Burlington and then adopted at the state level such as financing programs and supportive legislation. These creative efforts garnered national attention and results, including new programs or changes made to existing programs that now serve the rest of the country. So, one community can make a difference with a focus and strategy on CSEs.

CSEs provide an avenue for communities to grow more resilient, locally focused businesses and organizations that help support the goals of their communities. The efforts described in this chapter can serve as inspiration to other communities seeking to support growth and development of CSEs in their areas.

Note

1 For an in-depth exploration of the development of City Market, please see *Sustainable Communities, Creating a Durable Local Economy* by R. Phillips, B. Seifer and E. Antczak, Earthscan, 2013.

References

Benefitcorp.net. (2020). *Vermont Benefit Corporation How-To-Guide: Incorporating as a Benefit Corporation Step-by-Step.* Downloaded August 22 from: https://benefitcorp.net/sites/default/files/documents/Vermont_Benefit_Corp_How_To_Guide.pdf

Flora, C. B. & Flora, J. L. (2008). *Rural Communities: Legacy and Change* (3rd Edition). Boulder, CO: Westview Press.

Gonzales, V. & Phillips, R. (2013). *Cooperatives and Community Development.* London: Routledge.

Hewitt, B. (2010). *The Town That Food Saved: How One Community Found Vitality in Local Food.* Emmaus, PA: Rodale Books.

Jordan, H. L. (2020). Community Supported Enterprises. Quote downloaded June 5 from: https://ptvermont.org/our-work/cse/.

Kelley, C. L. & Eller, C. K. (2018). Understanding the Community-Supported Business Model, A Primer for Tax Professionals. *The CPA Journal*, April.

Mars, M. M. (2015). From Bread We Build Community: Entrepreneurial Leadership and the Co-Creation of Local Food Businesses and Systems. *Journal of Agriculture, Food Systems, and Community Development*, 5(3): 63–77.

Matthew, J., Thomas, D. J., Lumina, A. S. & Fitza, M. A. (2017). The Role of Community in Crowdfunding Success: Evidence on Cultural Attributes in Funding Campaigns to "Save the Local Theater." *Entrepreneurship Theory and Practice*, 41(2): 161–182.

National Center for Employee Ownership. (2020). Downloaded June 1 from: http://www.nceo.org/.

Neal, M. B. & DeLa Torre, A. (2016). *The Case for Age-Friendly Communities. Portland State University.* Downloaded from: http://pdxscholar.library.pdx.edu/aging_pub/20

Phillips, R. & Pittman, R. (2015). *Introduction to Community Development* (2nd Edition). London: Routledge.

Phillips, R., Seifer, B. & Antzcak, E. (2013). *Sustainable Communities: Creating a Durable Local Economy.* London: Earthscan/Routledge.

Phillips, R., Seifer, B. & Brennan, M. (2020). Connecting Industry and the Arts for Community Development: The Art Hop of Burlington, Vermont. In R. Phillips, M. Brennan and T. Li (Eds.), *Culture, Community and Development.* London: Routledge.

Preservation Trust of Vermont. (2020). Downloaded April 6 from: https://ptvermont.org/our-work/cse/.

Shuman, M. (2007). *The Small-Mart Revolution, How Local Businesses are Beating the Global Competition.* San Francisco, CA: Berrett-Koehler Publishers, Inc., pp. 46–50.

Shuman, M. (2015). *The Local Economy Solution.* White River Junction, VT: Chelsea Green Publishing.

Seifer, B., Antzcak, E. & Phillips, R. (2020). Achieving a Durable Economy: Lessons Learned from Burlington, Vermont. *Local Development & Society*, 1(1). https://www.tandfonline.com/loi/rlds20.

Tolbert, C. M. (2005). Minding Our Own Business: Local Retail Establishments and the Future of Southern Civic Community. *Social Forces*, 83(4): 1309–1328.

Vermont Employee Ownership Center (VEOC). (2020). Company Profiles. Downloaded June 1 from: http://www.veoc.org/vermont_companies#national.

Vermont Secretary of State. (2020). Limited Liability Corporations. Downloaded August 22 from: https://sos.vermont.gov/corporations/registration/domestic-registration/llc/#.

Walzer, N. (2019). *Guidebook and Resources for Starting CSEs.* East Lansing, MI: North Central Regional Center for Rural Development. Download from: https://www.cgs.niu.edu/Reports/cse-guidebook-final-2-8-19.pdf

Walzer, N. & Sandoval, J. (2016). *Emergence and Growth of Community Supported Enterprises.* East Lansing, IN: North Central Regional Center for Rural Development. Download at: https://www.cgs.niu.edu/Reports/Emergence-and-Growth-of-Community-Supported-Enterprises.pdf

White, T. (2013). *Seeds of a New Economy? A Qualitative Investigation of Diverse Economic Practices within Community Supported Agriculture and Community Supported Enterprise.* Dissertation, University of Massachusetts.

4

COMMUNITY-OWNED PUBS IN GREAT BRITAIN

Hubs of Community Enterprise

Stephen McCusker

Introduction

In the past ten years, there has been a growing revolution in the UK within Community Supported Enterprises (CSEs) as awareness and potential of Community Shares spreads from one location to another. There have been many studies about social economies, community businesses, and pubs during the same period of time. Some have focused on rural areas; some have compared rural and urban pubs; and a few have focused on community pubs or cooperative enterprises – all generally focusing on England.

This chapter, informed by those previous studies, focuses on local, community economies in three specific rural areas within Great Britain in an attempt to appreciate the role of Community-Owned Pubs (COPs) within that context and how the opportunities for these enterprises have been shaped and supported by evolving legislation and funding landscapes. The information available on, as well as the number of, established COPs shows that they are a clearly recurring theme of rural CSEs in the UK and therefore are a useful tool in discussing the narrative of this revolution over the last 20 years.

Some villages have expanded into Pubs after successfully running a village shop or Post Office but many start with the Pub before taking on further responsibilities. In 2019 and 2020, there were reports indicating that COPs were bucking the trend by maintaining a "100% survival rate." Notwithstanding the recent COVID-19 pandemic's impact on the economy, Britain's pubs have been in decline for more than a decade – sometimes nearly as many as 1,000 closing per year. However, in December 2019, the UK Office for National Statistics (ONS, 2020) reported a net gain of 320 pubs in the previous year – the first increase since 2009. This may be partly attributable to the dozens of COPs opening across England, supported by programs such as the Plunkett Foundation's

'More than a Pub.' Comparatively few have surfaced in Wales, but confidence is growing there with signs that this is taking hold in Scotland too (there are none recorded in Northern Ireland, the 4th country within the UK; therefore, the study is limited to Great Britain.)

Studies commissioned and published by national funding bodies such as the Plunkett Foundation and Power to Change highlight how these enterprises work and how they benefit the immediate, local economy. Academic research considers rural separation and community cohesion as significant factors in initiating these community enterprises with several specific studies on COPs.

As a practitioner, the author has worked on and previously written about a COP among other Community Share projects and has therefore been immersed in the reality of what these businesses face and how they overcome it. Using those experiences, this paper unites reflections on other research and extends the discussion to identify and compare three regional clusters (in Scotland, Wales, and England) to support previous research and demonstrate how these 'isolated' enterprises have evolved within three different but comparable rural landscapes during the past 30 years. The discussion is generally presented in a chronological sequence and is informed by interviews with individuals connected to the pubs and their locations. Each interview was identified through desktop and remote research into community pubs and their locality before focusing on three COPs that linked to other CSEs, some of which have operated for decades.

The research began prior to the COVID-19 pandemic declaration and did not take full account of how circumstances may have changed for these businesses, though it touches on them in places. Opportunities to meet people on the ground as originally intended have been limited as circumstances across the nation change, but contacts have been made in each region to discuss the research and observations with local entrepreneurs, promoters, or community participants. The discussion acknowledges this context in the conclusion and perhaps now is an appropriate time to reflect on successes of this movement.

In essence, the research sets out to clarify if COPs have a pivotal or catalytic role in stimulating other local initiatives or businesses in the three locations and to compare how different regional or national legislation may have affected them. The intent is that others may learn from these examples and perhaps consider how similar successes can be nurtured elsewhere.

Community Pub Context

Britain's pubs have been in steady decline for decades with as many as 1,000 closing in a single year. According to House of Commons Briefing paper released during the writing of this chapter (House of Commons, 2020), between 2000 and 2018, the number of pubs decreased from approximately 60,000 to 47,000. In January 2020, the ONS reported a change in the trend. There had been an increase rather than a decrease with data showing that the overall number of pubs and bars in the UK increased by 315 between 2018 and 2019. The same report highlights that people are buying less alcohol – so the turning tide is certainly about more than drinking.

This situation with a surge in independently owned pubs – they now exceed those owned by Breweries or Pub Companies – a trend that clearly emerged back in 2009 in the midst of the Global Financial Crisis (GFC; House of Commons, 2020) and is contemporaneous with a rise in the popularity and promotion of the COP across the UK.

Cabras has written several quantitative papers around the associated themes with a particular emphasis on the rural context and cooperatively owned enterprises. There were approximately 30 COPs in the UK in 2010 (Cabras, 2011), and this number has steadily increased with the Plunkett Foundation reporting 85 COPs trading across the UK at the end of 2017 (Plunkett, 2018). What is more notable is the spike in the rate of COPs emerging in more recent years. In 2019, the Campaign for Real Ale (CAMRA) reported more than 130 COPs (Ainsworth, 2019). By late 2020, this number had increased to 148, demonstrating significant growth with a similar number being established in the past few years as there were during the preceding seven years (CAMRA, 2020).

Sforzi and Bianchi (2020) identify a common process that gives rise to these specific community enterprises: a local pub closes, a few people devise the idea to promote a community development project. They find other locals willing to save the pub and then raise money together using their strong ties to find reliable people who trust them and will, therefore, believe in the goodness of the COP project. In turn, this process forges strong ties within the local community. Cabras (2011) also discusses the community cohesion that arises from such ventures in rural communities.

This process builds on the role of the village pub in the UK generally, not exclusive to COPs, and compliments the CAMRA research (Dunbar, 2016) that concludes with a series of recommendations for publicans and pub owners to address the business needs and decline in successful commerce in the sector mentioned previously. Some of the strongest recommendations are that they work closely with their community to develop a local community atmosphere. What better way to ensure a community atmosphere than to have the pub owned by that community? And perhaps, there is security in the knowledge that, as of fall 2020, no COP has ceased trading, bucking the trend and maintaining an impressive survival rate of 100% (Plunkett, 2018). Perhaps, it is both a resilient business model and a platform for other CSEs?

Pub Significance in UK's Rural Areas

Pub numbers appear to be relatively stable in Urban, Tourist, or Seaside areas when compared with areas on the edges of big cities or more remote parts of Wales and Scotland (ONS, 2018). As well as economic pressures arising from changing social habits and cheap alcohol available from supermarkets, the financial viability of public houses in rural areas is particularly noteworthy where declining populations and the lack of passing trade have without doubt had a significant impact (Dunbar, 2016).

If these rural communities lose their pubs, they lose an important asset – an asset that enhances and stimulates socio-economic activities within them such as business activities, volunteering organizations, charities, and leisure services (Cabras & Reggiani, 2010). The presence of pubs in rural parishes improves community cohesion, social integration, and ultimately well-being (Cabras, Canduela, & Raeside 2012; Mount & Cabras, 2016). This situation is underpinned by an unstated recognition that members of the same community are all members of the same club and are therefore likely to be more trustworthy than those who are not (Dunbar, 2016). Many of these rural locations are smaller and more intimate than urban pubs encouraging familiarity and the opportunity to get to know others nearby. Consequently, it seems that the existence of pubs in rural communities improve economic, social, and well-being prospects for the residents so, no wonder they become concerned when these facilities and businesses come under threat of extinction.

Asset Transfer

CSEs take many different legal forms in an effort to transform their local areas through engaging local people in the delivery of goods or services. As such, many have the potential or opportunity to save physical assets that may otherwise disappear. Though buildings are not always essential for pubs to exist, it is difficult to imagine that this will change much in the near future. Understanding how CSEs can acquire these buildings is therefore a key part of this discussion, especially when it comes to the capital required.

Clearly, the 2011 Localism Act created opportunities for community-interest organizations in England (e.g., Development Trust, Community Interest Company, and Social Enterprise) to transfer the management and/or ownership of community assets such as land or buildings from owners at less than market value (McCusker, 2018). Although this legislation usually concerns assets previously owned by a public body such as a local authority, this is not always the case.

In England, Pubs that are in private/company ownership may be listed as Assets of Community Value (ACV) under the Assets of Community Value (England) Regulations 2012. This can happen on the condition that it can be proven that the asset furthers the social well-being or social interests of the local community. A similar Community Right to Buy (CRtB) was legislated in Scotland through Part 2 of the Land Reform (Scotland) Act 2003 – further extended through the 2015 Community Empowerment Act to give communities first right of refusal to buy land that comes up for sale.

It should be clarified, however, that these rights to interest for communities in Buildings and Land do not necessarily prevent development or guarantee sale to the community. They are intended to facilitate community interest where there are opportunities and concerns. While they are often key in unlocking assets for CSEs and provide a supportive framework for this to happen, they are not essential. In fact, at the time of writing, Wales does not yet have a similar system, but, as will be discussed later, this has certainly not prevented Welsh rural communities from pursuing it nonetheless.

Promotion

There have been more than 1,200 successful applications protecting local pubs from conversion or demolition by developers (Dunbar, 2016). The growth in this model has not only been encouraged by legislation that focuses on the assets but also by supporting campaigns. In 2016, CAMRA mobilized its members to nominate their local pubs as ACVs, offering advice and guidance to other community groups looking to do the same after pubs with ACV status became protected by planning laws.

Policymakers have long recognized the potential of pubs in rural areas (Cabras, 2011) and supported through policies at the Government level, the creation of a designated Community Pubs Minister complimented by activities and promotion with various funding partners. This occurred in October 2010 after CAMRA's campaign following the loss of a minister for pubs – the title was also amended to add the word 'community.'

For example, the Plunkett Foundation announced a program of several million pounds in March 2010, with the aim of supporting 50 communities who wanted to save their local pubs. That specific program was funded by the UK Government's Department of Communities and Local Government (DCLG) and neatly coincided with the aforementioned Localism Bill, further expanding opportunities for ACVs (Cabras, 2011). Central government continued to steer DCLG funds in that direction in 2015 and 2016 helping communities take control of local pubs at risk of closure and supporting business development for existing COPs.

The latter, 2016 allocation, was jointly funded by Power to Change (an independent charitable trust, established in 2015 with National Lottery Funds). This initiative emerged as the very popular and well-known 'More than a Pub' program. Delivery of 'More than a Pub' has been by the Plunkett Foundation – a registered charity that supports rural communities across the UK to tackle the issues they face through community business. 'More than a Pub' was, and still is, a crucial campaign and support service within this narrative. It offers the opportunity to learn from existing community pub businesses and sector specialists to enable the community ownership of pubs. However, it is restricted to England.

The Plunkett Model Rules and associated resources have become significant contributors to supporting the growth of community pubs which they require to feature the following to access the program: Have a charitable purpose; Be for the benefit of the public; Address local needs; Trade for the benefit of the community; Be run democratically; and Have local support and investors. These principles underline how essential it is for the CSEs to demonstrate how they plan to benefit their community.

The Angler's Rest, a rural pub in Bamford, England, was one of the trailblazer projects featured in this launch and served as a precedent for others (McCusker, 2018). Not only did Bamford Community Society rescue the last pub in the village and save it from development. It also co-located the Post Office there, expanded into a successful café business, and facilitated other local facilities such as a mobile library and now has a small shop too.

It is not uncommon to find other CSEs such as Community Shops located at or near COPs. The two enterprises are so closely associated, and some might consider them symbiotic. It is, therefore, not a surprise that the Plunkett Foundation also supports community-owned shops. These rural shops lend themselves so easily to community-ownership models that they far exceed COPS with current numbers approximating 350. As with COPs, there was a very positive public campaign promoting the opportunities for community-owned in an effort to stymie the tide of hundreds of village shops closing each year. The Foundation was even referenced in the BBC's rural radio drama The Archers, the world's longest-running soap opera, as the village organized volunteers and began to run the shop themselves (Davies, 2009).

Informal and peer-to-peer knowledge transfer has played no small part in spreading the word on the value of CSEs. The independent and not-for-profit organization, Pub is The Hub (PiTH), has also played a key and complimentary role in this dissemination. PiTH materialized following a Countryside Agency report of the same title in 2001 along with the Vital Villages Grants Program that ran until 2005.

In those few years, the Countryside Agency awarded grants to small rural communities to assist them in meeting local service provision including transport needs while also promoting social inclusion and tackling problems associated with rural isolation. Since 2001, PiTH has been dedicated to improving pub-related community services and activities with a great deal of success, often in collaboration with the other bodies and funders referenced in this chapter.

PiTH's foundation clearly pre-dates the localism Bill and other government sponsorship that has taken place since this wave of COPs gained momentum circa 2010 but their role and expertise reach beyond COPs. It has been shown (Davies, Miscampbell, Barnard, & Hughes, 2017) that delivering multiple and different products or services helps some COPs by using the combined income streams to help cover operating costs (e.g., maintenance of old buildings). It can also attract greater custom than might have been achieved by a single service (Davies et al., 2017).

Since these conditions do not apply exclusively to COPs, PiTH considers other rural services and diversification opportunities for Pubs that may not be owned by a community but certainly benefit from their patronage. PiTH's success during the last two decades has attracted sponsorship from the pub and drinks sector as well other rurally focused or local government agencies. With a superb online resource and a wealth of case studies, PiTH's guidance takes the form of advice, signposting or links to relevant expertise, and the UK government has continued to invest in this initiative with significant funding boosts for PiTH announced as recently as 2019.

Funding Models

PiTH often leads in delivering small grants through local or national enterprise schemes that can be vital to make the leap from idea to reality in the embryonic stages of these CSEs. Research has shown that income from grants or subsidies plays only a small role in the finances among COPs with less than 20% of their income (Davies et al., 2017). This confirms research into the relationship between Industrial & Provident Societies (I&PSs) and rural village pubs (Cabras, 2011). Public sector funding is an important stimulus in the creation of I&PSs in rural areas, but in the cases identified in that research, the presence of grants was 'supportive' rather than 'necessary.'

Really, what local communities want to do is finance the purchase of their village pubs themselves (Cabras, 2011). This appears to be a recurring theme, echoed by COP board members and trustees who believe that the businesses were likely to be able to survive without grants or subsidies in the future trustees (Davies et al., 2017). Many get advice about financial models from supporting organizations such as the Plunkett Foundation, PiTH, and Co-operatives UK & Locality (among others). This can involve grants or tapping into business support, but it might also be about defining the most appropriate way to raise capital (e.g., cash that might be required to establish the business and/or secure a property). This is usually combined with galvanizing community support by seeking the main bulk of capital via the sale of shares to local people and donations from the community (Davies et al., 2017).

Early COP models discussed here set themselves up as Industrial & Provident Societies. This is a mutual model that originated in 1852. Incorporation in this manner allows people to buy shares in a society, the aim being that the I&PS existed for their benefit. Whether or not individuals earned dividends on their shares depended on that society, and generally, it seems that the COPs and shops discussed did not pay out profits as dividends. Instead, they generally chose to reinvest in the community.

The Co-operatives and Community Benefit Societies Act replaced the Industrial & Provident Societies Act in 2014, recognizing the need to evolve the legal structures and processes to support the growing popularity and potential of community-ownership models. The new Act makes a distinction between a Co-operative Society (which benefits its members and can pay out in relation to that membership) and a Community Benefit Society (which is focused on benefiting a community rather than members and reinvesting profits in the aims and purpose for which it was established). The latter model in many ways formalizes the practice that was already happening in many I&PSs. Both models enable ranges of investments but without proportionate control – in this way, all members remain equal despite the amount they invest.

The concept of issuing bonds or shares to raise funds is not new, but it has enjoyed a revival under the new banner of 'Community Shares' with a more focused and strategic purpose than its previous formats. This approach has made a real difference to communities across the country in the wake of the GFC. Starting circa 2009, the combined efforts of Locality (formerly the Development Trust Association) and Co-operatives UK reportedly attracted 60,000 investors to Community Shares in a period of five years (Community Shares Unit, 2015).

Backed by the UK government through the DCLG, these organizations established the Community Shares Unit. Development Trust Scotland and the Plunkett Foundation joined forces to launch Community Shares Scotland in 2014 and the Wales Co-operative Centre's Community Shares Wales Team followed in 2016. Community Shares focus on the ability to raise capital collectively for a benefit that reaches beyond the members of that legal society. Though shares could eventually be withdrawn, investors generally acknowledge that this might not happen. These new legal structures, share models, and support networks converged to establish a national platform that enabled community enterprises to benefit from up-to-date support and, perhaps key to the growth of Community Shares as a model, linked to other partners and funders which may have shared or overlapping interests.

As mentioned in previous articles, money begets money (McCusker, 2018) – or perhaps more appropriately, investment attracts investment. So, when funders observe clear commitment from individuals through raising of capital via community shares, they are more confident in the proposal. Similarly, when potential investors hear that funders might match their investment pound for pound (e.g., Through Power to Change's booster program), local investors become more confident about the CSE's potential and recognize that every unit they put in is effectively doubled by someone else. This is all very tangible and comprehensible, reaching beyond the face value of the capital invested and evidencing the social foundation required for potential success. COPs have highlighted the important role of Community Shares alongside donations, bank loans, and grants when planning finances for their businesses. It is also clear from this research that other successful COPs were key for inspiration and guidance (Davies et al., 2017).

It is perhaps, therefore, no surprise that COPs and community-owned businesses cluster in geographical areas. It is with this in mind that we turn to the three zones identified for the purposes of this narrative to understand how they benefit from each other and link to other CSEs beyond their local COP. Each zone is located in a distinctly different nation within the island of Great Britain, UK. Though some legislation unifies these countries, many of the funding pots, legal orders, or bills referred to in this discussion are devolved to each National assembly/parliament.

FIGURE 4.1 Regional clusters in Scotland, Wales, and England.
Source: Compiled by the author.

England

As with all the locations in this chapter, the research begins with a COP, using it as a point to link socially to other CSEs in the immediate geographical context. In the case of England, the focus is on the Northern part of Cumbria where the village of Hesket Newmarket is located, an example that has been written about in particular detail in other publications (Cabras, 2011). While some of the previously published details about this case are cited here, the information is presented in a different context to explore other links for current purposes.

Hesket Newmarket is a small village in Caldbeck Parish, Cumbria. It has a population of approximately 250 and is situated just inside the North Edge of the Lake District National Park. This area is more agricultural and population more dispersed than the popular tourist locations in the Lake District. Local village settlements historically benefited from mining in the area but, as similar to the area of Wales identified in the next section, these stopped in the 1960s. The economy has changed since then, but it is a relatively prosperous area with strong employment, household income, and economic activity when compared with other parts of England.

In 1999, the landlords of the local pub, The Old Crown, decided to narrow their business to the pub alone by retiring from the brewery business. The locals became sensitive to the fact that the brewery, which the Landlords had built from scratch, was a significant contributor to the local economy that they didn't want to lose – despite only it provided only a handful of jobs. So, they raised sufficient funds to buy it within eight days and set up an I&PS to manage their shares (Wainwright, 1999). Clearly, the brewery already had a ready-made and good outlet in the local pub so there was good business sense in retaining the jobs and enterprise locally.

At a similar time, healthcare workers in Caldbeck saw an opportunity to develop a community-led transport service, addressing social isolation and a lack of poor access to facilities such as shops, healthcare, and public transport. The local GP was successful in leading a bid for this new Northern Fells Group to become one of the three Prince of Wales Rural Revival Initiative Projects (the Prince of Wales also champions and supports the PiTH and the Countryside Agency work mentioned earlier).

It is a registered community charity and a Company Limited by Guarantee that began by identifying a gap in local statutory and voluntary provision. The practice nurse was seconded to the project initially as the Northern Fells Group coordinator before becoming employed part-time by them. After obtaining a minibus, the service was quickly able to provide a bespoke travel service for people with restricted access to, or ability to use, vehicles. This service is now available for shopping trips or hospital visits so in many ways is similar to a local taxi service.

In the author's discussion with a founder, the suggestion was made that taxis are not easy to establish in the area due to the limited income. Therefore, a service such as this can support a local community while also maintaining the local economy; it has now expanded to approximately 100 volunteers and a few part-time employees who are essential for organizing the roster writer and coordinating so many volunteers, among other things. It pays employees and encourages people to remain in the area by continuing to support them there. They do small and odd jobs for people where they can but limit this so that trades do not miss out on potential income.

Most of the Northern Fells Group's work addresses isolation and loneliness in this remote, rural Northern extremity of England. Inspired by a model in Gloucestershire, they secured further funding to employ Village Agents part-time to deliver essential services to older people. This is often done by providing companionship, practical support, and ensuring that those individuals are presented with opportunities to engage in a range of community activities. It supports groups such as Men in Sheds, walking/ramblers, and other social activities such as lunch clubs. In turn, these support local enterprises, re-investing in the immediate economy by using local shops for purchasing diesel and local caterers where there are no pubs/cafés in the many parishes it now supports. Where there are pubs/cafés, the group uses these also.

One such venue benefitting from this mutual support is the aforementioned Old Crown which became a COP in 2001. Almost to complete the circle, the village decided to buy the pub, as they had done the brewery, when it went up for sale, safeguarding more jobs at a time when the region was severely affected by the outbreak of Foot and Mouth disease in the UK. The outbreak led to significant loss of livestock and economic impact but, despite this or perhaps in spite of it, 125 shareholders were secured and, having already proven themselves with the brewery, they also secured grant funding from Cumbria County Council Rural Regeneration Fund and the Lake District National Park Sustainable Development Fund. As a result, they secured the mutual future of two village businesses not to mention the associated benefits for local villagers (Cabras, 2011). The Old Crown was officially registered as an I&PS in 2003 and has gained quite a reputation, serving as a very early precedent for others across England and featured in much publicity. But this has also had local impact, influencing other operations and enterprises.

As recorded elsewhere (Cabras, 2011), these successes influenced similar enterprises such as the Butcher's Arms, the only pub in Crosby Ravensworth. Concerned that the property would become housing after it was put on the market in 2009, the local Lyvennet Community Land Trust mobilized the community. This effort was not only about keeping an asset that would provide a service, but it was also intended to help local residents retain value in their own property. The village is a more attractive prospect if it has the pub too (Cabras, 2011). Adamant that they were not going to lose their community pub, surveys were undertaken, a prospectus developed, and a media campaign ensued. In addition to raising substantial capital, they secured more than 4,000 hours of volunteer time to assist with renovations before reopening in 2011 through Lyvennet Community Pub (LCP) Ltd – an I&PS with over 300 shareholders. As with the Old Crown, the pub is leased to tenants who are supported by the shareholding members.

It is clear that the message was spreading in the region – success followed success, and this was acknowledged by Cumbria County Council who had already launched the PiTH Rural Services Scheme in 2006. Continuing from the Vital Villages Program, it not only supported local communities but also encouraged breweries, pub owners, and licensees to work together to help retain and enhance local infrastructure by considering how new or essential services could be hosted by the pubs to increase access to rural services – something that has now become an established model (Lythe, 2006).

Indeed, there had been discussions in Hesket Newmarket about the community owning the village shop too, but it has now proven itself to be more than viable. It is a well-used business, complimenting other activities in the area. In other nearby locations where services were in jeopardy, the PiTH scheme stepped in to offer support. Only 14 miles from Hesket Newmarket, the licensee of the Kings Arms saw an opportunity to connect the local Post Office with the Pub when it looked like it was about to be lost in 2005. The landlord was able to draw on experience from the previous decade when they had relocated the village Post Office to the Horse & Farrier pub in Dacre.

Not only did the landlord recognize the significant role the Post Office can play in a rural community such as this but also the good business sense and advantages of co-locating services in one place. The proposal was well supported by the local community too, and as a result of relocation to the heart of the village, it was easier to access for local residents, and the service was extended with a shop selling a small range of goods (Pub is the Hub, 2020).

Similarly, the Black Swan in Ravenstonedale worked with the local community to establish a grocery store. It is an independently owned business within 40 miles of the other locations that took action when they became aware that approximately 20% of local residents were older than 65 years and that the nearest shops were 4–6 miles away (Pub is the Hub, 2020). Although these past three examples are not community-owned enterprises, they demonstrate the potential of community support for business in a rural economy and reassure community entrepreneurs that these are viable models.

Less than 30 miles from Heskett NewMarket, the villagers in Ennerdale Bridge also seemed to recognize this potential. Thanks to the Vital Villages Program, a fairly comprehensive Parish Plan was completed in the wake of the foot & mouth crisis. Despite disappointment at the shortfall of funding for some Community Room proposals, there was clear pride in the fact that the village had retained essential services such as the pub, shop/Post Office, church, and school. The study was emphatic that the Parish Council had no desire to compete with or manage commercial activity that is already being adequately provided but in doing so underlined that there was always a risk these services could be lost.

Unfortunately, these concerns were well-founded, and they progressively lost the shop and the Post Office. Their nearest shops were now 7 miles away, and as the local bus service became more diluted, villagers became reliant on cars. After a new study recommended that the restoration of the village shop was both needed and viable, funding was secured from a local action group made up of representatives from businesses, public agencies, and local community bodies. This Cumbria Fells & Dales funding enabled the village to start testing their ideas but no sooner had they started this exercise when the Fox and Hounds Inn closed. This must have been a real shock to the village, especially given the warnings from years before (Pub is the Hub, 2020).

Rather than this precipitating the demise of the village, this situation proved to be a great catalyst that propelled the community into action (Pub is the Hub, 2020); a business plan was written, an I&PS was formed, and 130 people attended a public meeting in the church (the village population is approx. 200). Sufficient capital was raised to take over the lease of the pub in less than two weeks. The scheme eventually attracted more than 200 shareholders, and the pub reopened in 2011, thanks to many volunteers and donated time to restore the premises.

Not content with exceeding their anticipated turnover in their first year of trading, the villagers reviewed the original plan and kept moving forward. Having proven their determination with the pub over a relatively short period of time, they secured further funding from the Copeland Community Fund to bring the village's facilities back to life. After much careful planning, fundraising, and investment, they opened The Gather in 2016 where they co-located the shop, café, and community rooms discussed years before. This was not a straightforward process and has since required further investment from the community in both 2016 and 2018 – and each time, the community responded constructively, raising further funds through donations, activities, and alternative membership schemes (Jenkinson, 2018).

It is not unusual to see further investment when the CSEs reach a new phase – perhaps because they had limited investment in the early days and just started running, perhaps because the business has grown, and sometimes because the model needs further finance to sustain it. It is not often that the investments are returned, but certainly in the case of the Old Crown, they have paid out dividends as and when they could afford it. The Old Crown is still trading, though it closed during COVID-19. The Butchers Arms recently reopened following its imposed hiatus, but most of the village shop services have continued. The Northern Fells Group's Village Agents took on new significance during the Pandemic lockdown by offering support to isolated members of the community and working with that key roster organizer to deliver essential foods and enable transport.

Wales

Although it has been suggested that the English Village of Hesket Newmarket is unique as a village with two separate cooperative businesses (Cabras, 2011), there are other locations that have had multiple community-owned businesses for some time that do not appear to have achieved the same publicity or reputation as those in England. Those in North Wales are worth further and more detailed study than the discussion in this chapter permits, but for the purposes of this study, the zone is generally limited to the Llŷn Peninsula where the oldest COP identified for this study, Tafarn y Fic, is located.

Llithfaen's Early Embrace of Community Ownership

Llithfaen is a small settlement in Gwynedd county with a population of approximately 250 that grew in the presence of local quarries that provided work in the 1800s and 1900s until the last one closed in the 1960s. The Llynn Peninsula is a beautiful, remote rural area that now has a different economy that depends less on one specific sector, and despite its growing tourist economy, salaries in this region are amongst the lowest in Britain. Weekly pay in the county was the lowest in Wales in 2019 with the remuneration at its worst in the rural communities.

Despite these conditions, the local community is strong. In 1988, when it looked like the Brewery did not foresee a future for the local pub, the only one in the village, 60 people from the local area got together and formed a company, raising sufficient capital in the process to purchase it and save it from closure. The repairs and work necessary were undertaken by the local community to help it survive. This was no mean feat. The pub has continued to survive to the present, enjoying an expansion that improved its offering a few years ago by adding a modern, multi-purpose community room that is available for hire for courses, meetings, or private parties. Its achievements are such that 2018 the Welsh Parliament recognized its 30th birthday, celebrating Tafarn y Fic, as the oldest community pub in Europe. But it is not just a pub; all the profits are reinvested in the community; it has created jobs, but it is also a key venue for the Welsh language and culture.

Only a few years after rescuing the pub, Llithfaen's only retail shop was put up for sale. It continued trading while waiting for a buyer, but after two years on the market, it had not attracted a purchaser, and the owners set a closure date in 1996. Once again, these resilient villagers grouped together, raising 50% of the funds needed to buy the shop. At a public meeting, 100 families backed the project. Market research undertaken to ensure viability of the project concluded that, if it remained open, villagers were prepared to spend 60,000 pounds a year there rather than travel 7 miles to a different location for their groceries. They set up a new company together, Menter Yr Eifl, and finally purchased the only shop in the village (Siop Pen-y-Groes) in 1999.

As with so many of these community enterprises, the purchase of the shop benefited from supporting grants to fill the gap. Similar to some of the models discussed earlier, it hosted the local Post Office and had continuous tenants for a while to keep it open. Although many felt that this service is critical for many financial and communication services, the postal service transferred to a mobile van, and the last tenant closed the shop due to lack of business in 2009. When asked about this, one of the villagers involved in the shop since the early days, said that it was very clear that there is a role and a need for shops like this within the community, but it is often a challenge to make sufficient profit to sustain a good living never mind a family.

Without a regular income from hosting a Post Office can be a precarious existence with little opportunity to take time off. Shops are more likely to be well used during tourist seasons. When asked why the community rallied around once again in discussion with the author, it seemed that there was a sense of panic without much time for thought or planning – only a few decades previously, the village had hosted a school, multiple shops, a chip shop, a surgery, pubs, a butcher, and a bakery, and now, they were on the verge of reducing everything down to the pub they had saved a few years before if something did not happen within a matter of weeks. They already owned the business at this point so, armed with a few hundred pounds thrown in by residents, a small group of about six people bought some stock and reopened as volunteers, concerned especially about elderly residents who relied on the local shop for basics.

They ran out of stock by lunchtime on the first day and used the profits gained to buy more stock, slowly re-building trade from there – reminiscent of the

Rochdale Pioneers who opened their first cooperative shop with some flour and butter. It seems that this is no coincidence since there was a cooperative branch shop of the local cooperative society a few generations before; the cooperative branch shop was also staffed by volunteers after daytime work had finished in the mines. It seems, therefore, that village life was echoing the past.

The new model of the shop, however, is different in that the shop is usually run by two part-time employees, and then volunteers help only during the afternoon. It makes sufficient money to more than cover costs without a need for grant aid but does rely on input and patronage from the local community to survive. But this is not an isolated case in the region. With more than 300 rural shops closing across Wales since 2009, local officials were keen to take action and support steps that could address the issues impacting the future of village life.

Growth of Cops in Wales

Less than 30 miles from Llithfaen (but in the same county, Gwynedd), The Pengwern Arms was the last of four pubs to shut in another quarrying village, Llan Ffestiniog. With help from the Wales Cooperative Centre, Pengwern Cymunedol registered itself as an I&PS in 2010, raising 320 community shares and sufficient funds to purchase the pub thanks to grants from Welsh Government and a local Social Housing Association.

The initial phases started with volunteers getting the basics completed so they could open. This allowed them to start opening for business and build on their vision by securing grants to help with further phases while they were trading. So, when it reopened in 2011, it wasn't just the pub reopened that was celebrated, just as important was the observation that local people were coming closer together. Like Tafarn y Fic, it too is committed to supporting local acts, local food, and Welsh Culture. This has helped to build a profile that extends beyond supporting local activities and taps into the tourist economy also, offering overnight accommodation and an authentic Welsh experience.

It should not be forgotten that many of these examples emerged against a backdrop of national austerity following the GFC. Regional and central government support enabled these rural communities to leap at the early stages of their projects in the same way the Cumbrian Councils and agencies nurtured the development of rural services a few years before in England. Recognizing what was already happening in Wales, a Welsh PiTH Co-operation Project was established for 2012–2014, working with the Welsh Government and Cadwyn Clwyd (A Welsh Rural Development Agency) across eight counties (including Gwynedd).

This initiative built on earlier pilot projects by Cadwyn Clwyd that explored economic opportunities for pub services in neighboring parts of rural of North Wales. Raven Mad Limited was one of those communal pilot projects. It adopted a COP model in 2009 when they took over Raven Inn in the village of Llanarmon-Yn-Ial. The model differs slightly in that they committed to a six-year lease instead of buying the premises. Then, after the business was established, they took on a new 20-year lease to secure its future. This model demonstrates that it is not always necessary to raise sufficient finance to buy the property – sometimes, the idea and the business are all that is required, and the owner may be happy to work with the community while also retaining ownership of the physical asset.

This effort has had that same catalytic impact found in other locations with further CSEs emerging in Llanarmon-Yn-Ial. As in Heskett Newmarket, the pub has a relationship with Cwrw Ial Community Brew Company, a social enterprise microbrewery established by two locals, inspired by the entrepreneurial spirit that resides in their village. The profits from both the brewery and the pub are reinvested in the business or benefit the community in the same way Tafarn y Fic pub operates.

However, the Raven also differs from Tafarn y Fic's model since it is ostensibly run and managed by 50 volunteers, though they do pay a small amount of staff to provide some training and employment for young people. As with some other examples discussed, the local Post Office service has been located at the Raven, and the experience of running these CSEs has enabled the community to take over operation of the village shop too. Llanarmon-yn-Ial's shop has been community-owned since 2012 (Pub is the Hub, 2020). Similar to the model in Llithfaen, the shop operates on a day-to-day basis with two part-time staff, and a group of volunteers while a committee (elected from the society's membership) provides oversight and management.

Other Welsh CSEs and Recent Growth of Cops

It is evident that once the community sees what is possible, more ideas emerge. This is certainly the case in Pen-y-groes, another small former mining settlement approximately 12 miles from Llithfaen and 25 miles from Llan Ffestiniog, nestled between the coast and Snowdonia. There is no COP there (yet), but as with other locations, villagers have rallied together to take responsibility for running the village hall and to support youth activities through Dyffryn Nantlle 20/20. This CSE has particularly focused on digital media since 2011, and with support from cooperative organizations and the Plunkett Foundation, it sets up a digital center in the rear yard of an old shop in the village. This will further enhance and support the digital activities, training and employment opportunities for local young people it had supported before.

When this shop came up for sale in 2016, more than 200 residents raised in excess of 80% of the funds required to purchase the building. The rest was sourced through grants, and Siop Griffiths Cyf was established as a community-benefit society later that year with more than 150 members participating in a community share offer. Again, it is perhaps not a coincidence that the premises had once been a local pub before becoming a hardware outlet. On a prominent corner location on the high street, it now hosts the Yr Osaf café having secured grants from the Rural Communities Development Fund.

Unfortunately, plans to open bed and breakfast accommodation were suspended due to the COVID-19 pandemic, but this setback has not stymied activities or aspirations in the village. They have also installed WIFI on the high street to support visitors and gather data about usage. This arrived just before the UK's lockdown and has proven a useful support service for people isolated in the area as things moved online.

As with Cumbria's the Northern Fells group, the gap in local transport provision is being addressed with the appointment of a Community Transport Co-ordinator, currently based at the Yr Osaf shop/café building. Their role changed dramatically as a result of the pandemic, switching to supporting local residents in a different way, similar to the village agents in Cumbria.

Local community leaders here certainly have vision and have earned the trust of residents through these ideas coming to fruition and working for the village community. Crucially, the CSEs across the region are learning from and supporting each other as they draw parallels with other community activism. The Pengwern Arms, referred to earlier in this section, are now part of Cwmni Bro Ffestiniog – a network of 14 social enterprises working together and promoting each other, acknowledging the benefits of mutual support to build a stronger place rather than working in individual silos. Listening to locals talking about this and their hopes for a Foundational Economy sounds similar to those of Llithfaen when they came close to losing their high street completely about 30 years ago. Another project network, Dolan, has been set up to link organizations, reaching further across the region to share information among CSEs.

With support from experienced CSEs in Llithfaen & Pen-y-groes, more than 500 investors bought enough shares to buy the Sportsman in Nefyn only a few miles down the road. Refurbishment work was suspended due to COVID-19 restrictions, but they hope to open for business soon, and the village is optimistic that this will stimulate their high street, something that really has been valued in the lockdown. Lltihfaen's shop has remained open throughout. Even when they struggled for supplies, it really was the vital resource that villagers thought it would be all those years ago.

The café reopened in Pen-y-Groes in August 2020 and continues to trade hoping to expand their other activities soon. Nefyn are already passing on their experiences and knowledge to Criccieth as they embark on a community share offer to convert The Feathers Inn to a COP. There is a pride and excitement in the CSEs here that will sustain future generations beyond those involved today.

Scotland

The changing legislative landscape through the Land Reform and Community Empowerment Acts in Scotland was highlighted earlier. There have been significant changes formalizing and preparing the way for CSE opportunities related to physical assets in Scotland, and yet, the scope for studying COPs in Scotland is very limited compared to the previous sections. The hope is that this research will expose other COP networks as it did in Wales given the many Scottish CSEs that comprise Distilleries, Cafés, Grocers, Halls, and other services. But there do not appear to be any longstanding COPs as in Wales or England – only three COPs appear to have been registered to date, and all of them opened in 2019/2020. Consequently, this section takes a slightly different approach being more discursive as it approaches the concluding observations for this chapter.

This situation is perhaps surprising, given Scotland's historic practice of crofting and managing communal assets. Ownership of land by rural communities is recorded as far back as 1923 with a renewed interest in community land purchase commencing in 1992 (Skerratt & Hall, 2011). There are conflicting records about exact numbers in recent years, but a report released during the development of this research identified 590 community-owned assets in Scotland, 63% of which were located in remote rural areas. This number has steadily risen during the last 20 years, but it is unclear if this is directly linked to legislation such as Scottish Government's promotion of the Asset Transfer Program through the Development Trusts Association Scotland (2009–2011) or the Community Ownership Support Service that has been ongoing since 2011.

Under Part 2 of the Land Reform (Scotland) Act 2003, communities who successfully register a community interest in land or buildings have the first option to buy when the registered land is offered for sale (CRtB). As noted earlier, the Welsh Assembly has considered introducing similar CRtB legislation, but one wonders if it is necessary to bring this in given how many Welsh communities have already negotiated the transfer of assets to community ownership without it.

Many communities in Scotland have also managed to proceed with similar purchases without their legislation. Glancing back at the perceptions of the high street in Nefyn, for that is what inspired villagers there to take action, it makes sense that Scotland has introduced a specific CRtB for abandoned, neglected, or detrimental land/buildings in 2018. This goes beyond some of the asset transfer legislation in England by giving community bodies a right to compulsorily purchase assets that are wholly or mainly, abandoned or neglected.

And yet, as far as could be ascertained during this research, these options do not seem to have led to any such purchases. Some critics have suggested that this is due to unclear definitions of terms such as 'abandoned' or 'neglected.' The same CRtB can be called upon if the use or management of the land is causing harm to the environmental well-being of the community, and a new CRtB Land to Further Sustainable came into effect during the course of this research, giving effect to Part 5 of the Land Reform (Scotland) Act 2016. So, there is no shortage of legislation in Scotland but what is unclear is if these are enabling change on the ground in the community.

There have been other campaigns alongside the changes in law. The Scottish Borders Council, in partnership with PiTH, launched an initiative in 2016 with the Prince's Countryside Fund to help rural pubs diversify and provide local services in communities. These are familiar partners for successful pub diversification programs in Wales and England. A wealth of business support is also available through Community Shares Scotland, Development Trust Association Scotland, Can Do network, and Co-operative Development Scotland (which is now part of Scottish Enterprise), mirroring similar organizations in other countries. However, the largest resource for these types of projects is probably the Scottish Land Fund. Founded by the Scottish Government in 2000 and delivered in partnership with the National Lottery Community Fund and Highlands and Islands Enterprise, it has granted millions in funding to enable communities to take ownership of the land and buildings that matter to them. All three Scottish COPs have received financial support from the Scottish Land Fund.

Scottish COPs

The COP most congruent with the clusters in Wales and England is in the village of Gartmore in the Scottish borders. The community there already operated both their village Shop and village hall before taking on the Black Bull Pub. The story, by now, sounds all too familiar. Not so long ago, Gartmore had two grocery stores, a baker, a tailor, a blacksmith, a joiner, and a shoemaker. The last shop in the village went for sale in 1997, and it seemed that nobody wanted to buy it. As was the concern in Nefyn or Ennerdale, it was at risk of becoming a residential accommodation and Planning consent had been secured to convert it.

A core group of about ten people organized a meeting attended by nearly half the village, and it was decided to set up a community shop. Subsequently, 130 people purchased shares, and in a manner similar to the more contemporary Power to Change Booster program, their investments were matched by a rural initiative fund. Within months, and after much volunteered time, the shop opened as a community cooperative in January 1998, staffed by a willing team of local people, and managed by a voluntary committee. Villagers are regularly encouraged to spend at least £5.00 per week to ensure the shop's future. It hosts the Post Office, as seen in other regions, and is a self-sustaining business with paid employees, but even the staff acknowledged that it is more than a job. When their longstanding manager retired, she was welcomed back to help out with the accounts and remains as valued as ever by the team around her.

The success of this shop made it much easier for the villagers to understand the value of purchasing the Black Bull in 2019, but there is much more to Gartmore than the pub & shop. It has its own heritage society, a theatre group, school, church (two churches unified in 1936 freeing up one church to be used as a village hall), and a Community Trust founded in 2002 after the first Community Action Plan was completed. Gartmore's Community Trust aims to work in partnership with the community to shape the future of Gartmore and its environs. Part of this work involves consulting local people to better understand village wants and needs.

The state of the village hall regularly emerged as a potential project on meeting agendas and a development group focused on its refurbishment circa 2008–2014. After more hard work and successful funding bids, an energy efficient hall was re-opened in 2014 featuring renewable energy sources and a new external appearance that was sympathetic to the Conservation Area at the heart of the village. It is well used for local performances, exercise classes and gathering events and complements other activities in the village community.

Talking these projects through with people from the village shows that there is a lot of trust in the community. Not that this is a given, but more that it has been earned by showing what is possible. These are not overnight successes but require vision, faith, and hard work. Attendance at public meetings is always good, and the community does not wait for a council to act on their behalf. In more recent years, the Community Trust has turned its attention to the 2018–2023 Action Plan, and there were many discussions about possibility of taking over the Black Bull Hotel though it was not put up for sale. Instead of using the CRtB registration process, the community approached the pub's owner and negotiated directly as seems to be the pattern in Scotland. In the course of this research, they were asked why this was. They acknowledged the role and aim of the legislation but were not persuaded that this was the correct way to approach an owner if it was to be sold back into the community for everyone's benefit. Rather than pursuing a legal route, they preferred to reach an agreement in person in the manner many other assets are acquired in Scotland and beyond.

From the outset, the community envisaged the pub as more than that and registered the new community benefit society as Black Bull Gartmore Hub & Pub Ltd in 2018. There have often been discussions about whether Gartmore CSEs should have shared ownership or overlap in some manner. The current preference is to keep them distinctly separate, but mutually beneficial entities, as observed in other locations discussed in this chapter – even if their customers and owners might overlap. With 250 community investors backing a share offer, they raised substantial funds.

When combined with their award from the Scottish Land Fund, they were able to reopen the pub in 2019. It is still in the early stages and largely dependent on volunteers – older members of the community work alongside younger residents. It remains open, and some refurbishment has improved their offer of overnight accommodation. A heritage room is dedicated to celebrating the life and past of the village (the pub is also a Listed Building), and the spaces lend themselves to activities for youth activities too. All of these address some of the key desires and challenges faced by the village. It certainly gives an outward impression of looking forward. The community pulled together during the COVID-19 lockdown and looked after each other, keeping the shop stocked and safe – sometimes turning over multiple times what they sold pre-lockdown as word spread about how safe it was to use.

Given that the other Scottish communities who have established COPs are less than 40 miles from Gartmore, this is perhaps a network of COPs and CSEs taking root as observed in other locations. The other two COPs also refer to themselves as hubs. The Merito Pub in Dunlop opened in early 2019 and the People United for Banton (P.U.B.) saved the Swan Inn from demolition in 2018 but are only now mobilizing the business after shutting for refurbishment in 2019 and reopening in August 2020 as the lockdown eases. Previously, there were three pubs in the village of Glenfarg with similar stories of conversion to residential development. Despite this, Glenfarg Community Company has been very resourceful and did not give up just because the physical buildings are no longer available.

Instead, the villagers started a pop-up pub open for certain hours in their village hall. They have been re-building the pub incrementally, in a virtual sense, whilst raising funds to secure some dedicated premises. This is a superb illustration of focusing on the idea and the CSE rather than become fixated by the building and a good place to consider what has been learned from these inspiring stories.

Conclusion

This research documents a trend for similar CSEs reaching back decades in all three regions. Though each cluster was not initiated by a COP, they have all involved at least one local COP, often located with a shop and/or Post Office that is owned by the same community.

COPs are not an essential requirement for the stimulation of other local CSEs, but it has been useful for those communities to have the COP established with them, a recognizable CSE model, as this often serves to demonstrate how such CSEs can play a vital role in community activism and how knowledge can be transferred both within and beyond a community. Some of this is actively supported through the same organizations and bodies who promote CSEs, but peer-to-peer support is often incidental too and more could be done on this nation-to-nation.

It is evident that COPs and associated CSEs have increased in each region in the past 20 years with the number much higher in England than in Wales. Scotland has only a few at the moment, and although they have many CSEs, very few of these are COPs when compared with England and Wales. However, we must also bear in mind that although its population is much larger than Wales, it is more widely dispersed, and this may affect the establishment of COPs in Scotland.

It is tempting to assume that the growth in COPs and associated CSEs is supported through legislature such as Community Rights to Buy. There is little evidence to suggest that this is the case. The growth of CSEs in both Wales and Scotland has occurred on a more informal basis, preferring negotiation with owners rather than pursuing a legal route. That is not to say that this legislation is not helpful – there are a number of locations in England where ACVs have become successful CSEs after employing such processes.

What cannot be denied is that CSEs such as COPs thrive when given the opportunity to get support through organizations that provide business or funding advice. COPs appreciate capital injection and funding support from central or distant bodies but really want to become self-sustaining businesses. Though not all CSEs or COPs are cooperatives, Community Benefit ownership structures and Community Shares offers are key to raising capital. This is particularly relevant if purchase of property is required, but, and perhaps more importantly, this model also empowers communities, allowing them to participate and invest in their own community by working together.

On this basis, some of the same funding bodies that have helped COPs in the past (Plunkett Foundation, The Prince's Countryside Fund, Power to Change) shifted their focus to supporting established CSEs trying to counter the impact of the Coronavirus pandemic within their rural community. Although COPs were generally closed during the COVID-19 lockdown period, a survey of nearly 50% of all COPs in Great Britain highlighted that many were remaining open but diversifying to serve their community in other ways. Sometimes, this was helping with food, being involved in coordination of local activities or acting as a physical hub for other community activities. Some even used closure as an opportunity to refurbish or clear out as it became safe to do so coming out of lockdown (Plunkett, 2020). Even if the COP was closed, there were other associated CSE activities in the zones identified in this study. Some combined the continuing provision of the shop with their own transport networks to get deliveries to the isolated members of their rural communities.

Clear from the discussions that informed this research is that local CSEs such as these are more appreciated now than they were before and the current global situation we find ourselves in will only make them stronger. Such resilience is at the foundation of these CSEs from the outset. Distant and detached from larger conurbations, they are used to making decisions for themselves and by themselves. It is therefore heartening, and it has been a privilege to hear how that has manifested during the pandemic of 2020, mirroring the audible pride these rural communities have in their self-reliance.

The examples of COPs and associated CSEs discussed here also serve to illustrate that they can become sustainable businesses, and even the use of some volunteers does not detract from that. After all, what is the difference between a volunteer who contributes time or skill and a volunteer who chooses to invest or spend in a CSE?

It is all too easy to become distracted by the buildings and places. Perhaps more so with COPs. That is not to say that they should be disregarded as mere physical assets – after all, they are where communities meet, eat, work, and buy. However, it is the people who are the real assets in these enterprises. Volunteers or staff, trustees or customers, promoters or investors. They are all stewards of their community, ensuring that these stories survive to serve the next generation.

References

Ainsworth, P. (2019). *Community Owned Pubs: A CAMRA guide*. Retrieved from https://camra.org.uk/campaign_resources/community-owned-pubs-a-camra-guide/

Cabras, I. (2011). Industrial and provident societies and village pubs: Exploring community cohesion in rural Britain. *Environment and Planning A*, 43(10), pp. 2419–2434.

Cabras, I., Canduela, J. & Raeside, R. (2012). The relation of village and rural pubs with community life and people's well-being in Great Britain. *German Journal of Agricultural Economics*, 61(670–2016–45940), pp. 265–274.

Cabras, I. & Reggiani, C. (2010). Village pubs as a social propellant in rural areas: An econometric study. *Journal of Environmental Planning and Management*, 53(7), pp. 947–962.

CAMRA. (2020). Retrieved from https://tinyurl.com/CommunityOwnedPubs.

Community Shares Unit. (2015). Inside the Market Report June 2015. Retrieved from https://communityshares.org.uk/sites/default/files/resources/community_shares_-_inside_the_market_report_-_june_2015.pdf

Davies, C. (2009 December 30). The Archers helps to save village shops. Retrieved from https://www.theguardian.com/uk/2009/dec/30/archers-village-shops-community-owned

Davies, M., Miscampbell, G., Barnard, M. & Hughes, S. (2017). *What works: Successful community pubs*. London: Power to Change. Retrieved from https://www.powertochange.org.uk/wp-content/uploads/2017/06/Research-Report-5-Pubs-DIGITAL-1.pdf

Dunbar, R. (2016). Friends on tap: The role of pubs *at the heart of the community*, CAMRA.

House of Commons Brief paper Number 8591 (May 28, 2020).

Jenkinson, L. (2018 June 21). Community Hub saved from closure after fundraising campaign. Retrieved from https://www.timesandstar.co.uk/news/17013313.community-hub-saved-closure-fundraising-campaign

Lythe, R. (2006 April 5). Pub is the Hub campaign launched. Retrieved from https://www.thewestmorlandgazette.co.uk/news/722810.pub-is-the-hub-campaign-launched/

McCusker, S. (2018). Learning through architecture and successful capital projects in the post-capitalist economy of Northern England. *Journal of Co-operative Studies*, 51(2), pp. 55–62.

Mount, M. & Cabras, I. (2016). Community cohesion and village pubs in Northern England: An econometric study. *Regional Studies*, 50(7), pp. 1203–1216.

Office for National Statistics. (2018 November 26). *Economies of ale: Small pubs close as chains focus on big bars*. Retrieved from https://www.ons.gov.uk/businessindustryandtrade/business/activitysizeandlocation/articles/economiesofalesmallpubscloseaschainsfocusonbigbars/2018-11-26

Office for National Statistics. (2020 January 16). *Economies of ale: Changes in the UK pubs and bars sector, 2001 to 2019*. Retrieved from https://www.ons.gov.uk/businessindustryandtrade/business/activitysizeandlocation/articles/economiesofalesmallpubscloseaschainsfocusonbigbars/changesintheukpubsandbarssector2001to2019

Plunkett Foundation. (2018). *Community pubs: A better form of business*. Retrieved from https://plunkett.co.uk/wp-content/uploads/PLUNKETT_BB_PUBS19_download2.pdf

Plunkett Foundation. (2020 June 17). *Call to support the community pubs which are diversifying to survive during the lockdown*. Retrieved from https://plunkett.co.uk/wp-content/uploads/Covid-19-More-Than-A-Pub-press-release-170620.pdf

Pub is the Hub. (2020). Case studies. Retrieved from https://www.pubisthehub.org.uk/case-studies/

Sforzi, J. & Bianchi, M. (2020). Fostering social capital: The case of community-owned pubs. *Social Enterprise Journal*, 16(3), pp. 281–297.

Skerratt, S. & Hall, C. (2011). Community ownership of physical assets: Challenges, complexities and implications. *Local Economy*, 26(3), pp. 170–181.

Wainwright, M. (1999 November 6). *Village clubs together to save tiny brewery*. Retrieved from https://www.theguardian.com/uk/1999/nov/06/martinwainwright

5

CORE COMMUNITY CAPITALS AND IMPACT ON SUCCESSFUL COMMUNITY DEVELOPMENT

Felix Sohnrey and Klaus Hegemann

Introduction

Two mega trends have challenged rural areas in developed countries: demography and digitalization. While the former results in fewer and older inhabitants in small settlements, the latter drives individualization and may therefore also reduce *physical* interaction. A possible remedy for these challenges (at least in rural areas) includes community-supported enterprises (CSE), where a collective effort is invested to fulfill community needs. One popular example includes community shops which address both hard (supply) and soft (social inclusion) needs.

General experience shows that some CSEs prosper and remain sustainably successful, while others fail for a variety of reasons. In hindsight, the reasons for failure are often easily attributed either to lacking financial or political support from the local government, insufficient built infrastructure and maintenance, or declining buying behavior of customers. So how can community initiatives maximize their probability of success? What factors are determining the success and failure of community development efforts?

The current study summarizes and highlights the work of the German Rhine-Waal University of Applied Sciences during the past approximately ten years. Voluntary initiatives in 55 villages in Germany and the Netherlands were accompanied and analyzed in various projects, such as the Interreg project "Krachtige Kernen/Starke Dörfer" (KRAKE), which is Dutch and German respectively for "Strong Villages." The goal of the KRAKE project was to further the self-management competencies of engaged volunteer citizens to improve the sustainability of their efforts.

The project had an applied character with moderated town hall meetings and methodological support provided, while ideas, initiatives, and investments originated from the respective community with the goal to increase local livability.

However, there was also a theoretical foundation for the work with the villages, namely the community capital framework (CCF) (Emery and Flora, 2006). An appreciative inquiry was used initially within the framework of a participatory bottom-up approach. The aim was to identify correlations based on the CCF, according to Emery and Flora, so that participating village communities can identify meaningful concepts for future measures to further develop their sense of community. In the long term, the model will be further developed so that both positive and negative effects are foreseeable.

This chapter summarizes action research and semi-structured group interviews of eight villages and examines their community capitals. Taken together with experiences during a three-year period, we distilled quantitative and qualitative correlations, narratives, and factors that drive both successes and failures of community development based on the seven community capitals. The most important, and maybe controversial, the finding is that it is not the hard factors, such as financial capital, that drive success; instead, it is the soft and complex factors such as social, cultural, and human capitals that seem to make the difference.

Every village is special, so each measure must be examined individually and adapted based on the findings. At the same time, however, the hypothesis is that, in every village, and also in every community, there is an identity that, as a strength in combination with other strengths, offers opportunities for active positive social shaping.

Best Practice Example: The Village Grieth

At some point, residents in the villages studied began to ask themselves what is to become of their properties. Many of their children had moved to the city, which apparently offers jobs, pubs, and culture. Some properties were already empty and did not find new owners. Who would want to buy here? The regional bank had closed the local branch, a pub in the town called "Vatican" on the outskirts of the town had been abandoned. The village of Grieth is in a rural area, which is in the process of aging, according to demographers.

Also, from a political standpoint, since it is technically described as a "rural area," it has long been little noticed. However, the fact that their village[1] would be seen too narrowly by this portrayal and since it is part of their identity that is perceived as valuable prompted the residents to become active by starting their own initiatives. Procedurally, this followed a bottom-up approach starting with town hall events.

In the search for professional partners, the city of Kalkar (the village Grieth is part of this city's administration) and the Rhine-Waal University of Applied Sciences were asked to provide further resources and methodological support. The topics that the residents identified as particularly urgent were tackled. For example, a small study of vacancies was conducted by the university and a real estate exchange with sponsorship by the city.

The focus, however, was especially on local supply or access to services, which the residents of Grieth lacked and missed severely according to a representative survey conducted by the university. After intensive preliminary work, discussions and analyses on behalf of the engaged community, a cooperative was formed to start a commercial retail trade – the '*Griether Hanselädchen*.' A German cooperative is a specific legal form for an enterprise that emphasizes democratic decision-making (One Member, One Vote) and intends to further aim for the community, rather than for profit. In an Anglo-Saxon context, this enterprise could be called either a CSE – USA (Walzer and Sandoval, 2016, p. 10; Walzer, 2019) or a Community Shop – UK (Plunket Foundation Report, 2019, p. 4).

Despite all the support provided by partners, it is obvious that the success of such measures depends to a large extent on the voluntary initiative of citizens. This is true in Grieth in an impressive way. However, to illustrate the systematic approach and to work out a model design, the context must be considered (see "The Community Capital Framework" section for methods used). What methodical approach – if any – is available here? And especially important: which factors can ensure the sustainable success of the local supplier? These questions, amongst others, will be answered and discussed later, along with the negative patterns of community development.

At this point, the ideal–typical character of Grieth and the initiative of the Hanselädchen should be emphasized. The strong civic commitment was accompanied at an early stage by the scientific community, which drew references to other foundations and developments in order to make criteria for success accessible and to point out mistakes that could be avoided and to contribute methodological skills (Arntz, Sohnrey and Vorwig, 2019).

Thus, an appreciative inquiry process was used at an early stage to direct the bottom-up-supported procedure to strengthen the existing identity. In addition, lessons learned from the CCF were also used as a central foundation (see the brief literature review on the CCF). It was important to consider the interactions of measures at an early stage so that predictions about the sustainability of the project were viable. In this respect, it was clear that when a community shop is founded, more is involved than a mere business calculation. It was no less important to find a participatory legal framework or low threshold access to make use of existing social capital. And, of course, it was also important to find a building that not only meets the spatial requirements of a retail business but also supports the structural or building capital of the community.

In Grieth, the Hanselädchen (Hanse[2] shop) is now located on the central market square. A café is part of the retail concept. From an economic point of view, the business is viable although it is certainly not profitable. Above all, however, the Hanselädchen is a social meeting place for the inhabitants of Grieth and for the people in the region as well as for tourists. Communication among residents in Grieth is clearly promoted as a small study of an interdisciplinary project of the Rhine-Waal University of Applied Sciences determined (unpublished study). Changes in the real estate market had occurred with vacancies no longer exist, and renovation work is also underway in the Vatican.

The Community Capital Framework

The community capital framework (CCF) builds the theoretical core of this study and therefore deserves a short introduction and literature overview since it can be used as a tool for the systematic identification of assets within a community for positive community change purposes (Emery and Flora, 2006; Flora, Flora and Gasteyer, 2016).

It does so, by dividing communities' resources into seven categories (capitals) to fully account for and distinguish between the respective capital strengths – as opposed to weaknesses – in order to continue the development on the existing foundations of the community. While the capitals do overlap and interact, it remains difficult to measure these links especially with respect to causation (Fey, Bregendahl and Flora, 2006).

It remains contested whether the CCF is a proper theoretical framework with causal determinants that, for instance, allows it to analyze community change from a systems perspective (Emery and Flora, 2006) or whether it is simply a "field theory," helpful in guiding community development practices (Pigg et al., 2013). Either way, the CCF was considered useful in the specific context of the KRAKE project since it uses an applied appreciative inquiry process to determine the status quo of the capitals in each respective village. However, going deeper into the model requires first to define and demarcate the concepts and terms used within this framework.

Capital Definitions

Natural capital serves as an important starting point in the CCF analysis because it forms the basis for the community since it is relatively simple to comprehend because it is observable and mostly descriptive – forests, lakes, rivers, landscape, animals, and parks (Emery and Flora, 2006). However, measuring how natural capital relates to community well-being and with the other capitals can sometimes be difficult (Fey et al., 2006). The natural environment of a community is most often related to cultural and social capital, that is, through organizing nature-related festivities and financial capital, that is, by the depletion of natural capital or the inflow of tourists and related revenues.

Built capital encompasses everything physically constructed by humans, such as infrastructure, buildings, information technologies, bridges, railroads, etc., with a focus on those structures that support the community (Emery and Flora, 2006). Critical, however, is that especially from an outside perspective, "new built capital is often equated with community development, [but] it is effective only when it contributes to other community capitals" (Flora, Flora and Gasteyer, 2016, p. 16).

Financial capital refers to resources that are available to support the community and/or invest in community capacity building (i.e., donations, sponsors but also general income levels). Such goals could entail, for instance, the ability to grant loans for new businesses, support social and civic entrepreneurial activities, and to save money for future purposes (Emery and Flora, 2006).

Political capital refers to access of power, organizations, and respective connections to resources. It also means that people can have a voice and thus create a democratic advantage, engaging in actions that benefit their own community (Emery and Flora, 2006).

Human capital includes education, skills, health, and self-esteem. It refers to the capabilities and potentials of individuals to develop and enhance the resources of their community. Moreover, "human capital addresses the leadership's ability to 'lead across differences', to focus on assets, to be inclusive and participatory and to act proactively in shaping the future of the community" (Emery and Flora 2006, p. 21, see also Becker, 1964).

Cultural capital within the CCF is defined as determining "how" a group views the world, what is valued, the written and unwritten rules of conduct, and more importantly, what is possible to change, which ultimately shapes how people act. It is expressed, for instance, through symbols, traditions, language, and festivities but also in terms of what "voices are heard and listened to, which voices have influences in what area and how creativity, innovation and influence emerge and are nurtured" (Emery and Flora 2006, p. 21). Thus, a "cultural hegemony" allows dominant social groups to impose their worldview over others (Bourdieu, 1986; Emery and Flora, 2006; Flora et al., 2016).

Social capital in the CCF is defined as "who" a group knows and "why" they interact with each other – it reflects the connections among people and organizations or the "social glue" to make things happen (Putnam, 1995; Emery and Flora, 2006; Westlund, 2006). It also includes mutual trust, reciprocity, associations, collective identity, willingness to join forces, and working together with a sense of shared future (Flora et al., 2016), which is characterized by a linear or exponential relation to distance due to lower interaction costs (Westlund and Larsson, 2016). Social capital can be further distinguished between bridging and bonding social capital, that is, how groups interact within their community and outside of it.

How Does the Spiraling-Up (Not) Work?

This framework, which builds on the concept of social capital as its foundation, was put forward by Emery and Flora (2006), who postulated that social capital, within the CCF, is the critical resource[3] to reverse a downward spiraling development (i.e., through industry loss and subsequent unemployment and poverty) into a spiraling-up development. In other words, social capital is considered as a main causal determinant of collective action and thus, a community's potential for spiraling-up. They build on Gutiérrez-Montes's (2005) finding that assets build on assets, or in other words, success builds on success. Such a spiraling-up process may be initiated, for instance, when assets flow across capitals. Meaning that when a community invests social capital in another capital, (un-)intended consequences of the said investment may therefore spillover to stocks of other capitals, such as cultural, financial, and others.

Emery's and Flora's notions of spiraling-up and the centrality of social capital are contested, however. In an empirical study, Pigg et al., (2013) find that the process among the various capitals is more complex than stated previously and that the narrative of upward and downward trends is too simple. Instead, the capitals interact amongst each other in different ways, and generalizations are both hard to establish and require further research. They interpret the CCF as a tool, which provides a framework to organize information and potentials for improvement. Participants in programs appear to "leverage the resources represented by the CCF among and against one another" (ibid., p. 492). Consequently, the conclusion is that the CCF, as a method for understanding the nature of and process(es) underlying community development, should be considered as an applied 'field theory,' instead of a generalized guideline to community development (Pigg et al., 2013).

Another study, while still supporting the spiraling-up narrative, posits that it is not only social capital at the core of community development but also cultural and human capital, which were a central requirement to mobilize political capital after a natural catastrophe required the rebuilding of an entire town. The political capital was necessary to acquire financial capital, which was a prerequisite to restore built and natural capital.

> Unlike previous research that emphasizes the role of social capital as the primary capital to be mobilized [...] this research adds cultural capital as a precursor to mobilizing social capital. Cultural capital determines how a community engages in collective action.
>
> *(Stofferahn, 2012, p. 1)*

These different findings should not be interpreted as contradictory. Rather they only highlight the uniqueness of each community and, consequentially, the impossibility to generalize causal capital origins of positive developments. What all of the successful communities have in common, though, is that they start with their strengths, that is, focus on their existing assets (see, for instance, Kretzmann and McKnight (1993) on their approach to asset-based community development [ABCD]).

Methodology

This section is kept brief intentionally to leave more room for the analysis and discussion of results. Yet, it remains important to highlight the methodological approach of the current study both from an applied (practitioners) and academic (researchers) perspective.

Applied – Practitioner's Perspective

As mentioned previously, researchers from the Rhine-Waal University approach communities using a bottom-up perspective. This means that any idea or initiative for change have to originate from within the community itself, as opposed to generalized best-practice examples, case studies, or governmental programs (top-down). This process allows each community to find the proper solution(s) for their respective and highly specific context.

Finding those specific and individual solutions requires establishing common ground on existing strengths. Focusing on assets through an appreciative inquiry is a useful tool to maintain a positive discussion and helps volunteers rediscover forgotten aspects about their community that they value very much. Moreover, taking a collective inventory of each of the seven community capitals generates a systemic overview of a community's foundations and allows it to identify connections among those capitals – which can be useful in later stages of project development and implementation.

Other important aspects of the process include participation and communication, which are strongly connected and interrelated. Bottom-up only functions when volunteers have a chance to participate in every step of the process – and they will only do so when they feel informed and knowledgeable about what is happening. This means that proactive traditional and modern forms of communication must be used to keep the community up-to-date and involved.

It is paramount that volunteers take over responsibility and accountability of the new undertaking from the start to achieve sustainable solution(s). Not only will this boost individual motivation and commitment but also increases identification and support from the collective community.

Academic – Researcher's Perspective

The current study follows an abductive approach, which is a blend of deduction and induction – deduction moves from theory to data and induction moves from data to theory. The deductive element of the current study relates to the investigation of the hypothesis testing whether spiraling-up is solely caused by existing social capital. The inductive element concerns its theory modification based on the analysis of villages' strengths.

The premise of this chapter is that villages' success in terms of their relative quality of life is caused by internal, rather than external, factors. In other words, the assumption is that 'complex' capitals (such as social, cultural, and human) have a stronger causal impact than 'descriptive' ones (such as natural and built). Generalizations will be attempted, although their external validity will be limited by specific regional and cultural factors of the study. *Data collection* (semi-structured group interviews) is used to explore a *phenomenon* (community development), identify *themes* and *patterns* (capital relations), locate these in a *theoretical framework* (CCF), and test it through subsequent *data collection* (action research and observation).

As described above, data collection was carried out in two ways. First, semi-structured group interviews were conducted to collect the status of community capitals per village, which allowed researchers to go in-depth where necessary while maintaining comparability due to an identical interview guide. Villages have long-standing traditions and history, which may prime participants about what may or may not be possible to achieve (cultural capital), which topics to discuss, and how to proceed. The interview guide has three parts. The first part deals with the (positive) perception of the village, the second and main part assesses each capital individually, and the third and the last part asks about future visions and goals.

To account for the authors' immersion and potential subjectivity, a qualitative content analysis is further combined with a quantitative analysis of code (capital) relations. In other words, qualitative data is *quantified*, meaning that "specific events in the data are counted as frequencies and numerically coded for statistical analysis" (Saunders, Lewis and Thornhill, 2019, p. 166).

Codes are applied to both positive and negative answers to fully reflect the current situation in the communities and to be able to draw conclusions regarding reasons for success and failure (research question). This implies that the sheer amount of codes distributed for one capital does not necessarily reflect the respective strengths or assets of the community in this capital. The researchers' task is to make connections between the quantitative amounts of capital codes and the qualitative nature of the conversation, which is supplemented by the analysis software MAXQDA that offers two functions, the code relation browser and code maps.

A total of eight villages were interviewed. The sample selection of the interviews is mostly contingent on the structure of the KRAKE project. To participate, a village, or rather a key leader, must sign a (somewhat formal) letter of intent. However, this document had no legal implications. Rather, it was meant to strengthen commitment between the involved parties. Invitations to the group interview were organized by contact persons within the community and are therefore not completely randomized.

Besides the semi-structured group interview, data collection for this study was also used through so-called action research and participant observations, which goes partially hand in hand. Action research has its roots in organizational learning and the production of practical solutions to real-world problems (Saunders et al., 2019). In the case of the KRAKE project, the social organization of a village community is considered as an "organization" that involves more about self-management competencies, hence the "learning," and the "practical solutions" refer to the implementations of projects to further livability "in the real world."

Participation is an important aspect of action research since it is also a social process in which the researcher works with members of a community as a facilitator and teacher (Greenwood and Levin, 2007). It also requires collaboration or building a democratic approach to communication and decision-making. The researcher passes on his or her own skills and capabilities to participants so that they effectively become co-researchers (Saunders et al., 2019).

This is exactly what happened in the KRAKE project, Volunteers are considered experts about their living environment and their community, not as research subjects or powerless people in need of external advice on how to solve their problems. Researchers in the project acted as incubators and moderators of community discussions (facilitator). The general input and specific ideas originated from the community (democratic) and inquiry into the functioning of their social processes made participants effectively co-researchers (Arntz et al., 2019).

Community Capital Connections

To remain within the scope of this chapter, detailed results of the data collection efforts are presented for only the village Grieth – simply because it is a very successful example of community development through a CSE (local supply). To provide deeper insight and analysis, aggregate results of sample data (n = 8) will be included in the following discussions.

Exemplary Case: Grieth

Grieth has roughly 830 inhabitants and is located directly next to the river Rhine, which is not just a stock of natural capital but also influences built, social and cultural capital. The villages' identity is still closely linked to its rich historic roots dating to the year 1250 when it was founded as a Hanseatic city. Thus, the built infrastructure resembles more of an urban city than a rural village, with houses being in very close proximity and without a typical garden. Since the main road runs outside the village, it has no negative impact on safety or social cohesion.

After the last pub closed in 2013, a group of volunteers, some of whom also were scientists at the Rhine-Waal University of Applied Sciences (human and social capital), created a research project to use Grieth as a field lab and test solutions for rural villages.

In 2016, the citizen initiative reintegrated a local supply of groceries in the form of a cooperative with an integrated social meeting space (café). Ever since then, a proper spiraling-up development could be observed with increased social interactions and communications[4] (social and cultural capital), which also made the village more attractive. After two years, no vacant building/apartment was left, and real estate prices increased slightly (built and financial capital). The goal for the KRAKE project was to realize the sustainability of the village store with the help of volunteers and to improve the social use of the central market space (black circle in the map) in front of the "Hanselädchen."

The interview process to collect the community capitals of Grieth was somewhat difficult to organize because the inhabitants were somewhat skeptical about the constant questioning and surveying from various researchers. Eventually, three local leaders, all over the age of 50, agreed to participate, which allowed a deep insight into the organization of the village. However, it does not fully represent the views of the average Grieth resident since younger generations are for instance not included. This limitation did not render the interview obsolete; however, it is an important factor to recognize when reviewing the relations among the community capitals.

Grieth's Assets

A highlight for the participants in the traditional culture of "robbers and pirates" (#01:33:55#) that stems from its Hanseatic roots and translates to "Whatever needs to be done, the village gets together and gets it done." This symbolizes the strong sense of self-efficacy and independence (cultural capital) as well as the dense social networks and mutual trust (social capital) to take care of their own village – both manifested in the current example of the new village store.

The local leaders (human capital) are another special asset of Grieth. One member stands out as a fitting example since she was heavily involved in the creation and day-to-day running of the cooperative. She is also a member of the parliament in the municipality (political capital) and worked in the context of the research project, which allowed her to obtain external know-how and financial resources (bridging social and financial capital).

Another connection lies with the close proximity of the buildings in Grieth's historic core (built capital) and social interactions since lively neighborhoods are often characterized by spontaneous joint activities (social capital), such as the "*Mauerbier*" (wall-beer, translated by author). In other words, since people are so close to each other physically, they are more likely to spend time together socially. Future wishes of the interviewees relate mostly to further their political and financial independence since they do not feel that their interests are properly represented by the administration, due mainly to the low number of possible representatives in the regional parliament.[5]

Yet, in the aftermath of the interview, it was revealed that there is also unresolved conflict between the most prominent local association and the newly established cooperative involving the "Hanselädchen." Because the village store receives much (media) attention and some financial consideration, other stakeholders in the community might fear missing out and thus do not cooperate at times. This may be a case where a high degree of social capital can be considered negatively since it may also function to exclude others (Portes and Landolt, 1996).

Grieth's Capital Connections

The interconnections and overlapping of capital codes from the interview are described and analyzed next. Table 5.1 shows the absolute times a capital has been

TABLE 5.1 Numerical code relation browser of community capitals in Grieth

	Political	*Financial*	*Natural*	*Built*	*Human*	*Cultural*	*Social*	*Sum*
Political	0	6	0	6	3	6	21	42
Financial	6	0	2	4	2	7	25	46
Natural	0	2	0	15	0	4	3	24
Built	6	4	15	0	7	10	26	68
Human	3	2	0	7	0	16	22	50
Cultural	6	7	4	10	16	0	46	89
Social	21	25	3	26	22	46	0	143
Relative (%)	9.1	10.0	5.2	14.7	10.8	19.3	31.0	100.0

Source: Compiled by the authors.

mentioned together with a different capital; the Sum column summarizes total capital connections, and the bottom row shows relative per-capital proportions of these connections.

The code relation browser for Grieth shows a strong connection of social capital with nearly every other capital, except for natural, while the closest relationship is with cultural capital. There are a total of 143 (31.0%) links to social capital, followed by 89 (19.3%) with cultural capital and 68 (14.7%) with built capital. This emphasizes the importance of social networks and organizations in relation to the village's activities and quality of life.

What stands out on the lower spectrum is that, despite the prominence of Grieth's natural environment (5.2%), it has hardly any connections to other capitals than built, which could imply that people use the natural surrounding privately rather than collectively. In light of the interview participants, it is not surprising that personal networks are strongly related to the ability to obtain external financial resources and support. While there is definitively a certain legitimization to characterize Grieth with a strong connected political and financial capital, it undermines the importance and abundance of human capital, which seems to have been somewhat underrepresented due to the circumstances of the interview since Grieth's human capital is 5% less connected than the average of all villages.

Political (9.1%) and financial capital (10.0%) are also strongly connected in Grieth when compared with the other villages and general averages. The code map (Figure 5.1) clarifies that the two capitals are in fact strongly interrelated. It also confirms the centrality of social capital relative to the other capitals. Especially interesting in the case of Grieth is the connection with built capital since the urban structures and proximity as well as the new village store seem to further social interaction in the village.

Another observation in the code map is that there seem to be certain groups or rather matches of two capitals that are particularly related to each other – such as built and natural; political and financial; and last but not least, human and cultural – with social capital at the center of it all (at least in Grieth).

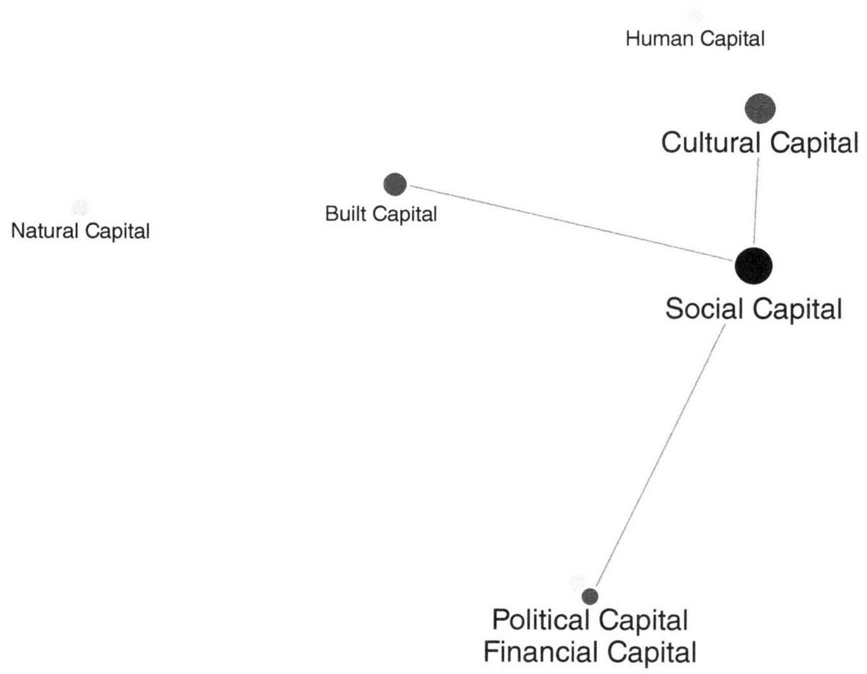

FIGURE 5.1 Code map of capital relations in Grieth.
Source: Compiled by the authors.

Aggregate per Capital Results

Grieth is, in many ways, a best-case scenario example in terms of spiraling-up development. Ultimately, however, not every community will be able to implement such a large-scale project and neither will every community need this specific solution. To generalize further, it is necessary to include the results from an aggregate perspective of the entire sample, which includes eight villages. While doing so, please keep in mind the limited external validity, especially the transatlantic.

The table below is an overview of each village's absolute sum of capital connections (i.e., the column on the far right in figure three above). Dark and light shades indicate the lowest and highest connections per capital, respectively. The bottom two rows display the arithmetic mean and the standard deviation per capital connection. Unfortunately, it is not possible to elaborate on the rich context of each of the eight villages, which would improve the reader's interpretation of the analysis, as these capital connections alone are not sufficient to draw meaningful conclusions. Therefore, the analysis below combines aspects of action research and participant observation with Table 5.2.

Natural capital, as well as geography in general, does not seem to have a significant influence on the outcome of community development efforts. It is more or

TABLE 5.2 Numerical code matrix browser per village and capital

Village	*Political (%)*	*Finance (%)*	*Natural (%)*	*Built (%)*	*Human (%)*	*Cultural (%)*	*Social (%)*
1	9.1	10.0	5.2	14.7	10.8	19.3	31.0
2	4.4	4.7	3.7	11.8	18.0	26.1	31.3
3	3.4	5.7	7.0	13.4	18.8	22.9	28.9
4	3.7	6.6	2.3	12.0	18.0	23.2	34.4
5	12.9	5.7	1.7	13.8	19.9	17.6	28.4
6	7.5	4.7	7.2	18.3	10.8	25.1	26.4
7	4.8	7.0	2.2	16.0	11.8	22.2	36.0
8	4.1	6.6	3.8	14.2	18.8	21.3	31.2
Mean	6.2	6.4	4.1	14.3	15.8	22.2	30.9
S.D.	3.1	1.6	2.0	2.0	3.7	2.6	2.9

Source: Compiled by the authors.

less evenly distributed among the villages, and there is apparently no relation to the eventual outcome. Some communities are more characterized by their natural environment and some are less, yet their development is not affected by either. Nevertheless, natural capital can be an important asset and may also have a positive influence on other capitals, such as cultural (identity) and financial (tourism).

Natural capital may also be considered as a foundation (Flora, Flora and Gasteyer, 2016) since many people stated that their decision to either remain or move to the village (human capital) was its beautiful natural embeddedness. However, its usage seems to be more individualistic and less collectively frequented. Natural capital has the lowest capital interconnections of all capitals – probably not because it is the weakest capital of the community, but more likely because it is less relevant for community cohesion and development and more relevant for personal recreation.

Built capital also seems to be foundational for a community since infrastructure in general, but more specifically, space for social gatherings are important assets. Built capital, therefore, has a strong connection to social capital, as it allows both formal and informal meetings. Grieth's story ultimately began with the closing of a pub, and the success of the local shop is to a large degree due to people being able to meet spontaneously in the café and/or to rent other rooms for a fraction of the "real" price. Community-owned buildings are also tremendous incubators of innovation and progress.

Another village has a "Citizen House," a self-organized place for the entire community and the church. It is frequently used as a source of pride and a place for the community to join forces. Yet, another village runs a "Citizen Hall," a self-organized assembly room for common purpose and dedication, which was renovated without external support, completely based on volunteers' engagements. The positive consequences of a collectively used built infrastructure are especially apparent in the Code Matrix Browser, relative to capital, where both Grieth and Wemb have a built capital that is strongly interconnected.

While there appears to be a certain relationship regarding village success and the abundance of *financial assets*, these results do not inspire sufficient confidence to draw meaningful conclusions. Given the project region, local circumstances are, on average, much more favorable than in other regions of Germany. The proximity to the job engine of the metropolitan Ruhr area and relatively well-earning commuters suggest that the sample's financial capital is likely to be stronger than the national average. Financial access is certainly a relevant, yet not causal determinant, of village development, which makes the abundance of financial capital an axiomatic assumption and a limitation of the study.

The strengths of communities in terms of *political capital* seem to be a valuable, yet neither a necessary nor a sufficient condition for successful community development. In one village, the vice-mayor participates as a volunteer in community development, and her personal contacts may help to speed up certain processes, yet there is no significant difference relative to similar efforts in other communities. One community created a unique "marketing association" that provides effective political leverage because it enabled the village voice to have more weight, yet this asset was not sufficient to prevent the local CSE from going bankrupt.

Last, in one village, the associations receive regular financial inflows from the municipality's fund (an asset no other village has), and the municipality also offered a guarantee for funding the cooperative at the bank and land to construct the CSE, free of charge. Yet, construction to date has not commenced and compared to Grieth, which had none of these supporting political factors for their CSE, shows that political capital may definitively support, yet is neither necessary nor sufficient for a village's successful development. At the same time, political capital, or rather its absence, may well deter positive developments when people feel left alone, their interests not represented and/or are powerless about their own fate – without a perspective, people will not invest their "free time" for the future of their community.

Human capital is the great 'unexpected' in the table, with no discernible relation between its assets and village development. Although this might also be due to methodological flaws in the interview guide, as interviewees were often unable to grasp the concept of "human capital" and how it is related to their community. Traditionally, human capital would be defined as education and skills of inhabitants, making schools very important in this regard (even more so as they attract young parents).

Paradoxically though, it is not the existence of an elementary school, but its absence that seems to stand out – as some villages without a school yield much better results than those who still have a school in the village. Maybe closing a school acts as a kind of "wake up call" to volunteers in villages who are "*too well off*" (see the next section) and provides the necessary urgency (nudge) to bundle their forces. This is pure speculation, of course, but an interesting observation, nonetheless. So, all in all, despite no quantitative relation between human capital and villages' success, it still appears that qualitatively, human capital could be labeled as a necessary condition for positive spiraling-up developments of communities. Why? Because more often than not, it is the key leaders who are emerging and who contribute not just their skills but their networks and engagement for their community that spills over to other areas of community development.

In our sample of villages, *cultural capital* has a linear relationship with village success. This is especially interesting since Emery and Flora (2006) did not mention the importance of cultural capital for spiraling-up at all, yet Stofferahn (2012) did. How may this be explained? The three top-achieving villages have associations (link to social capital) that define themselves as an open, welcoming, and integrating village that appreciates "newcomers" and allow them to contribute (link to human capital) while possessing high degrees of confidence in their own ability to shape their future (self-efficacy).

Three villages with moderate success have a slightly traditional understanding of how associations are supposed to function and while they are also very much open toward "newcomers," it might be slightly more difficult for them to convince others of their ideas. They are also confident to shape their future, but not as unconditional as the top-performer above. Two villages remain; they have a rather traditional understanding of associations functioning and existing factions in their community, that is, due to historical disagreements that dominate their (un)willingness to cooperate (link to social capital). Both villages experience a sustained culture of low self-efficacy, where citizens do not believe that they are able to realize new ideas to further their livability. Overall, it seems as if cultural capital is an important link between social and human capital, thus a necessary condition for a village's success, yet not sufficient. Moreover, cultural capital appears to have more explanatory power in terms of why villages fail rather than why they succeed.

As suggested by Emery and Flora (2006), *social capital* does, from a qualitative perspective, seem to be an important determinant of successful community development. Well-connected networks of associations with excellent external contacts (bridging social capital) and internal cohesion and cooperation (bonding social capital) allow communities to initiate a spiraling-up development. The three top-performing villages stand out in particular in this regard. On one hand, each village has well-connected individuals that enable the community to tap into external funds, expertise, and resources. On the other hand, each village has a "roof organization" (coordinating committee) for its associations or rather, for the entire community, with a strong sense of togetherness (link to culture) and coordination to solve, for instance, collective action problems (bonding).

Yet, one village from the middle and top group, respectively, also has a coordinating committee of their associations (bonding) and well-established external contacts to provide resources when necessary (bridging) – with a minor difference compared to the aforementioned villages in the intensity of the strength of togetherness (link to culture). One village stands out as the only one with weaker social capital as they have no coordinating committee to deal with collective action problems and factions that block each other's progress, and thus, there is no feeling of mutual trust among the different parties.

Interestingly, in contrast to cultural capital, there is not the same "perfect" relationship between assets and successful development. Therefore, we must conclude that social capital is indeed a necessary condition for successful development, but it is neither sufficient nor the only necessary condition, as the full potential of social assets can only be realized when connected to a strong cultural and human capital.

Patterns in Capital Map(s)

Figure 5.2 is another aggregate construct, here of all eight code maps together (i.e., see Figure 5.1 from Grieth). It shows that on average, the very core of a village community is made up of social and cultural capital, which are interconnected to a large extent, with supporting pillars of human and built capital. Although natural capital is somewhat isolated, political and financial capital are very close to one another with a distant link to human capital.

The aggregate code map further corroborates the above findings. It appears that there is not a single capital that qualifies as a sufficient criterion, which (in the absence of all other capitals) would still enable successful community development. On the contrary, findings from our data hint toward the possibility that it is, in fact, the interrelation of mostly cultural and social capital, with supporting casts from human and built capitals, their connection and synergies, that allow for a successful spiraling-up development. The nucleus of a community is made of its social and cultural capital, and together, they form the basis for successful village development.

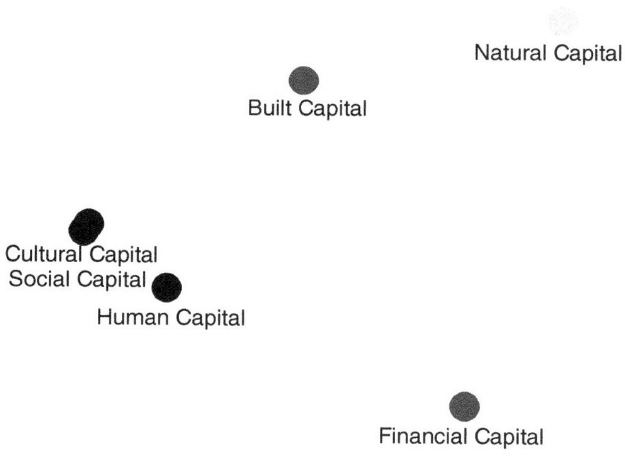

FIGURE 5.2 Code map of capital relations for eight villages.
Source: Compiled by the authors.

Negative Patterns of Community Development

"*Ghosts from the past*": Small villages, in which a low degree of anonymity defines social life, where knowledge and experiences are passed on and are lived on from generation to generation, are well aware of what works (not) in their community (Cultural capital). This may, however, also turn into a negative perception, especially if past efforts did not succeed. All villages experience setbacks at some point in the process; yet, in three circumstances, it feels as if a "*ghost from the past*" would haunt the volunteers and their self-efficacy until today. An interviewee in one village literally said that nothing ever succeeds in this village, another community is extremely skeptical after the village store went bankrupt, and the third is still hung up on projects that were not realized 20 years ago. Interestingly, these three villages have relatively high interconnections with cultural capital in the code matrix browser.

"*Too well off*": Some villages, at least in this region of Germany, are very well off indeed. Their built infrastructure provides for every possible want and need, with an elementary school, community spaces, local supply, and other assets. Yet, (demographic) change is inevitable and be it key leaders who are retiring or festivities that are no longer visited, every village community must be proactive regarding its development. Two villages were characterized by an insufficient urgency among the volunteers. However, if suddenly, something external changes, people are quick to demand action and participate actively in the process. In one of those villages, capital relations are always within one standard deviation of the aggregate relations, hence no outlier. This may be interpreted as no special excitement and/or resentment about a specific capital, in other words, a certain satisfaction with the status quo.

"*Opposing factions*": In Germany, it is (traditionally) the responsibility of local associations to trigger village development and/or run CSEs. They are well-established, have a very specific and clear set of (un-)written rules on how to approach projects, or rather, how to approach whom in which hierarchical order, and they also have a social understanding of people in terms of those who were born in the village (old-timer[6]) and those who moved there (newcomer).

In Grieth, a new initiative was established to start a cooperative and consequently, a local supply shop – but the key personnel involved were people who moved to the village. Although the founders were also somewhat integrated in the associations, this project was rather considered as "external" during the inception phase, and today, the relative success of the stores overshadows the traditional associations and their power to shape the community. As a result, tendencies are emerging that are somewhat associated with less cooperation and coordination.

The existence of factions within a community is more directly noticeable in villages, where a demarcation between old-timers and newcomers exists. In one village, people who wanted to become engaged in and for their community, contingent on being able to do so outside the "traditional approach" from the associations, invited the KRAKE project team for a citizen debate. Yet, two of the most influential associations were not willing to join forces in this specific kind of participatory and collaborative environment.

A different, but significant, demarcation exists in yet another village. When no successor was willing to take over the position as president of the home association, a 24-year old woman[7] took over. She went through the traditional ways of the various associations from Boy Scouts to the Heimatverein, and she literally succeeded her father as president and still – perhaps because of age, gender, or even new ideas and approaches, or possibly a combination of all, causes the other main association to withdraw and even intimidate the new leader indirectly. Ultimately, she did not nominate for the position again after the first two-year term because the opposition was driving a further wedge in the community, and the volunteer effort should definitively contain an enjoyable part as well.

Lessons Learned

Two questions are necessary to discuss based on the findings. First, how do we translate these rather abstract and theoretical findings into practical advice and general lessons learned? And second, are these findings, which relate more to general community development, applicable to efforts of CSEs and if so, how?

One main take away is that the community capitals, and with them the community's assets, are highly interconnected and even interdependent, meaning that the capitals build on each other. Therefore, when any community wants to create change[8] to further its own livability, it may be a useful starting point to inventory local strengths. This process allows different perspectives and stories to be shared and thus new insights to be gained from various community members. A heterogeneous mix of skills and knowledge makes for an effective team!

Having taken such an inventory, it may at first become rather obvious and straightforward that capitals are underserved and therefore need further investment. In Grieth, for instance, the built capital was in decline, so it made sense to invest in it. Yet, our experience shows that success in community development is not necessarily this linear. Descriptive capitals especially built and financial are often identified as weaknesses, yet standalone investments in these capitals will unlikely result in sustainable improvements. Community development starts from the *community's core* – such as social, cultural, and/or human capital. Having included community needs that relate to the core, one can then attempt to address further and likewise important capitals, such as built and financial – but it should not serve as a starting point.

In other words, while a community shop (which would be defined as built capital) may always help improve the local livability, the social and cultural aspects of the store and the café are the underlying reasons for success. Increased quality and quantity of communication through a central meeting spot allows for random and planned personal interaction. After the pub closed, this was what the citizens were longing for the most!

This is precisely the reason why the other village that has been attempting to open a community shop, failed (thus far) despite stronger assets in financial and political capital. The underlying problem in the village is a fragmented community due to different factions (cultural capital) as well as the built structure of the village, making the social cohesion difficult. Therefore, any kind of individually designed solution must be aware of the preliminary inventory and attempt to include the most prevalent and current community need regarding the core capitals (social, cultural, and human) since those have the strongest correlation to successful community development. In other words, any implementation should aim to influence at least two capitals directly, which may then spill over to other capitals as well.

Another main finding from the KRAKE project and the data collection has been that no community is equal to another one. Each village is unique in its respective capital structure, meaning that each village must work out individual solutions to their specific situation – starting with the inventory.

Finally, we need to determine whether these results apply to CSEs as well. The short answer is yes; we believe that they do simply because any collective community effort (be it development or enterprise) is ultimately designed to improve local quality of life based on voluntary citizen engagement. Thus, community development, as seen in the example of Grieth, can take the form of a CSE (community shop) since a CSE is meant to develop the community.

Conclusion

The key finding in this chapter is that a village's success in terms of relative quality of life is caused by internal, rather than external, factors. In other words, it is assumed that 'complex' capitals (such as social, cultural, and human) have a stronger causal impact compared to 'descriptive' ones (such as natural, financial, and built). Generalizations were attempted, although external validity is limited due to specific regional and cultural factors in the current study. Data collection (semi-structured group interviews) is used to explore a phenomenon (community development), identify themes and patterns (capital relations), locate these in a theoretical framework (CCF), and test through subsequent data collection (action research and observation). These findings should be, at least in our assumption, directly applicable to the context of CSEs – if your understandings might vary, we would be interested in a discussion about different experiences.

Notes

1 The terms village and community are used synonymously/interchangeably throughout this chapter.
2 The Hanse is a historic German association of sea traders, which Grieth used to be a part of due to its vicinity to the river Rhine. It therefore still provides a strong sense of belonging and identity to the community.
3 "Our contention is that the best entry point to spiraling-up is social capital" (Emery and Flora 2006, p. 23).

4 A student research project compared the social interactions and communications of Grieth and its neighbor village Wissel in the Winter of 2016. It found a significant positive structure of both categories in Grieth as opposed to Wissel due to common and central store as a meeting point.
5 This is, of course, a testament to the specific backgrounds of the interview participants.
6 These generalizing terms are created for easier legibility only. 'Old' and 'new' are not to be understood as value laden.
7 Technically an "old-timer," since she was born in Hommersum (this is why there is no value statement in connection with the term 'old-timer', as it may also apply to young people).
8 This implies that, for effective community development, the residents need not only to be involved, but they shall be in charge of the design of projects and their individual solutions. Top-down solutions are hardly sustainable because of a lack of identification with and commitment for the implemented assignment – meaning that nobody feels responsible for maintenance.

References

Arntz, B., Sohnrey, F. and Vorwig, A. (2019). Starke Dörfer: Nachhaltige Entwicklung in den "kleinen Kernen" durch Bürgerbeteilung, in: Hegemann, K. and Sohnrey, F. (eds.): *Soziale Verantwortung. Eine vergessene Selbstverständlichkeit?*, pp. 106–122, Augsburg: Rainer Hampp Verlag.

Becker, G. (1964). *Human Capital: A Theoretical and Empirical Analysis with Special Reference to Education*, New York: Columbia University Press.

Bourdieu, P. (1986). The Forms of Capital, in: Richardson, J. (ed.): *Handbook of Theory and Research for the Sociology of Education*, pp. 241–258, New York: Greenwood Press.

Emery, M. and Flora, C. (2006). Spiraling-up: Mapping Community Transformation with Community Capitals Framework, *Community Development*, 37(1), 19–35.

Fey, S., Bregendahl, C. and Flora, C. (2006). The Measurement of Community Capitals through Research, *Online Journal of Rural Research & Policy*, 1(1), 1–26.

Flora, C. B., Flora, J. L. and Gasteyer, S. P. (2016). *Rural Communities: Legacy and Change* (5th Ed.), Boulder, CO: Westview Press.

Greenwood, D. J. and Levin, M. (2007). *Introduction to Action Research* (2nd Ed.), London: Sage.

Gutiérrez-Montes, I. (2005). Healthy Communities Equals Healthy Ecosystems? Evolution (and Breakdown) of a Participatory Ecological Research Project towards a Community Natural Resource Management Process, San Miguel Chimalepa (Mexico), PhD Dissertation, Iowa State University.

Kretzmann, J. P. and McKnight, J. L. (1993). *Building Communities from the Inside Out: A Path toward Finding and Mobilizing a Community's assets*, Chicago, IL: ACTA Press.

Pigg, K., Gasteyer, S. P., Martin, K. E., Keating, K. and Apaliyah, G. P. (2013). The Community Capitals Framework: An Empirical Examination on Internal Relationships, *Community Development*, 44(4), 492–502.

Plunket Foundation Report. (2019). *Community Shops: A Better Form of Business*, available online at: https://plunkett.co.uk/reports/

Portes, A. and Landolt, P. (1996). The Downside of Social Capital, *The American Prospect*, 26, 18–21.

Putnam, R. (1995). Bowling Alone: America's Declining Social Capital, *Journal of Democracy*, 6(1), 65–78, available online at: http://archive.realtor.org/sites/default/files/BowlingAlone.pdf (accessed at February 23, 2020).

Saunders, M., Lewis, P. and Thornhill, A. (2019). *Research Methods for Business Students* (8th Ed.), New York: Pearson.

Stofferahn, C. (2012). Community Capitals and Disaster Recovery: Northwood ND Recovers from an EF 4 Tornado, *Community Development*, 43, 581–598.

Walzer, N. (2019). *Guidebook and Resources for Starting Community Supported Enterprises*, East Lansing, MI: North Central Regional Center for Rural Development, available online at: https://www.cgs.niu.edu/Reports/cse-guidebook-final-2-8-19.pdf

Walzer, N. and Sandoval, J. (2016). *Emergence and Growth of Community Supported Enterprises*, Center for Governmental Studies, Northern Illinois University, available online at: https://www.cgs.niu.edu/Reports/Emergence-and-Growth-of-Community-Supported-Enterprises.pdf

Westlund, H. (2006). *Social Capital in the Knowledge Economy: Theory and Empirics*, Berlin, Heidelberg and New York: Springer.

Westlund, H. and Larsson, J. (2016). Social Capital and Regional Development: An Introduction, in: Westlund, H. and Larsson, J. (eds.): *Handbook of Social Capital and Regional Development*, pp. 1–23, Cheltenham: Edward Elgar.

6

ST. PAUL, KANSAS' CITY-OWNED GROCERY STORE

A Variation of the Community Supported Enterprise Approach

David E. Procter

Introduction

In 2006, Kansas State University (KSU) created the Center for Engagement and Community Development (CECD) with a mission to facilitate campus/community partnerships that would address the salient challenges and needs facing Kansans and communities worldwide. The university sought to expand campus engagement beyond the traditional Extension service and work in areas of need not necessarily addressed by K-State Research and Extension. CECD staff spent 2006 attending meetings and conferences, listening to Kansans' goals, dreams, and concerns. It was clear from these listening sessions that maintaining local, independently owned grocery stores in rural Kansas was a salient need and a significant challenge. Kansans discussed the rural grocery store issue as both a community sustainability and healthy food access crisis.

To address these challenges, the KSU CECD launched the Rural Grocery Initiative[1] (RGI) in 2007. RGI is a multi-state, multi-university, campus/community partnership involving food access and community development non-profits, state and federal funders, rural grocery store owners, food distributors, grocery-affiliated businesses, state and federal government agencies as well as university faculty, staff, and extension professionals. RGI's work has been guided by five goals including (1) cataloging and understanding challenges faced by these small businesses, (2) developing evidence-based responses to the identified challenges, (3) building both virtual and face-to-face networks for rural grocers and rural food access stakeholders, (4) increasing rural access to healthful foods, and (5) identifying and supporting sustainable models of rural grocery operation.

The RGI's research identified six general organizational structures used by rural Kansas grocery operations. These ownership models include resident-owned operations, cooperatively owned grocery stores, school-owned grocery businesses, sole proprietorships, 501c3 grocery operations, and city-owned grocery businesses. Interestingly, five of these six models are some form of a community supported enterprise (CSE).[2]

This chapter focuses on one specific model of a community supported grocery enterprise, the city-owned grocery operation. Using primary and secondary source data and qualitative interview data, the analyses examine how rural communities work to build, launch, and sustain a grocery store owned and operated by the local city government.

Beginning with a general discussion of the value grocery stores provide rural communities, discussions then move to a specific case study of St. Paul, Kansas as it worked to launch and sustain its city-owned supermarket. The analyses also draw on the experiences of other rural communities moving to a municipally owned grocery store model, including Erie and Caney, Kansas and Baldwin, Florida. The chapter concludes by distilling principles and lessons learned from the St. Paul process along with how these practices can be generalized to other rural communities. The experiences of St. Paul highlight how a city-operated grocery store is both similar and yet, in some ways, distinct from other forms of CSEs.

The Community Need for Rural Grocery Stores

Grocery stores are a vital part of the fabric of rural communities and a central piece of the infrastructure sustaining communities in rural regions. These stores are an important element of the local food system, providing a supply of fresh fruits, vegetables, dairy, breads, grains, and meats. They are a cornerstone business, functioning as an important part of the economic engine that drives most rural areas. These stores are also important as a social and civic anchor, functioning as a site for social capital and a community asset in recruiting and retaining residents.

Rural Grocery Stores as Source of Healthful Food

A primary function of retail food outlets is to provide healthful food for local neighborhoods, towns, and the surrounding market areas. Unfortunately, large geographic tracts in rural America have food deserts. According to the United States Department of Agriculture (USDA), 2.3 million rural residents live in food deserts (USDA, 2011) that are especially prominent throughout the western portion of the Great Plains states (Morton & Blanchard, 2007). Rural regions qualify as a food desert if the rural census tract meets certain low-access and low-income criteria. If a rural census tract has at least 500 people and 33% or more of its population resides more than 10 miles from a supermarket or large grocery store, then the region is considered a food desert. Likewise, if the tract has at least 20% of its residents below the federal poverty line, the tract is designated as a rural food desert (Dutko, Ver Ploeg, & Farrigan, 2012; Morton et al., 2005, USDA, 2011).

As rural retail food access has declined, convenience stores, dollar-type stores, and gas stations have increasingly filled this grocery void. Research, however, has consistently found that these alternate food outlets supply high-priced, nutritionally diminished foods (Bitler & Haider, 2009; Ford, 2009; Morris, Neuhauser, & Campbell, 1992; Morton & Blanchard, 2007; Ver Ploeg, 2009).

Research also shows a relationship between those residents living in food deserts and health-related diseases. High rates of obesity positively correlate with life in food deserts (Morland, Diez-Roux, & Wing, 2006; Whitacre, Tsai, & Mulligan, 2009). Jackson et al., (2005) specifically note that the prevalence of obesity is higher in rural counties than in urban counties, while Jilcott et al., (2011) report that the prevalence of grocery stores in non-metro counties is inversely associated with the incidence of obesity. Ford (2009) points out that the increase in obesity has significant implications for public health since it is associated with increased risk for many other diseases, including high blood pressure, high blood cholesterol, type 2 diabetes, and coronary heart disease.

Larson, Story, and Nelson (2009) specifically found that residents of low-income, minority, and rural neighborhoods have the most health effects related to poor access to supermarkets and healthful food. Likewise, Whitacre et al., (2009) report that these expanding food deserts especially affect the elderly and poor, who represent high proportions of rural communities.

Nevertheless, rural grocery stores remain as the primary source of healthful foods in rural regions of the US (Liese et al., 2007). Not only do these retail food outlets sell a variety of produce, dairy, grain foods, and protein options from their corporate food distributor, they also represent an important piece in local food systems. These stores are a significant distributor of locally sourced food. Seventy-one percent of rural, independently owned grocery stores reported in a 2008 survey that they sold locally sourced foods, including 41% of store owners who reported selling locally grown fruits and vegetables (Clark, Tsoodle, & Kahl, 2008).

Rural Grocery Store as Economic Driver

Beyond the vital function of providing healthful food, rural grocery stores are also an important economic driver powering rural America (McDaniel, 2001; The Reinvestment Fund, n.d.; Treuhaft & Karpyn, 2010). These stores are a significant source of local taxes that fund city services, promote neighborhood improvement, and expand local community development (Cunningham, 2010). In a 2011 sample of six Kansas rural grocery stores, the Kansas Department of Revenue reported that 20% of all community sales tax receipts came from the local grocery store (Kansas Department of Revenue, 2011). These important tax dollars help fund city services, support local libraries and the arts, promote neighborhood improvements, sustain and improve local parks, build swimming pools, and facilitate a host of local community development initiatives.

Besides supplying important local tax revenue, rural grocery stores provide significant employment opportunities. Miller (2013) conducted an economic impact study of 163 small town Kansas rural grocery stores and found those independent grocers employed an average of 17 employees (see also Clark et al., 2008). Her study found that these small businesses, on average, employed 5 full-time and 12 part-time grocery workers. The jobs provided – managers, food distributors, office and administrative support staff, butchers, cashiers, bakers, and stockers – often offer young people their first job, adults a full-time job, and seniors the opportunity to continue to be active and productive.

Grocery stores also support economic development in a variety of other ways. Treuhaft and Karpyn (2010) describe grocery stores as a "high-volume anchor," meaning that people who visit the local grocery store also shop at other nearby businesses such as cafés, banks, and pharmacies. Small town grocery stores support a myriad of other local jobs, including local growers, plumbers, electricians, general contractors, accountants, lawyers, and more (McDaniel, 2001).

Purchasing from small, independent businesses such as rural food outlets keeps more local dollars circulating in the community than purchasing from out-of-town or national chain food sources. Known as the "local multiplier effect," this concept refers to how many times a dollar re-circulates within the local economy before leaving that community. While estimates vary on how much more locally invested dollars re-circulate, research indicates that it is clearly higher than dollars invested out of town or with corporate chains (Civic Economics, 2002; Cunningham, 2010).

Miller (2013) found that local food retail businesses had economic multipliers ranging from 1.17 to 1.57. These multipliers indicate that every dollar spent at these local grocery stores meant an extra .17 cents and .57 cents of economic activity within the community, respectively. Local business owners also report a "reduction effect" when the local grocery store struggles and closes. Reports from economic development directors and numerous local businesses indicate that as grocery stores fare, so do other local businesses. When local food access outlets struggle and close, local economies suffer (Keen, 2011).

Miller's study (2013) is the most comprehensive examination of the economic contribution of rural grocery stores to the communities served. The research estimated the jobs created, compensation provided, tax implications, and the value of production and services provided by these rural food retail outlets. Her analysis found that these stores contributed, on average, $644,413 annually to local rural economies.

Rural Grocery Stores as Social Anchor

According to Clopton and Finch (2011), when community institutions act as a support for the development and maintenance of social capital and social networks, they become social anchors. These physical institutions and locally familiar places provide spaces of "personal identification" for participants. In other words, the locale creates a place for community members to come together for a purposeful reason that ultimately provokes the formation of a collective identity (Alonso & O'Shea, 2012). These businesses provide a sense of cultural and civic identity to a community (Tolbert, Lyson, & Irwin, 1998). Just like schools, post offices, restaurants, and churches, grocery stores are gathering places – places to meet friends, catch up on the latest news, and build and sustain bonds of community interconnectedness. Rural grocery stores often serve as public spaces for meetings and socializing.

Oldenburg (2001) refers to these sites as "third places" or public places on neutral ground where people can gather and interact. In public and neutral places, people can put aside their concerns and simply enjoy the company and conversation around them. These sites "host the regular, voluntary, informal, and happily anticipated gatherings of individuals beyond the realms of home and work" (Oldenburg, 2001). They are the heart of a community's social vitality and the foundation of a functioning democracy. They promote social and political equality by leveling resident status, enhancing citizen interconnectedness, providing a setting for grassroots politics, and creating habits of public association (Mencken, Bader, & Polson, 2006).

These physical spaces promote face-to-face interaction and informal gatherings to extend and develop social networks. Furthermore, these spaces are places of pure association, meaning that there are no restrictions determining who is allowed to participate. With a focus on discussion and interaction, third places and social anchors allow participants to relax and ignore goal-oriented conversations. Instead, communication serves to enhance trust and bridge individuals across demographic lines. These components all work together and result in the construction of a strong network and community.

Yet, rural grocery stores struggle to remain viable, and there are numerous reasons why these businesses are so difficult to sustain. Walzer and Sandoval (2016) argue that rural areas, especially in the Midwest, have experienced stagnant economies and that small stores such as restaurants and grocery stores that for many years have been mainstays in the community are closing due to pending retirements, shrinking markets, and lack of investment capital. Return on equity on businesses in rural areas may not compete effectively in the capital market for new investment.

Grocery stores operate on a slim profit margin per item, with profits usually between 1% and 3%, depending on the item. It's not unusual for a grocery store to make just a few cents per item and they make money on volume (Bean-Mellinger, 2018). Consequently, small town grocery stores are highly challenged since a lack of a significant population base limits the volume of groceries likely to be sold. Others point to the consolidation of the wholesale food distribution industry as a significant cause of rural grocery closures (Bitto et al., 2003; Morton & Blanchard, 2007).

Indeed, the numbers confirm a steady decline in rural grocery stores. Since 2008, in Kansas, 54 grocery stores in communities with populations smaller than

2,500 have closed. Thirty-nine of those grocery operations have not reopened (Center for Engagement and Community Development, 2019).[3] There are only 98 rural grocery stores left in North Dakota (Abrahamson, 2020). In the past six years, North Dakota has lost more than 20% of its rural grocery stores, and nearby states face similar issues (Schlecht, 2019). According to US Department of Agriculture data, between 2010 and 2015, 135 counties in the Ohio Valley increased in the percent of the population with low access to grocery stores – 51% of counties in Kentucky, Ohio, and West Virginia (Boles, 2020).

Because grocery stores are such important rural businesses, providing access to goods and services considered essential to the quality of local life, community leaders are often very determined to find ways to keep a local store open or to find ways to reopen a store if it has closed. Increasingly, rural communities are looking at CSE models to own and operate grocery stores. St. Paul, Kansas provides a case study of how one small town responded to the need for a local grocery store.

The St. Paul Supermarket Story

In many ways, St. Paul is similar to other Kansas rural communities. The town, located in southeast Kansas, is laid out on a perpendicular grid extending one mile east to west and one mile north to south. It is a deeply religious community with a significant majority of residents attending the local St. Francis Catholic Church. In fact, the town was established only after the Catholic Church and school were built in the mid-nineteenth century.

St. Paul highlights St. Francis Catholic Church on its official webpage proclaiming that the town is known as "the little town with the big church." The community also boasts that a town of its size has been able to retain its elementary school, junior, and senior high schools (http://stpaulks.us/history). Like so much of rural America, St. Paul is politically conservative, consistently supporting Republican candidates including presidential candidates Mitt Romney (68%) in 2012 and Donald Trump (71%) in 2016.

St. Paul also struggles to retain its population. According to Census data, St. Paul had a population of 646 in 2000 and 629 in 2010. Its population has declined another 5% since the 2010 census, leaving only 597 residents in 2019 (https://www.biggestuscities.com/city/st-paul-kansas). The town also struggles to keep its businesses open. Nearly all of the businesses on the historic main street have closed, leaving only a bar, thrift shop, construction company, post office, and city offices downtown.

The heartbeat of the town now resides along its southern edge on state Highway 47. Sitting along this two-lane Kansas highway is the Catholic Church, the elementary school, the junior and senior high schools, and the county historical museum. Most businesses have also migrated to the highway, including two auto shops, the St. Paul Café, the Farmer's State Bank, the Git and Split convenience store, a car wash, and the St. Paul Supermarket. It is this 10,000 square foot grocery store that makes St. Paul unique among rural communities both in Kansas and across the United States. The St. Paul Supermarket is a very distinct version of a CSE since it is one of only a handful of city-owned and operated grocery stores.

The old St. Paul grocery store that had for generations operated in a building located on the town's historic main street closed in 1985. That closure left the St. Paul café and a local convenience store as the only places to purchase food in town. To access groceries such as fresh meat, varieties of fruits, vegetables, and dairy, St. Paul residents had to travel 32 miles round trip to the nearest supermarket in Parsons, Kansas.

In 2004, the local school board voted to close the community's public schools and consolidate their schools with a nearby community's schools. This decision sent shock waves through town. They perceived that anchor institutions – schools, grocery stores – were closing and took this decision as a sign that their town was in trouble. The school board vote was a catalyst for a group of residents to gather and discuss strategic actions to save their town. Together, these residents formed a 501c3 named the St. Paul Community Development Corporation (CDC). The first priority for the newly formed CDC was opening a grocery store.

Rick Giefer was elected mayor of St. Paul in 2005 and met with the CDC to express his support for opening a grocery store. He believed that access to food, like access to water, is a public good and something that should be supported by public dollars. In addition, like the CDC, he saw the community at a crossroad. The town was continuing to lose population and rumors were that the local schools might permanently close. To keep people in the community and, in order to draw people to town, the mayor believed that St. Paul needed a food source other than a convenience store (Giefer, 2020). He met with the CDC and other local residents, and all agreed that the town definitely needed a grocery store (Giefer, 2020).

St. Paul's leaders recognized that location would be important for a store to survive, so the decision was made that the former downtown grocery location was not viable. Recognizing that there was not enough traffic driving downtown to shop, the city identified and purchased land along Highway 47, where locals and commuters would pass by regularly.

The mayor and the CDC reached out to a nearby USDA Rural Development regional office for help. USDA encouraged St. Paul to apply to the zero-interest Rural Economic Development Loan and Grant (REDLG) program.[4] The REDLG program requires that USDA loan funds go to a local electric cooperative, and then the coop passes the funding onto the local organization that will create jobs in a rural area. The local Heartland Rural Electric Cooperative stepped forward and agreed to apply for the loan. However, the rural electric coop wanted the loan guaranteed, and so Mayor Giefer and the city commission decided to ask the town's residents to approve the city guaranteeing the REDLG loan from USDA. This proposal was placed on the ballot in 2005 and passed overwhelmingly (Giefer, 2020; Smith, 2020; Willey, 2013). Funding from the loan passed from the Heartland Rural Electric Cooperative to the CDC. REDLG loan funding was used to prepare the land, install a parking lot, construct the grocery facility, and purchase the equipment necessary to operate the store.

Once the grocery facility was built, the town needed a grocery distributor. The CDC identified and contracted with Affiliated Foods Midwest, a food wholesaler for independent grocers in Nebraska.[5] Affiliated Foods is a wholesale food cooperative. Grocery stores paid a membership fee to join the coop and then paid for their weekly grocery deliveries. The initial cooperative membership fee was $5,000, and the CDC raised money for this entry membership fee. Consequently, the CDC became the initial "owners" of the St. Paul Supermarket.

The city now owned the property. The St. Paul CDC owned the business and had secured a food wholesaler. The CDC also equipped the grocery facility. Still, the grocery operation had to purchase a grocery inventory and needed managers to run the operation. The city identified a couple who managed a nearby grocery store and had indicated an interest in moving to St. Paul. They did agree to purchase the grocery inventory and also manage the store. Thus, the St. Paul Supermarket opened in 2008 to great fanfare. Public dollars from the residents of St. Paul had purchased the property and were also guaranteeing the USDA loan. A volunteer group of St. Paul residents (the CDC) invested their money to buy the business and secure a wholesaler. Finally, a local couple used their funds to buy the grocery inventory. This public/private CSE lasted from 2008 until 2013.

By 2013, the couple that owned the grocery inventory and managed the store was having health issues. Both were increasingly unable to properly manage the grocery operation and were looking to retire. The city commission decided that the time had come for the city to take over the entire operation. The city's elected leaders decided, without a public vote, to buy out the CDC, thereby owning the business, and to purchase the grocery inventory from the previous owners. The city identified and hired another local couple to manage the operation. Both were long-term residents of St. Paul with significant experience in the grocery business. The St. Paul Supermarket was now a city-owned business with 15 employees (5 full-time and 10 part-time). Public dollars now financed the grocery retail operation, and the full-time employees were city employees with city-funded benefits.

Lessons Learned

After researching numerous examples of various CSEs from several states, Walzer and Sandoval (2016) and Walzer (2019) distilled useful lessons learned when establishing CSEs. The authors note that when creating CSEs, communities must (1) communicate that a vital community need exists to build local interest and community support for a CSE; (2) have a local champion to communicate that need and to spearhead the CSE effort; (3) identify a crucial, viable local business enterprise that is sustainable and financially viable and will adequately address the vital community need; (4) identify suitable organizational structure (LLC;

coop; sole proprietorship; city-owned) for the CSE business enterprise; (5) have access to technical assistance; and (6) stay in touch with investors and keep them engaged in the CSE effort.

This previous work on CSEs is very instructive. However, the case of a city-owned CSE is significantly different from other forms of CSEs. While the CSE principles offered by Walzer and Sandoval (2016) and Walzer (2017) are very relevant, city-owned CSEs present a different community dynamic and thus result in some different lessons learned – either lessons not discussed by previous authors or variations on their identified principles.

RGI's research of city-owned grocery operations in general and the St. Paul Supermarket in particular revealed critical lessons about this form of CSE. Some of these lessons were similar to the general learnings from earlier CSE research, while other principles were either variations of previous findings or new, unreported lessons. The principles identified in the current work include: (1) build support for a city-owned organizational CSE structure, (2) identify an entrepreneurial champion, (3) work collaboratively with a leadership team, (4) community support of the grocery operation is vital, and (5) identify and secure an experienced and committed manager/operator. To help facilitate a successful transition from a private business to a city-owned operation, proponents of a city-owned CSE must be sensitive and responsive to local culture as well as specific social, economic, and political events impacting the local community.

Build support for a city-owned organizational structure. The decision of a city government to buy and operate a business that has traditionally been a private enterprise is one with substantial risks and consequences and requires significant public support. Securing public support for a city-owned CSE is perhaps the most important lesson to be learned, and there are multiple steps involved with this principle.

The first step in securing support for a city-owned CSE is establishing that a vital community need exists. In order to justify the city government taking over a private business, the community must believe that an existential community threat exists that the livability and sustainability of the community are at stake. St. Paul's mayor and his allies at the time argued that access to groceries was vital for the town to survive given two significant community threats.

Initially, those in favor of the city becoming financially responsible for the grocery operation argued that the lack of a grocery store was a significant reason for a continuing decline in the town's population. Certainly, it is a challenge for communities with dwindling populations to attract new residents (Farzan, 2019). Potential residents see a town with a declining population and question its vibrancy and sustainability. St. Paul's mayor contended that in order to draw people to town, they needed a food source other than a convenience store (Giefer, 2020).

Others argued that without a grocery store, it would be difficult to attract younger people to town (Voorhies, 2020a). Without younger families, the number of children necessary to populate the local schools would also decline. St. Paul had recently seen its school consolidated with another nearby school district. Fortunately, the school physical plant and students remained in St. Paul. However, the perception persisted: the town was losing population, and as the population decreased, there was the increasing possibility that the public schools could permanently close, and remaining students would be bused to locations away from the town.

Once an existential need is established where the threat can be mitigated by government response, the case has to be made for running the business as a city entity. This is necessary for several reasons. Initially, conservative rural America traditionally resists government intervention into business sectors long considered the domain of private enterprise. Second, questions arise as to why local government is willing to purchase and run some private businesses but not others. Finally, there is concern about government intervention functioning as merely a bailout for poorly managed private businesses.

To make the case that the city should run the grocery store, proponents not only must make the case that the expressed need threatens community sustainability but also point out that the need falls into an area that may be legitimately seen as a responsibility addressed by a governmental response. In the case of city-funded grocery stores, food is constructed by proponents as an essential public good that may be rightfully provided by the government.

The mayor of a small town in Baldwin, Florida, where the local municipality bought the grocery store, argued that "We take water out of the ground, and pump it into your house and charge you. What's the difference with a grocery store" (Farzan, 2019). St. Paul's mayor echoed this sentiment stating that "the city owned the water department, to furnish water for the citizens of the community. Why could we not own our grocery store to furnish food for the citizens of the community?" (Giefer, 2020). This "food access as government responsibility" speaks to critics who might ask why the city doesn't also buy and run furniture stores or antique shops or some other non-essential business.

The case also must make why private ownership (e.g., sole proprietorship) cannot run the grocery enterprise. In the case of rural grocery operations, the case is pretty clear. It is becoming increasingly difficult to attract national grocery operations, regional supermarket chains, family operators, or sole proprietors to rural communities to buy and run a grocery store. Rural citizen leaders report that it is increasingly difficult to attract private investors (Farzan, 2019; Walzer, 2017) as rural grocery businesses are too small, there is a lack of available capital, the market area is not large enough, and profit margins are not sufficient enough to risk private investment. Both Baldwin, Florida, and St. Paul, Kansas, for example, tried to find private operators but were unsuccessful. Rural communities often work through a process of searching for private investors and a variety of CSE models before coming to the city run option.

Evidence from the Kansas Healthy Food Initiative (KHFI) illustrates this trend.[6] KHFI is a statewide financing vehicle to provide funds to emerging or expanding healthy food retail operations in Kansas. Since 2017, this initiative has provided funding to 14 new or existing grocery stores. Six of those 14 funded projects have been to CSEs – two cooperatives, two public/private ownership examples, one public school-based model, and one not-for-profit owner. In addition, the KHFI is currently working with two emerging projects (Erie, Kansas and Caney, Kansas) that are proposing city-funded grocery stores. While private ownership is still the most prevalent ownership model, it is just slightly so with CSEs becoming more and more popular.

To secure community support for a city-owned grocery operation, advocates must also demonstrate that the business is likely sustainable. Local residents are wary of the government propping up struggling businesses or investing public dollars in an enterprise that will fail, thereby necessitating even more government intervention. Consequently, city ownership proponents often finance and report on positive market analyses that demonstrate the business' viability. Supporters also often argue that the city-owned CSE will not be held to the same profit goals as a private business, but rather, the business will merely seek to break even, to try and cover expenses and that any profits will simply be funneled back into the grocery operation.

Finally, after proponents have made their case for a city-run grocery store, argued that the city is the only viable owner and that the business will most likely be sustainable, city leaders seek public confirmation of that support. Often, this public support comes in the form of a survey (Erie, KS; Caney, KS), where residents are asked if they are supportive of the city government buying and operating the grocery store. At other times, this issue is placed on a city ballot (St. Paul). This public affirmation of support provides necessary evidence for elected officials to commit the public resources required to acquire and operate the formerly private business.

Identify an entrepreneurial champion. While securing community support for a city-owned CSE is vital, a local champion or spark plug is necessary to effectively lead the advocacy regarding this significant community decision (Walzer, 2017). This individual must have the ability to effectively communicate the need and express the vision so as to marshal the financial and human capital necessary to advance the vision toward action. Walzer (2017) notes that:

> As with most local initiatives, the chances of success are higher when a local champion or leader is willing to spearhead the effort. In the case of CSEs, it is especially important that this person or group has credibility within the community and can convince investors of the soundness of the venture and its potential contributions to the area.

St. Paul's mayor at the time played this important champion role. It was his vision that food – as is water – is a public good. As noted previously, the mayor and the regional Kansas USDA Rural Development office identified the REDLG program as a funding vehicle to finance much of the proposed plan with participation by the Heartland Rural Electric Cooperative in transferring the monies. He also worked with staff at a small business development center at a local college to develop grocery business plans and marketing analyses. He negotiated with a local bank to secure a revolving loan fund as well as continually communicated with other city council members and regularly interacted with the volunteer St. Paul CDC. The chair of St. Paul's CDC affirmed that "99 percent of this probably wouldn't have happened without Rick Giefer so we have to give him more credit than probably anybody" (Smith, 2020).

Work collaboratively as a leadership team. While a local champion is critical, it is not enough. Securing community support and organizing city run grocery businesses are complex issues. Multiple voices advocating to multiple audiences are vital as is the technical information a leadership team can bring to the CSE effort. Leadership teams in rural communities often come from a variety of business and community interests. In St. Paul, the CDC served as the local leadership team in support of Mayor Giefer and the initiative to run the grocery store as a government operation. There were five members of the CDC. The chair of the CDC was a co-owner of a large chain of carpet stores. CDC members included a clerical employee for a southeast Kansas inter-local school consortium, a manager of a grain company, and two local ranchers. Interestingly, none of the CDC members' businesses were located within St. Paul.

In addition to the CDC, other technical assistance came from a small business development center at a nearby university. That SBDC provided the community with business planning assistance and marketing help. USDA Rural Development, Heartland Rural Electric Cooperative, the CDC, and the Farmer's National Bank all provided technical assistance and funds for the project. Associated Wholesale Grocers (AWG) and their grocery consultants provided technical assistance regarding the size, layout, and design of the store as well as a suggested inventory for the new store.

Community support of the grocery operation is vital. Securing community support to initially make the decision that a municipality will purchase and operate a local grocery store is incredibly important. Three surveys conducted in the Great Plains show that the issue of community support consistently ranks as one of the significant challenges rural grocery stores face. These surveys were conducted by KSU's RGI (Clark et al., 2008), by North Dakota's Association of Rural Electrical and Telecommunications Center (Capouch & Stumph, 2015), and by the University of Minnesota Extension (Lanthier & Draeger, 2015).

However, for that city-run CSE to survive, the community must also support the business with its patronage. There are numerous examples of financially successful, small town grocery stores across the United States. While there are certainly many reasons why these stores thrive, one critical factor is that the community broadly supports the grocery operation. Rural communities demonstrate this grocery support in several ways. Governmental support, for example, is obviously demonstrated by the purchase of the grocery operation but can also be seen via city or county tax incentives or exemptions.[7]

Financial support can also come through private investment from some coalition of local residents. Walzer and Sandoval (2016) show that financing CSEs involves many approaches ranging from donations to crowdfunding – raising capital through the collective effort of friends, customers, and individual investors. Some community investors may financially support the grocery operation with the expectation that, for their money, they will receive some form of discount or dividend. Others may financially support the grocery store simply to ensure that the retail food business survives and provides a needed service to the rural community.[8]

In St. Paul's case, the volunteer CDC functioned as an investment group. CDC members used their funds as collateral for the USDA loan to buy grocery store equipment and to officially purchase "the grocery business" by paying the membership fee for entry in the Affiliated Food Midwest Cooperative. This group of investors used their financial resources to ensure the grocery operation opened and had a chance to succeed. This volunteer non-profit, in fact, disbanded when the city purchased the entire operation in 2013.

Other community support includes volunteer labor to help in operating the store. There are numerous rural grocery stores where locals come to the grocery store and help with a variety of tasks. Residents in Cuba, Kansas, for example, meet at the store on food delivery day to help unload the groceries and stock shelves (Tanner, 2014). The St. Paul Supermarket manager tells of a St. Paul fix-it man who volunteers to help maintain the supermarket. He's "a local guy who can pretty much fix anything – he helped us set up the coolers. He stops in here all the time to check on things, and it doesn't cost us a thing" (Voorhies, 2020a).

Ultimately, however, community support is demonstrated by how committed local organizations and residents are in patronizing the store. Sufficient demand for the goods or services is the main determinant of CSE success (Bailey, 2010b; Walzer, 2017). Mayor Giefer noted that "the biggest challenge is getting people to shop locally" (2020), while Kelly Voorhies, one of the St. Paul Supermarket managers, bluntly stated, "Number one, you have to have your community behind you, or you won't succeed" (2020b).

Patronizing the local grocery store comes in many forms. Residents shopping at the store for a significant portion of their groceries rather than treating the grocery store as a convenience store is especially important. The store also needs businesses and organizations to regularly purchase grocery products. This trade may be just as, or even more, important than individual grocery shopping since businesses and organizations have the capacity to regularly purchase large quantities. Many rural grocery stores enter into partnerships with other institutional buyers, negotiating purchase agreements with such businesses as local cafés, schools, hospitals, assisted living centers, and government offices.

Small town grocery stores, such as St. Paul, also function as small distribution hubs, purchasing food from their national food wholesalers and then distributing that food to even smaller communities running limited grocery operations. Indeed, the St. Paul store has built its own network of institutional food buyers. The store serves a few nearby small grocery stores and provides food to local businesses and organizations, including the town's only café, the community's retirement center, the public schools, the local library, and St. Paul's Country Club.

But, perhaps, the organization most important in financially supporting the supermarket is the local Catholic Church and its affiliate organizations. As Voorhies (2020b) pointed out, "A lot about St. Paul is faith. We have a big Catholic Church, and this is a Catholic town. Faith is a support system." Indeed, the church serves as an important lifeline to the grocery store.

Father Pinkerton, St. Francis' pastor, spoke of the "principle of subsidiarity" to ground the church's support of the local grocery store (Pinkerton, S. (Fr), 2020).[9] Subsidiarity urges Catholics to address wicked issues[10] – issues such as food security, food access, community sustainability – at the most local level possible, and so perhaps it should not be surprising that St. Francis and its parishioners patronize the St. Paul Supermarket.

Indeed, St. Francis has a history of purchasing food for various meetings, an annual auction, and its annual bazaar that feeds 600–700 people (Voorhies, 2020b). In addition, St. Paul's local Catholic service organizations, the Knights of Columbus and Altar Society, purchase all their food and supplies from the St. Paul Supermarket.

Based on RGI's 2020 interviews with the store managers, two city commissioners, a past mayor, and the former chair of St. Paul's CDC, the St. Paul Supermarket is holding its own. The store's food distributor requires a minimum weekly food order of $10,000, and according to the supermarket's manager, the St. Paul store regularly orders between $13,000 and $14,000 of groceries per week. A current city commissioner stated that "sales have steadily increased a little bit" (Van Leeuwen, 2020) since the change in managers in 2013. The current store manager also said that the store makes about a 3% annual profit in an industry, where profit margins range from 1% to 3% (Bean-Mellinger, 2018). He summed it all up saying, "we have a good community backing."

Identify and secure an experienced and committed manager/operator. Fundamentally, a CSE is an organization, venture, or business started to address a local community need and maintain access to goods and services considered essential to the town's quality of life. While these enterprises are not always created with the primary goal to make a profit, they face market tests as do other small businesses. They cannot lose money and stay in business long. This means that CSEs need a sound business plan, marketing strategy, and competent individuals to run the operation. While city governments, investment groups, and outside technical assistance stakeholders can build the CSE, equip the business, and put a business plan in place, competent managers/operators are needed to ensure its success.

Perhaps, the most vital role in sustaining a CSE grocery store is an experienced operator who will manage the day-to-day operations. The St. Paul Supermarket initially found a couple that had been managing a grocery store in a nearby community and were interested in moving to St. Paul. They agreed to both purchase the initial grocery inventory and manage the store. This arrangement worked for six years, but health issues and management problems emerged.

A city-owned CSE offers advantages as well as potential concerns for managers/operators. A city-run business, much like other city departments, provides a reliable salary as well as defined and stable benefits. In fact, one of the reasons the current St. Paul grocery managers were attracted to the position is because of the city health benefits.

However, a city-owned CSE also poses risks for both the staff and the community. Critics of this form of rural CSE point out that operators hired to manage these businesses do not necessarily have the same motivation or drive for excellence as an individual or family running a business they own. The managers of city-run CSEs are also at risk as they must respond to elected officials who are now "owners" of the business. Consequently, these managers are now tied to the political winds of the local community.

Conclusions

This chapter describes the experiences of a rural southeast Kansas community as they worked to establish and sustain a retail grocery operation. After years of unsuccessful attempts to identify and secure a private owner/operator, the town explored and ultimately pursued a city-owned and operated grocery store – a specific and unique form of a CSE.

The research identified five lessons for those communities considering or seeking to establish a city-owned grocery enterprise: (1) build support for the city-owned organizational CSE structure, (2) identify an entrepreneurial champion, (3) work collaboratively with a leadership team, (4) community support for the grocery operation is vital, and (5) identify and secure an experienced and committed manager/operator.

In addition to the five principles necessary when forming this type of CSE, it seems that the decision to invest public dollars to purchase and run a grocery business depends also on local culture and the shifting socio-economic and political conditions within that community. Local values, community history as well as significant day-to-day events will influence community thinking and constrain city decision-making (Braden & Mayo, 1999). A town's perception of the role of government, its history of independence versus collaboration, and its focus on the common good versus individual success impact how residents and elected leaders perceive government involvement in business and private lives. Also important in civic decision-making are major local events that capture local attention and seemingly demand some type of response.

The St. Paul grocery store example illustrates this process. While there may have been a history of independence and individualism, the continued lack of a grocery store and the dramatic 2004 school board decision to close the public schools focused community attention. It catalyzed residents to think strategically and communally about how to preserve their town. The stark reality of no grocery store and potentially no public schools led to determined community discussions regarding re-establishing a long-lost grocery store. As a St. Paul city commissioner stated, "If you don't have a grocery store and a school, you can't bring any younger people into town" (VanLeeuwen, 2020).[11] A trusted entrepreneurial champion (former mayor) along with the volunteer leadership of the St. Paul CDC raised the idea of a city-owned grocery store and broached the topic with the community, an idea that probably would have been an anathema just a few years earlier. These city leaders certainly appeared to do their due diligence by working with USDA Rural Development, the local small business development center, and representatives of a national food wholesaler to prepare business plans, marketing analyses, and customer patronage projections. However, it seems clear that the existential threat perceived by the community spurred the community into action. This event combined with a community culture grounded in faith and public education facilitated a positive vote from both the city commission and community residents when deciding to operate the grocery store as a city-owned business.

The chapter also provides a process roadmap and a set of lessons learned for opening a city-owned and operated grocery store, using St. Paul, Kansas as the primary case study. It has added to the research of Walzer and Sandoval (2016), Walzer (2019), and other CSE scholars. The current research identified principles similar to building other forms of CSEs but also revealed some variations. Perhaps, the most significant is securing support for a city-owned organizational structure. In a city-owned and operated CSE, obtaining community support is an essential, multi-step process.

Without public support, city decision-makers are unlikely to pursue this form of a CSE. The other variation is the importance of the manager/operator. It is challenging for rural communities to find qualified and committed grocery managers. The pay is generally low and the hours long. However, with a city-owned CSE, the operator/manager becomes a city employee, paid on a city rate scale with city benefits. Conversely, the manager must also be willing to deal with elected officials as his or her employer as well as be part of the local political environment and the subject of political discussion.

As rural grocery stores continue to transition via retirement or declining profits, community leaders and residents increasingly look to alternative ownership models to run these businesses. CSEs are an increasingly popular option. The case of St. Paul, Kansas and other communities working to own and operate a grocery store as a city department offers towns another potential path to preserve access to groceries and sustain the rural community.

Notes

1 For more information about the Rural Grocery Initiative, see www.ruralgrocery.org.
2 For case studies of the various models of grocery operation, see https://www.ruralgrocery.org/successstories/successstories.html.
3 Each year, K-State's CECD has worked with the Kansas Department of Agriculture to determine the grocery stores that have closed during the previous year. Our office confirms closed stores versus stores that close briefly only to re-open under new

ownership. When the RGI began in 2007, there were 213 independently owned rural grocery stores. Since that time, 54 stores have closed. Thirty-nine have not re-opened (Center for Engagement and Community Development, (2019). "Rural grocery closures." Unpublished Research).

4 The REDLG program provides funding for rural projects through local utility organizations. USDA provides zero-interest loans to local utilities, which they, in turn, pass through to local businesses (ultimate recipients) for projects that will create and retain employment in rural areas.

5 In 2016, Affiliated Foods Midwest merged with AWG and now operates under the AWG name.

6 For more detail regarding the Kansas Healthy Food Initiative, see www.kansashealthyfood.org.

7 See Healthy Food Policy Project (www.healthyfoodpolicyproject.org) database for policy and regulation examples.

8 See the example of Walsh, Colorado where residents bought shares in increments of $50.00 to raise working capital to build and run a community-owned grocery store (Booth, 2014).

9 The "principle of subsidiarity" is a commitment to address social issues such as food insecurity, food access, or community sustainability by working with those closest to the issue, in other words. This principle directs the Catholic Church to work at the most local level available – local governments, local community organizations, local businesses – to address societal issues for the public good. For a more complete discussion of the Principle of Subsidiarity and its focus on lowest level of decision-making for the public good, see Clark (2012).

10 To read more about the definition, history, and examples of wicked problems, see Cooper, K. (2017). "Wicked problems: What are they, and why are they important to NNSI researchers."

11 See also Farzan (2019) as she reports on a city-owned store in Baldwin, Florida. The mayor of Baldwin reflected that "Should local governments be in private enterprise all the time? Maybe not. But for situations like this (a closed grocery store, a town unable to attract private operators), yeah, definitely I believe they should."

References

Abrahamson, W. (2020). Fight is on to keep rural grocery stores open. *NewsDakota.com*. https://www.newsdakota.com/2020/02/13/fight-is-on-to-keep-rural-grocery-stores-open/

Alonso, A.D. & O'Shea, M. (2012). "You only get back what you put in": Perceptions of professional sport organizations as community anchors. *Community Development, 43(5)*. 656–676.

Bailey, J.M. (2010). *Rural grocery stores: Ownership models that work for rural communities*. Lyons, NE: Center for Rural Affairs.

Bean-Mellinger, B. (2018). What is the profit margin for a supermarket. *Chronicle*. https://smallbusiness.chron.com/profit-margin-supermarket-22467.html

Bitler, M. & Haider, S. (2009). *An economic view of food deserts in the United States*. USDA Economic Research Service Conference. Washington, DC: National Poverty Center.

Bitto, E.A., Morton, L., Oakland, M., & Sand, M. (2003). Grocery store access patterns in rural food deserts. *Journal for the Study of Food and Society, 6(2)*. 35–48.

Boles, S. (2020). Coal country struggle to stay in business. *Resource*. January 17, 2020. https://ohiovalleyresource.org/2020/01/17/grocers-in-rural-coal-country-struggle-to-stay-in-business/

Booth, M. (2014). *Walsh grocery co-opts the future while other Colorado stores falter.* Colorado Health Foundation. Retrieved from https://www.coloradohealth.org/insights/stories/walsh-grocery-co-opts-future

Braden, S. & Mayo, M. (1999). Culture, community development, and representation. *Community Development Journal, 34(3).* 191–204.

Capouch, L. & Stumph, M. (2015). *North Dakota's independent grocers: Report on the opportunities and challenges for the long-term success of community businesses.* Mandan: North Dakota Association of Rural Electrical and Telecommunications.

Center for Engagement and Community Development. (2019). *Rural grocery store database.* Unpublished raw data.

Civic Economics. (2002). *Economic impact of local merchants and chain retailers.* Retrieved from http://www.civiceconomics.com/

Clark, M. (2012). Subsidiarity is a two-sided coin. *Catholic theology.* Retrieved from https://catholicmoraltheology.com/subsidiarity-is-a-two-sided-coin/

Clark, P., Tsoodle, L., & Kahl, D. (2008). *Rural grocery sustainability project: Owner survey.* Retrieved from http://www.ruralgrocery.org/survey/

Clopton, A., & Finch, B. (2011). Re-conceptualizing social anchors in community development: Utilizing social anchor theory to create social capital's third dimension. *Community Development, 42(1).* 70–83.

Cooper, K. (2017). Wicked problems: What are they, and why are they important to NNSI researchers. Retrieved from https://nnsi.northwestern.edu/wicked-problems-what-are-they-and-why-are-they-of-interest-to-nnsi-researchers/

Cunningham, D. (2010). *Community support for rural grocery stores.* Second National Rural Grocery Summit: Saving America's Critical Infrastructure. Manhattan, KS: Kansas State University. June 4.

Dutko, P., Ver Ploeg, M., & Farrigan, T. (2012). *Characteristics and influential factors of food deserts.* Washington, DC: United States Department of Agriculture: Economic Research Service.

Farzan, A.N. (2019). "When a deep red town's only grocery store closed, city hall opened its own store. Just don't call it 'socialism.'" *The Washington Post*, November 22, 2019. https://www.washingtonpost.com/nation/2019/11/22/baldwin-florida-food-desert-city owned-grocery-store/?utm_campaign=morning_mix&utm_medium=Email&utm_source=Newsletter&wpisrc=nl_mix&wpmm=1

Ford, P. (2009). *The local food environment and its association with obesity among low-income women across the urban-rural continuum.* Doctoral Dissertation, Kansas State University.

Giefer, R. (2020). Personal interview with author. February 20.

Jackson, J.E., Doescher, M.P., Jerant, A.F., & Hart, L. (2005). A national study of obesity prevention and trends by type of rural county. *The Journal of Health, 21(2).* 140–148.

Jilcott, S., Keyserling, T., Crawford, T., Guirt, J., & Ammerman, A. (2011). Examining associations among obesity and per capita farmers' markets, grocery stores/supermarkets, and supercenters in US counties. *Journal of the American Dietetic Association, 111(4).* 567–572.

Kansas Department of Revenue. (2011). Unpublished research study.

Keen, J. (2011). Small towns try to save vital grocery stores. *USA today.* Retrieved from http://www.usatoday.com. July 8.

Lanthier, K. & Draeger, K. (2015). Anchors of main street: Results from the 2015 rural grocery survey. Fifth National Rural Grocery Summit. Wichita, KS. June 6.

Larson, N., Story, M., & Nelson, M. (2009). Neighborhood environments: Disparities in access to healthy foods in the U.S. *American Journal of Preventive Medicine, 36(1).* 74–81.

Liese, A.D. et al. (2007). Food store types, availability, and cost of foods in a rural environment. *Journal of the American Dietetics Association, 107(11)*. 1916–1923.

McDaniel, K. (2001). *Small business in rural America*. Center for the Study of Rural America. Federal Reserve Bank of Kansas City.

Mencken, F., Bader, C., & Polson, E. (2006). Integrating civil society and economic growth in Appalachia. *Growth and Change, 37(1)*. 107–127.

Miller, H. (2013). *The economic contribution of rural grocery stores in Kansas*. Thesis. Kansas State University.

Morland, K., Diez-Roux, A.V., & Wing, S. (2006). Supermarkets, other food stores, and obesity: The atherosclerosis risk in communities study. *American Journal of Preventative Medicine, 30(4)*. 333–339.

Morris, P.M., Neuhauser, L., & Campbell, C. (1992). Food security in rural America: A study of the availability and costs of food. *Journal of Nutrition Education, 24(1)*. S52–S58.

Morton, L.W., Bitto, E.A., Oakland, M.J., & Sand, M. (2005). Solving the problem of Iowa food deserts: Food Insecurity and Civic Structure. *Rural Sociology, 70(1)*. 94–112.

Morton, L.W. & Blanchard, T. (2007). Starved for access: Life in rural America's food deserts. *Rural Realities, 1 Rural Sociological Society*: 1–10.

Oldenburg, R. (2001). *Celebrating the third place: Inspiring stories about the "great good places" at the heart of our communities*. New York: Marlowe and Co.

Pinkerton, S. (Fr). (2020). Personal interview with author. February 12.

Schlecht, J. (2019). Access to healthy food important in keeping people healthy. *Ag-Week*. December 23, 2019. https://www.agweek.com/business/agriculture/4692390-access-healthy-food-important-keeping-people-healthy

Smith, M. (2020). Personal interview with author. March 2.

Tanner, B. (2014). Cuba, Kansas: A town of Doers. *The Wichita Eagle*. Retrieved from https://www.kansas.com/news/local/news-columns-blogs/the-story-of-kansas/article1055535.html

The Reinvestment Fund. (n.d.) *The PA fresh food financing initiative: Case study of rural grocery store investments*. Retrieved from http://www.trfund.com/resource/downloads/policypubs/FFFI_Impact_RuralPA.pdf

Tolbert, C., Irwin, T., & Irwin, M. (1998). Local capitalism, civic engagement, and socioeconomic well-being. *Social Forces, 77(2)*. 401–428.

Treuhaft, S. & Karpyn, A. (2010). *The grocery gap: Who has access to healthy food and why it matters*. Oakland, CA: PolicyLink.

USDA. (2011). *Food deserts*. Retrieved from http://apps.ams.usda.gov/fooddeserts/food-Deserts.aspx.

VanLeeuwen, J. (2020). Personal interview. January 30.

Ver Ploeg, M. (2009). *Access to affordable and nutritious food: Measuring and understanding food deserts and their consequences*. A Report to Congress. Washington, DC.

Voorhies, J. (2020a). Personal interview. January 30.

Voorhies, K. (2020b). Personal interview. January 30.

Walzer, N. (2017). Community supported enterprises as a local investment strategy. *Illinois Municipal Policy Journal, (2)1*. 35–48.

Walzer, N. (2019). *Guidebook and resources for starting community supported enterprises*. East Lansing, MI: North Central Regional Center for Rural Development. Retrieved from https://www.cgs.niu.edu/Reports/cse-guidebook-final-2-8-19.pdf

Walzer, N. & Sandoval, J. (2016). *Emergence and growth of community supported enterprises*. DeKalb, IL: Center for Governmental Studies.

Whitacre, P., Tsai, P., & Mulligan, J. (2009). *The public health effects of food deserts*. National Academic Press.

Willey, J. (2013). St. Paul to take over grocery. *Parsons Sun*. August 15. Retrieved from https://www.parsonssun.com/news/article_7d697d6c-0626-11e3-961f-001a4bcf6878.html

7

COMMUNITY ENGAGEMENT OR COMMUNITY SERVICE?

Case Study of Italian Community Co-Operatives and Networks

Michele Bianchi

Introduction

In the international debate around community-supported enterprises (CSEs), the experiences of Italian community co-operatives can make a serious contribution for several reasons even though they are quite recent and require more investigation. Nevertheless, the debate between practitioners and policymakers on the definition of the main characteristics of community co-operatives re-opens the discussion regarding the proper nature of this form of social business (Peredo & Chrisman, 2006; Somerville & McElwee, 2011; Walzer, 2017).

The definition of CSEs seeks a balance between the effective participation by local residents and the relevance of the enterprise's services to community development. Therefore, it is important to examine how spontaneous bottom-up initiatives, supported by a national confederation of co-operatives (Confcooperative and Legacoop), have reformed the co-operative legal form bringing it into the "community economy" field (Wilkinson & Quarter, 1996).

After several years of economic crises and drastic public spending cuts, Italian communities have looked for new models to help them regenerate their economies and local societies. Public authorities closed many services and reduced spending on infrastructure, leaving numerous assets abandoned (Visco, 2018). In addition, the private market did not respond sufficiently in many communities and deprived them of basic services due to inadequate profit margins or business shutdowns (Bianchi & Vieta, 2019).

For several centuries, the Italian co-operative movement has proven to be a valuable instrument in leveling of social inequalities, allowing people to access basic resources, and having adequate living conditions (Zamagni & Zamagni, 2008; Bianchi, 2019). This chapter examines how co-operatives can become CSEs when they simultaneously favor collective actions, economic activities, and community development. Previous studies illustrate how these organizations manage local services with a community development mission (Bartocci & Picciaia, 2013; Mori & Sforzi, 2018; Teneggi & Zandonai, 2017).

The current research builds on past work to provide new insights on this innovative form of CSEs and shows how local networks with key partners have a fundamental role in their operations and poses several questions. How do local groups adapt the co-operative form to a community development mission? How does this support contribute to achieving community development objectives? Is the community's participation or the service for community the main enabling factor for CSEs? The intent of this discussion is to determine which factors facilitate the community development process through the co-operative legal form and how relationships with local partners help these co-operatives achieve their objectives. The findings propose an interesting argument in the debate on CSEs, emphasizing the relevance of their services over the requirement to involve shares of local population as widely as possible.

Community-Supported Enterprises: International Perspective and Framework

As a new phenomenon in the field of community development, Italian community co-operatives' analysis must adopt a solid and accepted framework based on the international literature on community-supported enterprises (CSEs). In this way, a comparison between the empirical evidence from the Italian context and the theoretical knowledge from the academic debate can provide communalities with general theories on CSEs and the Italian co-operatives' peculiarities.

In general, one can define a "community supported enterprise" as an enterprise with social purposes for the interest of its community which is the basis for this organization or one it strongly supports (Wilkinson & Quarter, 1996; Peredo & Chrisman, 2006; Somerville & McElwee, 2011; Walzer & Sandoval, 2016; Walzer, 2019). This enterprise form is clearly different from the traditional firm model. A CSE results from peoples' willingness to promote bottom-up initiatives to fulfill needs that otherwise will remain unsatisfied because they cannot find an adequate response from public agencies or a private market solution (Somerville & McElwee, 2011; Bianchi, 2019). Thus, it is necessary to consider these organizations as a sub-group of social enterprises (Bailey, 2012).

Wilkinson and Quarter (1996) note in their analysis of community economy that various aspects play a role in creating bottom-up initiatives and engaging communities in participatory processes for local development. "Supportive structures" play a key role in allowing the realization of community-based initiatives along with the "community consciousness" and the "empowering activities."

Indeed, the enterprise formal structure can be enriched with the other two elements to become a CSE. The "community consciousness" refers to people's awareness of being part of a community due to their cohabitation in a specific place and social networks that connect them. Also, community economy initiatives promote "empowering activities" that involve strategies for obtaining maximum participation from the community in developing strategies for self-reliance. These activities enhance the direct control over local assets, which allow the creation of services and strategies to tackle socio-economic issues and promote opportunities designed by community members (Kretzmann & McKnight, 1993).

Therefore, CSEs are an evolution of the for-profit firm model into the non-profit sector. Their capacity to operate for social purposes and especially conditions of "market failures" is due to their non-profit nature (Borzaga & Santuari, 2001). These businesses are not created for return on capital invested or profit maximization. Instead, they operate to generate revenues that provide communities with useful services and resources (Tracey et al., 2005; Lang & Roessl, 2011; Bianchi & Vieta, 2019).

CSEs have grown and diversified thanks to their capacity as multifunctional organizations able to engage in the holistic regeneration of the local economy and promote community development objectives (Tracey et al., 2005; Bailey, 2012; Bianchi & Vieta, 2019). Thus, CSEs are not defined by types of services but by their mission toward the community, with every local resident as a potential beneficiary of the enterprise service (Mori, 2017).

The governance model enables CSEs to succeed as non-profit enterprises and community-focused organizations (Wilkinson & Quarter, 1996; Lang & Roessl, 2011). The for-profit structural modification requires adaptation of the governance structure to re-calibrate the enterprise's priorities for community development objectives. CSE governance does not limit its stake regarding efficiency, but it also involves inputs from external subjects such as key local stakeholders (Lang & Roessl, 2011; Borzaga & Sacchetti, 2015; Walzer & Sandoval, 2016). Differences in governance allow the expansion of relationships within local communities, with these collaborations bringing both material and immaterial benefits. Table 7.1 summarizes the main elements that compose the research framework for the current analysis.

TABLE 7.1 Framework structure

CSE Components	
Community mission	CSEs arisen from collective processes that acknowledge the state of need or local opportunities for development. The community mission converts the community consciousness into an operative structure.
Multifunctional organization	In order to fulfill various necessities and take advantage from diverse opportunities, CSEs are multifunctional and provide different services and goods. This is how they promote empowering activities which can either directly service local needs or generate resources for community initiatives.
Open governance	CSEs adopt legal form and the consequent governance structure (e.g., elected board for co-operatives). Nevertheless, they open their governance to inputs from the external stakeholders and partners.

Source: Compiled by the author.

The intention here is to use this framework to examine recent initiatives in several Italian regions that have merged community economy characteristics with the co-operative legal form. Important information about Italian co-operatives and past attempts to intertwine community development practices and co-operative structures is provided next since it is useful in understanding how and why community co-operatives have grown in Italy recently.

Italian Co-Operatives and Changed Role in Community Development

Co-operatives offer a business model that allows members to collectively manage it with democratic mechanisms in order to provide members, who gather the necessary resources to start the enterprises, with specific benefits. These reciprocal relationships are called "mutuality" (Casale, 2005) that permits groups of people with few funds and similar economic needs to create an adequate and permanent organization – not-for-profit maximization but for the collective interest.

Co-operatives have proven to be able to level social inequalities allowing people in marginal economic conditions to acquire sufficient resources to maintain themselves, obtain employment with safety conditions, and access market opportunities such as collective purchases or assets sharing (Borzaga & Tortia, 2004; Zamagni & Zamagni, 2008; Ianes, 2013; Bianchi, 2019). MacPherson (2013) underlines how the "concern for community" has always been considered a collateral effect of the co-operative firm. Therefore, it is important to understand why in the past ten years, the Italian movement witnessed both a return to a co-operative form strongly stressing the value of mutuality plus an innovation in this mutual system that enlarges the array of beneficiaries even to non-members (Bianchi, 2019).

Since the beginning of the economic crisis in 2008, the socio-economic system has been weakened due to several factors. First, the Draconian spending to reduce the national deficit and public debt deeply cut the public investments for services and infrastructure, leaving thousands of public assets in a state of abandonment (Visco, 2018). Critical conditions are especially harsh in those areas situated at long distances from cities. In these cases, a steady process of depopulation closed many businesses and public authorities to reduce local services, compromising livelihood possibilities (Carrosio, 2015). In urban areas, social inequalities have significantly increased, and local institutions have few resources to meet the growing social unrest (Fazzi, 2013; Ranci Ortigosa, 2018; Leno et al., 2019).

Prior to these dramatic conditions, a new wave of civic activism had emerged. This phenomenon arose in areas where public authorities withdrew and the private market did not find a profitable interest (Bartocci & Picciaia, 2013; Teneggi & Zandonai, 2017). Because of the economic crisis and limits of public authorities, local civic groups actively searched for possible solutions to complex issues. Given the structural nature and magnitude of these issues, a stable and continuing response became fundamental. That outcome had to involve a permanent structure able to generate resources focusing on local community interests.

As Mori and Sforzi (2018) explain, these co-operatives use assets with a special value recognized by local communities to generate resources and services for the "community interest." Previous researchers (Bartocci & Picciaia, 2013; Mori & Sforzi, 2018; Bianchi & Vieta, 2019) illustrate how these organizations manage local services and focus on community development. The current research advances this understanding with new information on local networks with the community. The intent is to identify which factors led local groups to choose the co-operative legal form, how communities support them through relationships with local partners to help these enterprises, and why service to community underlies effective community participation as a key element in defining CSEs.

The Role of National Confederations for Co-Operatives and Regional Legislation

Since the early stages of the Italian co-operative movement, participants have seen the necessity to develop national organizations to coordinate their activities and improve their effects on other economic sectors and on public institutions (Zamagni et al., 2004). Thus, national confederations for co-operatives are key actors that support their members and new co-operators. The main organizations, with branches in every province, are Confcooperative and Legacoop. The following findings are based on conversations with managers from both confederations, where they explained visions, strategies, and processes behind the national bodies' actions for implementing community co-operatives across the country.

During the past ten years, there has been an increase in strategies of the confederations for implementing the number of community co-operatives in Italy. Indeed, the concept of "community co-operative" started in 2010 when the former president of Legacoop, Mr. Poletti, visited the Valle dei Cavalieri co-operative. In 1990, a group of young residents had decided to stop the depopulation process and keep their village Succiso Nuova alive. They formed a social co-operative on Apennines in Emilia-Romagna. For 30 years, the co-operative has re-opened a small grocery, started a local bar and a new restaurant, and began a B&B inside the former primary school closed because of too few students.

By regenerating a local abandoned asset, the co-operative provided the community with basic services that re-launched the village destiny. Based on this success, Poletti declared Valle dei Cavalieri a "community co-operative" because it showed an innovative approach in the interpretation of its mutual action, a new attitude toward the community, and capacity to be multi-functional and adaptive to the deprived context in a remote area (Bianchi & Vieta, 2019).

Based on that encounter, both national bodies saw a possibility to reactivate the original spirit of co-operatives repositioning the mutuality as a core value and re-igniting the model with a strong and clear mission toward community interests.

At the same time, both Confcooperative and Legacoop had to face the deep consequences of economic crises within their membership. They recognized the aspirations of both informal groups and local authorities to form new co-operatives with innovative economically sustainable ways to manage public assets and generate opportunities for socio-economic development. For several years, the two confederations have tailored programs to help new co-operative entrepreneurs start businesses:

- *Coop Start Up Rigeneriamo Comunità* in the past six years, Legacoop activated a project for entrepreneurial ideas from young and unemployed people. Selected projects receive support in terms of business plan and marketing tutoring. Each local branch of Legacoop follows projects in its area, including the first stage of crowdfunding followed by expert assistance in organizing a business plan. The confederation has already supported seven co-operatives through this program.
- *Centro Italia Reloaded* is another project initiated by Legacoop in 2017. The aim is to support areas in central Italia hit by the 2016 earthquake and create community enterprises that support the populations in the Abruzzo, Marche, and Umbria regions. Legacoop has invested €235,000 creating grants and financing professional tutoring for seven new community co-operatives along with nine other worker co-operatives.
- *Confcooperative* has allocated resources that sustain other operative community co-operatives; the first call for financing projects for the implementation of their services and assets was in 2018 with a fund of €50,000. The program has been confirmed for 2020 with a fund of €1,000,000.

Along with the considerable economic efforts, the two confederations lobby for members' interests at both regional and national levels. Indeed, for years, co-operators have wondered about the necessity of regional and national legislation on community co-operatives. Even if a national law on community co-operatives is currently only an idea, many regions have already promulgated regulations in this field.[1] These laws demonstrate the widespread interest in this new form of local co-operation; each act includes the "community co-operative" as a legal definition applicable to the traditional co-operative form (art. 2511 Italian civil code). Thus, in those regions where a legal framework exists, co-operators can adopt an already codified form for co-operatives (e.g., workers, services, or social co-operative) and define it as "community co-operative" when the intention is to achieve community development objectives.

Of special interest are the Puglia and Abruzzo regions' laws regarding minimum community presence in co-operatives. These regional legislators specify a percentage of local residents as members in order to classify the organization as a community co-operative:

- 10% (in both regions) of the population in towns, villages, and districts of under 2,500 people.
- 7% (Puglia) or 8% (Abruzzo) of the population in towns and districts of under 5,000 people.
- 3% (Puglia) or 5% (Abruzzo) of the population in towns, cities, and districts of over 5,000 people.

These requirements for effective participation by the local population triggered a wide debate inside the co-operative sector regarding ways to properly define the nature of "community co-operatives"; are they community enterprises due to their services for community or for the actual community's involvement in them?

Methodology

This section introduces the research design and objectives of the current project and addresses key topics in the discussion about Italian community co-operatives and their work with local territories. The research draws on findings from an electronic questionnaire used to collect information from a broad range of co-operatives. Bechhofer and Paterson (2000) show that a survey approach is a useful research tool to collect information from a large number of subjects to standardize the results. The aim was to obtain information from an adequate number of co-operatives widely spread across the country. The online platform, Google Docs, was used to send the questionnaire via email and store the information directly on an online Excel sheet.

The questionnaire asked for general information about each enterprise using both open and closed questions (Gillham, 2008). The questions included the year of foundation, municipality where co-operative operates, number of members, how co-operators interpret their community development works, co-operative's activities, the founders, how they got the idea for the co-operative, whether the co-operative has or not collaborated with a national confederation and an assessment of local collaborations. Lack of national law and registry made it impossible to obtain an official number of co-operatives, so the analysis relied on estimates from the two confederations. In February 2019, the number of community co-operatives in Italy was estimated at 60 units. By the completion of the research (July 2019), 45 co-operatives were contacted with 29 agreeing to complete the questionnaire. This response (50% of the universe) is considered successful, and Table 7.2 summarizes information about the respondents.

Despite the risk due to the self-selection by voluntary participation (Bechhofer & Paterson, 2000), there is an adequate representation from each geographical area and a fair diversification in terms of legal form, size, and year of foundation. After the first stage of data collection, the analysis followed two

TABLE 7.2 Participant characteristics and information

Geographical Position	*North Italy*	*10*
Subdivision of co-operatives' location according to their geographic area	Centre Italy	13
	South Italy & Islands	6
Legal form	Agriculture Co-op	1
The "Community Co-operative" label can be applied to various legal forms of co-operatives listed in the Civil Code	Workers Co-op	15
	Service Co-op	4
	Social Co-op	9
Size	Micro (fewer than ten members)	4
Subdivision on the base of co-operatives' size determined by number of official members	Small (from 10 to 49 members)	16
	Medium (from 50 to 249 members)	7
	Large (over 250 members)	2
National bodies membership	Confcooperative	8
How many community co-operatives are members or not of national confederations	Legacoop	5
	Both	2
	Other	2
	None	12

Year of foundation										
1991	1999	2001	2003	2008	2011	2015	2016	2017	2018	2019
1	1	1	1	1	3	2	4	3	10	2

Source: The author's survey.

approaches. Information from closed questions were ordered in tables and diagrams for examination. Data from open-ended questions were analyzed with Nvivo[2] and key information on community development and work in partnership with local actors labeled.

Main Features of the Italian Community Co-Operative Phenomenon

First step in the analysis of Italian community co-operatives was to understand the founders behind these projects and the reasons that led them to start these enterprises in their territories. Past research discussed the "activation of community" for creating CSEs (Bandini et al., 2014; Walzer & Sandoval, 2016; Mori & Sforzi, 2018), and specific actors are likely to participate in forming community co-operatives. Table 7.3 reports answers from the questionnaire about the category of groups responsible for the co-operatives' foundation.

Community co-operatives are independent bottom-up initiatives that arise from civic initiatives. Nevertheless, some cases show possibilities for alternatives

TABLE 7.3 Community co-operatives founders

Categories	*No. of Co-ops*
Informal group of citizens	24
Public–private partnership	2
Local enterprise	1
Third-sector organization	1
Local citizens and migrants	1

Source: Compiled by the author.

TABLE 7.4 Reasons for community co-operatives

Co-operatives' Aims and Objectives	*No.*
Local economic development	19
Revitalize rural and mountain areas	14
Local services management	9
Promotion of territories	8
Actions for young residents	7
Protection of local traditions and heritage	4
Common goods	4
Social integration	3
Networks among local firms	2
Sustainable energy production	1
Migrants' integration	1

Source: Compiled by the author.

motivations for these co-operatives, including initiatives by local authorities, collaborations among local enterprises, a project from the third sector, or an initiative to integrate migrants into the local community. This first finding illustrates the preeminent civic nature of community co-operatives. Namely, community members organize to promote a project for their community. These initiatives are self-activation efforts designed to be outside the formal schemes of other organizations, namely, an autonomous response to local issues through an independent initiative.

The second step in the analysis is to determine the reasons behind the formation of community co-operatives based on summary answers provided by co-operators regarding motivations for starting the co-operative enterprise. Each co-operative gave multiple reasons for its activities. Open questions were labelled and categorized with diverse responses and results presented in Table 7.4. Sometimes, it is possible to trace how various reasons intertwine with objectives demonstrating the complexity of the views of co-operators on local issues and resources.

> Create a sustainable lifestyle in our mountain area, valorizing our resources, recuperating the old agricultural traditions, helping people in need, utilizing local commons.
>
> *(Respondent no. 1)*

> We want to provide people with basic services and avoid the depopulation of our village and hope to keep young generations here.
>
> *(Respondent no. 7)*

> The encounter of two dreams, the one of who wants to keep alive the community and the one of who has had to emigrate.
>
> *(Respondent no. 10)*

> We have an enormous touristic potentiality unexpressed, we want to manage local commons, and provide the community with basic services.
>
> *(Respondent no. 19)*

In spite of homogeneity in co-operator groups at the start of projects (mostly informal groups of residents), reasons vary from case to case (Table 7.4). First, it is clear how the aims and objectives of co-operatives are outcomes of processes that address local issues and potentialities. Solutions arise from critical socio-economic situations embedded in the structure of these communities. Notwithstanding, there is a general awareness that solutions can also come from local communities and territories.

Moreover, these responses demonstrate the broad scope of community development issues in economic development but also include a more general sense of community well-being and social inclusion. Since their foundations, these enterprises have been devoted to improving conditions in the communities, enhancing them through a multi-dimensional approach recognizing the complex nature of issues affecting their localities. Clearly, the most often cited objective is economical and looks at the development of local economies.

Second is the revitalization of rural and mountain areas, where most actions by CSEs can affect the livelihood conditions in these areas. Along with this intent is the service management that enables opportunities for a new service provision model. Of special interest are the "actions for young residents" that reflect co-operators' aims to improve the possibilities for younger generations. Of special interest is the category "protection of local tradition and heritage"; co-operators expressed a desire to embrace local culture in their businesses. These co-operatives recognize the value of local traditions as a core element of a community's identity and want to protect and pass on their activities.

This motivation causes co-operators to enrich their services with local characteristics such as traditional food and wine, both religious and other celebrations, a rediscovery of old peasants' lifestyles, conservation of tales and narratives, and historic heritage protection. Co-operators mix them with their innovative services and provide local people and clients with embellished products that transmit the identity of the communities. For example, co-operatives that run restaurants use local products. Those that serve tourists offer primary local cultural attractions and promote events for sharing local traditions with visitors. For those in agriculture, it means the rediscovery of old crops.

Co-operators' interpretation of their work provides further confirmation of how these co-operatives fit in the field of community economy. Indeed, higher than other critical aspects of their territories such as depopulation, few job opportunities, and decrease of services, these community members see their initiatives as collective solutions for the community's benefit. This priority is confirmed by their survey responses which addressed this topic in the question "*How would you define your role in the development of your community?*" Replies prove the communality among all cases. These co-operatives are CSEs because they put the community's interest as a core element in their mission.

> We are a point of reference for the innovation of our community.
>
> *(Respondent no. 2)*

> The presence of our co-operative represents a factor for the survival and dignified life of our community. We propose basic services and an alternative idea of tourism.
>
> *(Respondent no. 3)*

> With our work we take care of our community's future. We want to tackle the depopulation and improve our citizens' living conditions.
>
> *(Respondent no. 7)*

> What we do is a great help for both the economic and social development.
>
> *(Respondent no. 9)*

> We do a dual key work: we seek solutions for community and territory problems through the intermediation between individuals and public entities. Alongside, we improve the network among local businesses in order to enhance the tourist offer.
>
> *(Respondent no. 14)*

> We re-evaluate local heritage richness and the importance of co-operating for achieving advantageous results for the community.
>
> *(Respondent no. 20)*

> We have a strategic role in developing networks for triggering innovative processes for local development.
>
> *(Respondent no. 22)*

> We do not want to see our village end.
>
> *(Respondent no. 25)*

> We aim to create a network for a circular economy and be the main landmark for it in the territory.
>
> *(Respondent no. 27)*

These responses clearly show how the community consciousness guides the organizations.

Moreover, in co-operators' views, their enterprises must be at the center of a local network for collaborating and achieving these common objectives. Therefore, another step in these collective processes is gaining an awareness that only an entrepreneurial organization, connected to the community and embedded cultural elements from its locality, can be a solution.

Co-operators emphasize that their community suffers from structural socio-economic issues so they must implement permanent solutions to address them. By examining co-operators' words, it is possible to see the further steps by the co-operatives sector toward the achievement of common good. Acknowledging the capacity of this firm model to enhance members' conditions and engage a multitude of people in the management process (Zamagni & Zamagni, 2008), local groups translate this capacity into a wider mission toward the community. Using many local cultural elements can create strong bonds with people and create effective relationships to define co-operatives' strategies for the largest share of local population. Therefore, the co-operative model is the most suitable enabling structure (Wilkinson & Quarter, 1996) for regenerating local socio-economic contexts (Bailey, 2012) according to these civic groups discussing community commitment (Phillips & Pittman, 2015).

As in any other business, co-operatives need funds to initiate activities and proceed with the start-up phase. Community co-operatives present a dual way for accessing adequate resources to start their activities (Table 7.5). A significant number have opted for the most traditional solution for collecting enough funds – membership contributions. In addition, many other co-operatives took advantage of one or more funds or programs designed to foster new co-operatives. In these cases, the role of national confederations is key because they help founders find the most suitable financial solution for projects. Indeed, 9 of 12 co-operatives that are not members of any confederations (see Table 7.2) had no access to funds or programs and only 2 of 11 co-operatives that raised funds only from their members are members of a confederation. Therefore, it is plausible that membership in a confederation can help co-operators access resources over and above members' contributions. Table 7.6 reports co-operatives' business activities by category.

TABLE 7.5 Resources used for starting up the co-operative

Funding Source	*No. of Co-ops*
Only members' shares	11
National bodies for co-operative initiatives[a]	10
Regional funds for co-operative development	7
European funds	3
Foundations' support	2

a Programs listed in the previous paragraph.
Source: Compiled by the author.

TABLE 7.6 Community co-operatives' business activities

Sector	*Activities*	*No.*
Tourism	Hotel, B&B, diffused hotel, info-point, website, tourist entertainment	23
Culture	Events for promoting local cultures and heritage, museum and historical sites management, theatre and music shows	10
Child care	Babysitting and summer camps	10
Agriculture	Cultivation, rearing animals, product transformation	9
Assistance for individuals	Support and assistance for physical and psychological needs	9
Green activities	Gardening, green spaces maintenance, forest services	9
Commerce	Store and minimarket management	8
Property management	Sites of interest (e.g., historic buildings or public parks) management on behalf of others	6
Education	Projects with schools	5
Food services	Bar and restaurant management	5
Maintenance	Plumbing, electrical, carpentry, repair services	3
Cleaning	Cleaning services and laundry	3
E-commerce	Sales of local products on the internet	2
Water services	Water resources management	2
Energy	Energy production with solar panels	1
Migrant services	Accommodation and support in cultural integration	1

Source: Compiled by the author.

They can generate resources, create jobs, and initiate related processes to develop their local economies. It is especially interesting that these co-operatives operate as multi-functional organizations able to create a variety of services and diversify their forces in multiple fields. These results explain how the community development mission becomes complex as it involves activities that directly address local issues or others that mitigate them through their work. The list of activities in Table 7.5 allows grouping the activities into two types: those "direct to the intern" and others "direct to the extern" of the community. The first refers to those activities planned for local residents; the second to those services provided to people from outside the community (e.g., tourists).

A grouping such as this is relevant to the analysis of community development initiatives because it is necessary to assess where resources for these activities come from and how these organizations address their services (Phillips & Pittman, 2015). This analysis examines income sources to see how these enterprises create a mix between services that can provide a direct benefit to their communities and others that generate profits from interactions with external groups. The first category includes services that specifically target the local population, their needs, and aim to achieve a local self-reliance. This category includes activities such as "child care," "assistance for individuals," "green activities," "maintenance services," "water and energy services," and "bar and restaurant" that also serve tourists. These activities help local populations to enhance their livelihood by directly addressing people's needs.

By comparison, services "direct to the extern" of communities generate incomes from transactions with outsiders such as "tourism" that brings visitors, resources, and more opportunities to the community.

> We offer an alternative idea of tourism, a more sustainable offer.
>
> *(Respondent no. 2)*

> We want to improve our citizens' future with our services.
>
> *(Respondent no. 6)*

> We work in network with other tourist businesses for creating a better territorial offer.
>
> *(Respondent no. 13)*

> Improve the circular economy.
>
> *(Respondent no. 26)*

Moreover, these services contribute directly to people's everyday lives in many cases; alternatively, they are used as tools to attract external resources to the community, as in the case of tourism activities. As explained earlier, community co-operatives show a tendency to intertwine local cultural elements with their services and present themselves as rooted businesses in their communities committed to historical heritage, traditions, and culture conservation.

Firming Community Support

This section describes the dynamics that gain community sustainment for these enterprises by evaluating networks around community co-operatives and identifying key local partners and co-operators' assessments of these collaborations. The community development literature emphasizes (Wilkinson & Quarter, 1996; Lang & Roessl, 2011; Phillips & Pittman, 2015) that networking with local partners is key to the success of community organizations. Therefore, this research examines how Italian community co-operatives establish relationships. Social connections give community developers many advantages such as access to information, more contribution to resource collection, inputs from different perspectives regarding community's issues with the partnerships advocating for these organizations (Mori & Sforzi, 2018; Bianchi, 2019).

Several points should be addressed at this point. First, it is important to examine how local populations participate directly in community co-operatives by becoming members and supporting them by purchasing shares. Table 7.7 provides key information regarding the involvement of local population with the relationships between the number of members and residents as percentages.

TABLE 7.7 Percentage of local population involved in community co-operatives

Co-operative	*Members*	*Town*	*Local Population*[a]	*Percentage*
L'innesto	252	Gaverina Terme (BG)	855	29.47
Valle dei cavalieri	55	Ventasso (RE)	4,130	1.33
Brigì	14	Mendatica (IM)	180	7.77
Briganti di cerreto	11	Ventasso (RE)	4,130	0.26
Tavola rotonda	76	Campo di Giove (AQ)	793	0.95
La mosca bianca	29	Corfinio (AQ)	1,025	2.82
Le fonti	46	Fontecchio (AQ)	342	13.45
Melpignano	269	Melpignano (LE)	2,211	12.16
Tralci di vite	12	Chianche (AV)	480	2.5
Montagne della duchessa	12	Borgorose (RI)	4,435	0.27
Cadore	163	Valle di Cadore (BL)	1,868	8.72
Anversiamo	60	Anversa degli Abruzzi (AQ)	310	19.35
100 laghi	8	Corniglio (PR)	1,842	0.43
Terre del magra	72	Ameglia (SP)	4,316	1.66
San Zeno	3	Galeata (FC)	2,500	0.12
A menzalora	22	Petrizzi (CZ)	1,103	1.99
Beverino	6	Beverino (SP)	2,350	0.25
Fuoco	13	Comano Terme (TN)	2,963	0.43
Germinale	58	Demonte (CN)	1,959	2.96
Sant'onofrio 3.0	75	Sant'Onofrio (VV)	3,035	2.47
Viseras	3	Mamoiada (NU)	2,498	0.12
Borgo di fiume	13	Fiumefreddo Bruzio (CS)	2,918	0.44
Comunità dei monti sibillini	12	Montemonaco (AP)	551	2.17
Vivi petroio	84	Trequanda (SI)	1,228	6.84
Vara	42	Follo (SP)	6,317	0.66
Mulazzo ospitalità e ambiente	4	Mulazzo (MS)	2,398	0.16
Ecosistema comunale castell'azzara	97	Castell'Azzara (GR)	1,408	6.88
Vallecchia	77	Castelnuovo Magra (SP)	8,381	0.91
Giovani orme	19	Corna Imagna (BG)	925	2.05

a Istat January 1, 2020.

These figures must be assessed carefully because there are no restrictions for community co-operatives to also enroll non-residents in the municipality where they operate. Thus, not all co-operative members are necessarily residents in the town.

The proportions shown illustrate relationships between the actual size of each co-operative and the community where it operates. The figures clearly show that none of these co-operatives has a significant participation in terms of the percentage of local population enrolled as official members. Only one co-operative engages more than 25% of the local population; 25 of 29 co-operatives are less than 10%; and 21 do not reach even 5%. This is a fundamental finding because it points out how many co-operatives struggle in reaching percentages required by regional laws.

Nevertheless, these co-operatives, despite the marginal formal participation of local population, have defined views and objectives for their community development missions. Thus, the analysis must focus attention on how these organizations create effective networks with their communities by collaborating with other local entities. Previous results from the questionnaire showed how small groups of residents provided proposals for socio-economic development through collective firms.

Then, Table 7.7 shows that their organization does not achieve significant critical mass in local population that can qualify them as community co-operatives by specific criteria as a community enterprise. Consequently, their ability to develop a project for the community's benefit and to implement solutions for local issues must use other approaches or processes. In this sense, it is useful to investigate collaborations with other organizations, both public and private, and examine how they support the community development realization.

Every co-operative has more than one collaboration demonstrating a general tendency toward partnerships with other local organizations. Moreover, these collaborations are with both public and private agencies showing a capacity to collaborate with a wide range of interlocutors; indeed, public authorities and private businesses are the most common partners.

Local authorities see promoting a community co-operative as a valuable way to support socio-economic development. During times of shortage of public resources and disempowerment of public institutions, they find a reliable partner that can operate outside the bureaucracy to improve the public service. In many cases, these authorities engage co-operatives in regenerating local assets that otherwise must be abandoned (Bianchi & Vieta, 2019).

The authorities can also support community co-operatives with commissions to provide basic services to the population such as snow shoveling, green areas maintenance, or heritage conservation. Collaboration with private-sector agencies is fundamental because these enterprises operate in the same locality and

TABLE 7.8 Community co-operatives' local collaborations

Main Collaborations	*No. of Co-ops N = 29*
Collaboration with local public authorities	25
Collaboration with private businesses	25
Collaboration with third sector	23
Collaboration with religious organizations	14
Collaboration with political parties	2

Source: Compiled by the author.

enhancing socio-economic conditions can affect every business in the area. It is for this reason that many co-operatives engage other firms in planning common strategies for territorial promotion or marketing products. One co-operative is the result of a private business collaboration that created a dedicated organization to promote local products and assets (Table 7.3).

Also of crucial importance are collaborations with the third-sector and religious organizations. In these cases, communality is the path toward non-profit objectives and the community's interest. These categories of partners operate in the community with various purposes such as charity, volunteering, social promotion, and altruism. Their missions overlap with community co-operatives' objectives and are a basis for collaborations that can benefit the community. In the end, co-operatives avoid relationships with political parties, perhaps to avoid political disputes that could compromise connections with other parts of the community. Staying apolitical can be an effective strategy because it does not create barriers with other residents having opposing views or with local authorities.

What emerges from co-operators' responses is the contribution that these networks give to their businesses undergirding the main factor of the community's support in this model. Having direct contact with various subjects, both individuals and organizations allow the co-operatives to expand their view of the community. These connections can provide key information about the socio-economic status of the territory as well as form new collaborations with other subjects that have common objectives. Even the simple supply of information can become strategic because it enables the co-operatives to assess what the community needs.

This also confirms the deep difference between CSEs and for-profit organizations. The latter prioritize investors' interests and are guided by metrics used by for-profit maximizations, CSEs manage their business activities to address local issues based on contextual settings. Therefore, community co-operatives develop a multi-stakeholder governance approach (Borzaga & Sacchetti, 2015) to consider this wide plethora of collaborators and to fulfill multiple socio-economic issues.

After mapping local collaborations, it is useful to examine how co-operators assess relationships with local partners. Figures 7.1 and 7.2 report responses by co-operators that assess local collaborations with partners in their communities. Definitely, these social networks are key elements in realizing community development objectives. Considering the aim of community development processes, as the community well-being and socio-economic development (Wilkinson & Quarter, 1996; Phillips & Pittman, 2015), expanding networks inside the community facilitates the comprehension of both local problems and potentialities.

Figure 7.1 shows the agreement about relationships with partners helping to understand problems – 27 of 29 co-operatives share this idea. Likewise, 28 of 29 co-operatives consider these connections as key tools for assessing local potentialities in problem-solving. These results point out several community co-operative

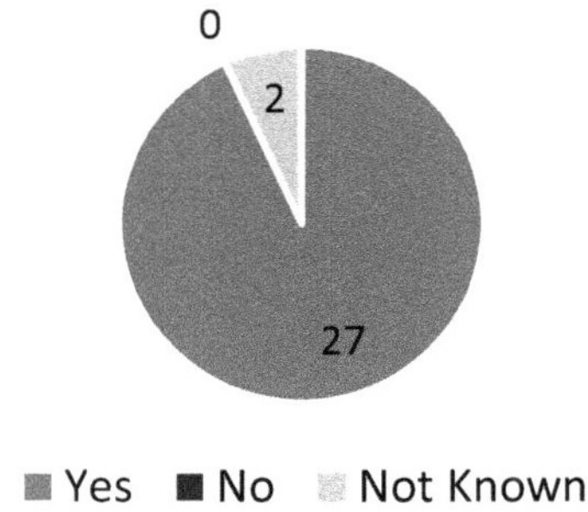

FIGURE 7.1 Understanding local problems.

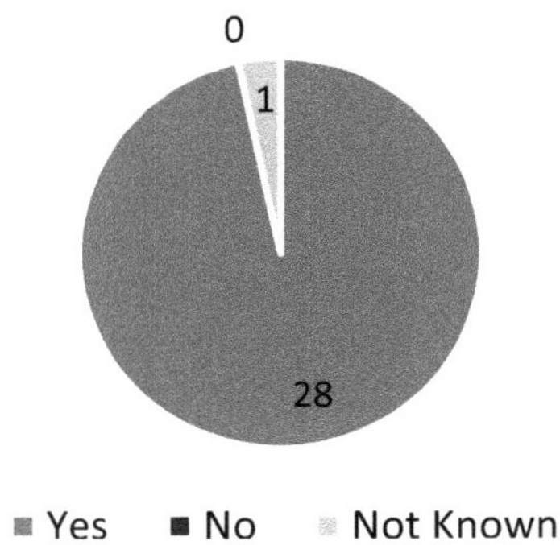

FIGURE 7.2 Understanding local potentialities.

views. They might not engage large shares of local populations, but they develop networks with key actors and stakeholders, both public and private, to delineate strategies and actions for community development. Indeed, 28 of 29 respondents confirm their intentions to work toward implementing these relationships by creating new collaboration opportunities such as programs, projects, services, or contracts with local partners.

Main Features of Italian Community Co-Operatives

In various parts of Italy, local groups congregate to respond to concerns created by diverse socio-economic factors. These initiatives are part of the wider field of "community economy" (Wilkinson & Quarter, 1996) because they aim to create new enterprises strongly intertwined with local societies and economic systems. Moreover, these enterprises operate with the community's interest as the core element in their mission. Therefore, they cannot be considered as traditional business establishments. So, they assume the status of "community enterprises" due to their clear choice to benefit the local population under its various forms (Somerville & McElwee, 2011).

The decision to use the co-operative legal form is fundamental because it embodies key values such as democracy and solidarity. Also, it has proven its relevance in spreading mutual benefits among both members and non-members (Zamagni & Zamagni, 2008). For this reason, it has been selected as a unique form for developing community economies in Italy.

This specific aspect highlights the significant evolution of the model managed by local groups. Usually, co-operatives arise from groups of people with homogenous needs and few resources (Zamagni & Zamagni, 2008) who decide to start-up a co-operative to provide mutual benefits to their groups.

Results from the questionnaire present a different situation; residents with a strong community commitment need an enterprise model to enhance their endeavors and stabilize them in a permanent organization able to generate resources. Moreover, since the start, these co-operatives consider the relationships with local partners a key part of their community development work because they have the community's interest as a core element of their mission. Therefore, the second key evolution of the traditional co-operative model was to abandon members' personal interest as the main goal and make the community's well-being the main focus.

Furthermore, the co-operative model is innovative because Italian community co-operatives are independent bottom-up initiatives created by a few community members in partnership with key local actors, both public and private, to propose new solutions using local resources, both material (public assets, commons, infrastructures) and intangible (information, culture, traditions). This is progress from the goal to be a private, even if collective, enterprise with specific scopes of production to focus on the community's mission in partnership with other local actors.

Community co-operatives compensate for the limits of both public and private sectors. As co-operators explain, most of the partnerships with public authorities see collaboration for service management using co-operatives as outsourcing at less cost to the public sector. Municipalities can work with community co-operatives by transferring public assets for regeneration or using them as providers.

Moreover, the collaboration with local public authorities opens other options for organizations. Public institutions can discuss general issues about the community and give the co-operative a better understanding about important topics. They can involve community co-operatives, as key players in socio-economic development, to co-design a restructuring of local services such as park and green area maintenance and management, services to people in a state of need, commons management, and cultural heritage conservation. These are areas where public actions are essential, but public authorities no longer can adequately manage them (Ostrom, 2012; Fazzi, 2013; Borzaga & Zandonai, 2015).

The co-operatives can find reciprocal support in this sense providing necessary services in economic conditions where private markets normally do not invest (Borzaga & Tortia, 2004). Indeed, the local town hall is the most common partner in the sample. In general, local public authorities recognize the value of these initiatives and sustain them as an accomplishment of their mission for the community. Also, the collaborations with other private and non-profit organizations strengthen the networks around the co-operative projects and allow access to other sectors and privileged points of view regarding communities.

Community co-operatives tend to establish relationships with partners that share the same interests, the well-being, and wealth of the community even if from diverse perspectives. Therefore, a community's support in Italian community co-operatives comes from multiple sources and takes different forms. As previous figures show, it is not a matter of effective community participation in the co-operative membership, but rather it is the co-operators' capacity to establish networks with key local partners that constitute the community's support. In many cases, a small informal group of residents decides to take action to tackle an issue or provide a potential benefit using local resources that triggers a collective process for establishing a community co-operative.

The business firm model *per se* already represents a valid tool for implementing social services and constraining social inequalities (Borzaga & Santuari, 2001; Zamagni & Zamagni, 2008). The new initiatives translate the co-operative model into the "community economy" and definitely accomplish the "concern for community," which has been underestimated for decades in value and importance (MacPherson, 2013). National confederations clearly work in this direction; their efforts in spreading this new concept of co-operation have resulted in new projects and relevant achievements in legislation. Notwithstanding, politics will drive the main debate on Italian community co-operatives in the next few years. Some regional lawmakers have already taken a clear stance on their definition of community co-operatives and decided that community participation is the basic and unequivocal element that is the essence of a "community enterprise."

Findings from this research show how enterprises can develop a structure for implementing community development work even without a major enrollment of local population. This debate recalls the opposition highlighted by Somerville and McElwee (2011) in their critic of Peredo and Chrisman (2006), who points out that most communities cannot participate in their entirety in these enterprises. This situation is possible only in small communities with a homogenous ethnic composition and a strong social capital.

Therefore, Somerville and McElwee suggest that "community enterprises" are those that can provide residents with key services through entrepreneurial activities designed in accordance with the community's needs and resources. In the future evolution of this sector, legislators must keep this key concept in mind and consider how to assess the effective contribution of these CSEs instead of the percentage of local population involved.

Conclusion

It is possible to see Italian community co-operatives as CSEs. They represent a specific sub-category in this field because they adopt a precise legal form that determines key characteristics of the Italian model. First, these community enterprises are co-operatives, which means that they must operate within specific boundaries and take a distinct form. Despite this restriction, the Italian cases show typical aspects of CSEs, and they confirm residents' willingness to improve community well-being due to their community spirit.

Thus, these organizations are deeply rooted in their communities because local people created them. Furthermore, they are multi-functional because they interlink diverse business areas inside the same firm structure to develop a range of services for both direct and indirect community benefits. They work with both residents and external groups to address their business goals regarding external and internal resources always with the aim to generate positive outcomes for their communities. Instead of engaging as many people as possible, community co-operatives opt for establishing wide networks with a variety of local partners, both public and private, who share same objectives.

Despite the absence of a national law, which can provide a unique definition and fix the terms for community co-operatives, many local groups have already decided to take action and improve this solution in their territories with varying results. National confederations play a key role in institutionalizing a common idea of community co-operative and help sustain new co-operators by providing projects. In the end, community co-operatives devote their organizations to the community's commitment because they solidify some local members' willingness to foster innovative solutions for key issues and make local resources more central in addressing local issues.

Notes

1 List of regional legislation on community co-operatives: Toscana Regional Law no. 24 May 8, 2014, article 11bis. Puglia Regional Law no. 66 May 26, 2014. Emilia Romagna Regional Law no. 12 July 17, 2014, article 2. Basilicata Regional Law no. 12 March 20, 2015, article 12. Liguria Regional Law no. 14 April 7, 2015. Lombardia Regional Law no. 6 November 6, 2015, article 11. Abruzzo Regional Law no. 25 October 8, 2015. Umbria Regional Law no. 1 June 19, 2019.

2 The text of each answer has been examined with Nvivo, a software for content analysis. Labels were created to select information for each analytical category of this study.

References

Bailey, N. (2012). The Role, Organisation and Contribution of Community Enterprise to Urban Regeneration Policy in the UK. *Progress in Planning* 77:1–35.

Bandini, F., Medei, R., &Travaglini, C. (2014). Community-Based Enterprises in Italy: Definition and Governance Model. *SSRN Electronic Journal*. doi:10.6092/unibo/amsacta/3980

Bartocci, L., & Picciaia, F. (2013). 'Le "Non Profit Utilities" Tra Stato e Mercato: L'esperienza Della Cooperativa Di Comunità Di Melpignano.' *Azienda Pubblica* 3:381–402.

Bechhofer, F., & Paterson, L. (2000). *Principles of Research Design in the Social Sciences*. London and New York: Routledge.

Bianchi, M. (2019). With Members and for Members? A Theoretical Analysis of Mutuality in Co-Operatives, Its Evolution and Re-Formulation through the Italian Community Co-Ops. *Argomenti* 12:85–103.

Bianchi, M., &Vieta, M. (2019). *Italian Community Co-Operatives Responding to Economic Crisis and State Withdrawal. A New Model for Socio-Economic Development.* Geneva: United Nations Task Force for Social and Solidarity Economy.

Borzaga, C., & Flaviano, Z. (2015). Oltre La Narrazione, Fuori Dagli Schemi: I Processi Generativi Delle Imprese Di Comunità. *Impresa Sociale* 5:1–7.

Borzaga, C., & Sacchetti, S. (2015). Why Social Enterprises are Asking to be Multi-Stakeholder and Deliberative: An Explanation around the Costs of Exclusion. Euricse Working Paper no. 75.

Borzaga, C., & Santuari, A. (2001). From Traditional Co-Operative to Innovative Social Enterprise. In Borzaga C., & Defourny J. (Eds.), *The Emergence of Social Enterprise.* London: Routledge, pp. 161–181.

Borzaga, C., & Tortia, E. (2004). *Dalla Cooperazione Mutualistica Alla Cooperazione Sociale. AICCON Working Paper.* 6-2004. Associazione Italiana per la Cultura dellaCooperazione e del Non Profit.

Borzaga, C.& Flaviano, Z. (2015). Oltre La Narrazione, Fuori Dagli Schemi: I Processi Generativi Delle Imprese Di Comunità. *Impresa Sociale* 5:1–7.

Carrosio, G. (2015). 'Economia civile e gestione delle risorse ambientali nelle aree interne'. *Territorio* 74(3):115–221. doi:10.3280/TR2015-074020.

Casale, F. (2005). *Scambio e Mutualità Nella Società Cooperativa.* Milano: Giuffré.

Fazzi, L. (2013). *Terzo Settore e Nuovo Welfare in Italia.* Milano: Franco Angeli.

Gillham, B. (2008). *Developing a Questionnaire.* London: Continuum International Publishing Group.

Ianes, A. (2013). *Introduzione Alla Storia Della Cooperazione in Italia (1854–2011): Profilo Storico-Economico e Interpretazione.* Soveria Mannelli: Rubbettino.

Kretzmann, J., & McKnight, J. (1993). *Building Communities from the Inside Out: A Path toward Finding and Mobilizing a Community's Assets.* Northwestern University: Asset-Based Community Development Institute, Institute for Policy Research.

Lang, R., & Roessl, D. (2011). Contextualizing the Governance of Community Co-Operatives: Evidence from Austria and Germany. *VOLUNTAS: International Journal of Voluntary and Nonprofit Organizations* 22(4):706–730.

Leno, K., Monni, S., & Tomassi, F. (2019). *Le Mappe Della Disuguaglianza Una Geografia Sociale Metropolitana.* Roma: Donzelli Editore.

MacPherson, I. (2013). Cooperatives' Concern for the Community: From Members towards Local Communities' Interests. *Euricse Paper No. 46/13.*

Mori, P. A. (2017). 'Community Co-Operative and Co-Operatives Providing Public Services'. In Michie, J., Blasi, J., & Borzaga, C. (eds.), *The Oxford Handbook of Mutual. Co-Operative, and Co-Owned Business.* Oxford: Oxford University Press.

Mori, P. A., & Sforzi, J. (2018). *Imprese Di Comunità. Innovazione Istituzionale, Partecipazione e Sviluppo Locale.* Bologna: Il Mulino.

Ostrom, E. R. (2012). *The Future of the Commons: Beyond Market Failure and Government Regulations.* London: Institute of Economic Affairs.

Peredo, A. M., & Chrisman, J. J. (2006). Toward a Theory of Community-Based Enterprise. *Academy of Management Review* 31(2):309–328.

Phillips, R., & Pittman, R. (2015). *An Introduction to Community Development.* London and New York: Routledge.

Ranci Ortigosa, E. (2018). *Contro La Povertà. Analisi Economica e Politiche a Confronto.* San Giuliano Milanese: Francesco Brioschi.

Somerville, P., & McElwee, G. (2011). Situating Community Enterprise: A Theoretical Exploration. *Entrepreneurship & Regional Development* 23(5–6):317–330.

Teneggi, G., & Zandonai, F. (2017). *The Community Enterprises of the Appennino Tosco-Emiliano UNESCO Biosphere Reserve, Italy: Biodiversity Guardians and Sustainable Development Innovators. SSRN Scholarly Paper ID 3095544.* Rochester, NY: Social Science Research Network.

Tracey, P., Phillips, N., & Haugh, H. (2005). Beyond Philanthropy: Community Enterprise as a Basis for Corporate Citizenship. *Journal of Business Ethics* 58(4):327–344.

Visco, I. (2018). *Investimenti Pubblici per Lo Sviluppo Dell'economia Intervento Del Governatore Della Banca d'Italia Ignazio Visco.* Keynot Speech at "64° Convegno di Studi Amministrativi Sviluppo economico, vincoli finanziari e qualità dei servizi: strumenti e garanzie", Varenna.

Walzer, N. (2017). Community Supported Enterprises as a Local Investment Strategy. *Illinois Municipal Policy Journal* 2(1):35–48.

Walzer, N. (2019). *Guidebook and Resources for Starting a Community Supported Enterprise.* East Lansing, MI: North Central Regional Center for Rural Development. Available at https://www.cgs.niu.edu/Reports/cse-guidebook-final-2-8-19.pdf

Walzer, N., & Sandoval, J. (2016). *Emergence and Growth of Community Supported Enterprises.* East Lansing, MI: North Central Regional Center for Rural Development.

Wilkinson, P., & Quarter, J. G. P. (1996). *Building a Community-Controlled Economy: The Evangeline Co-Operative Experience.* Toronto: University of Toronto Press.

Zamagni, S., & Zamagni, V. (2008). *La Cooperazione. Tra Mercato e Democrazia Economica.* Bologna: Il Mulino.

Zamagni, V., Battilani, P., & Casali, A. (2004). *La Cooperazione Di Consumo in Italia: Centocinquant'anni Della Coop Consumatori.* Bologna: Il Mulino.

8

TAIWAN COMMUNITY-BASED ENTERPRISE AS DEVELOPMENT STRATEGY TOWARD COMMUNITY CAPACITY BUILDING

Chaimei Hsia

Introduction

The magnitude of the economic impact on society that is increasing at an unprecedented scale due to the Coronavirus crisis revealed the fragility of the modern economy and urges us to scrutinize economic practices in a more comprehensive way. Capitalist markets, monopoly, globalization, and pragmatism all contribute to an enormous economic growth in the world. Nevertheless, the economic inequality, social exclusion, bipolarized society, and social conflict combined are reaching a tipping point. The COVID-19 pandemic brings a backlash of globalization in terms of dependency on international supply chains and monopoly businesses. It also exacerbates the chronic problems of economic inequality and social exclusion. Marginalized groups and disadvantaged populations especially are in dire situations as people, including the middle classes, suddenly struggled to procure basic products and materials in the pandemic crisis. Alleviating the acute problems elicited from an unbalanced economic system calls for structural changes and systemic solutions.

Numerous scholars and social activists have advocated other streams of economic practices as alternatives to the dominant capitalist economy and seek sustainable approaches to create a more equitable, independent, resilient, and sustainable society. Solidarity economy (Miller, 2006; Castells et al., 2017), time banking (Cahn & Rowe, 1992; Seyfang, 2002, 2004), co-operatives, feminist critique of mainstream economy (Gibson-Graham, 2006), women's empowerment through micro-credit or small loans (Begum, 2007), community-supported enterprises (CSEs) (Walzer & Sandoval, 2016), and community-based enterprise (CBE) (Peredo & Chrisman, 2006) all provide ways, methods, or motivations to promote different economic practices that foster human dignity, equity, social inclusion, self-determination, and empowerment.

Drawing on the perspective of economy as culture extends the discussion of economic practices to social justice, gender issues, politics, and democracy issues (Banet-Weiser & Castells, 2016). Rather than the production, consumption, and exchange based on financial value as conventional economic practices often focus, the contemporary radical socio-economic activists leverage economy as a vehicle for social transformation (Miller, 2006). To characterize this specific feature, the term "social-value based economic practices" serves as an umbrella concept to cover a wide range of economic practices with social intentions.

To better understand the notion of social-value-based economic practices, two cases of CBEs in Taiwan are discussed to explore the social purposes of CBEs by analyzing their context, mechanism, practices, and impacts. In response to the challenge of globalization and competition of capitalist market, a modified CBE model is also suggested through a conceptual framework. The following sections advance the concept of CBEs and explore the potential of utilizing them as a development strategy for community capacity building.

Community-Based Enterprise

Drawing on the networks and social bonding rooted in the local context, CBE is defined as "a community acting corporately as both entrepreneur and enterprise in pursuit of the common good" (Peredo & Chrisman, 2006). Treating the community as an endogenous resource to the enterprise, the development of CBE is the entrepreneurial process in which the community "acts entrepreneurially to create and operate a new enterprise embedded in its existing social structure" (p. 310).

Given they are rooted in a community, CBEs are often based on available community skills and local assets, depend on social capital that provides a trustworthy network, and they seek an incremental learning process grounded in collective experience. Characterized as community industry in Taiwan, community enterprises often connect to the inherent cultural heritage and place-specific resources that provide materials for inspiration and serve as creativity reservoirs for entrepreneurial innovation and local identity formation (Chen, 2019).

Different from the mainstream entrepreneurship tendency to pursue mainly economic goals in a new venture, CBEs differ from existing entrepreneurship models by emphasizing community issues and concerns. The community economic considerations may be secondary to other interests, such as cultural, educational, or environmental preservation. In most CBE cases, profit-making typically is not the primary purpose of the enterprise. Often, CBEs emphasize the necessity of addressing social, economic, cultural, and environmental goals simultaneously to achieve sustainable local development.

Given the collectiveness, local networks, and empowerment in management and operation, the CBE approach is not solely defined by proprietorship, nor does it rely only on the support of its residents. Instead, it is characterized by members' substantial engagement and commitment to the enterprise. CBE members play important roles in the organization by acting as owners, managers, supervisors, employees, and even volunteers. In some scenarios, unsalaried work or unpaid service contributed by local volunteers in support of the community enterprises is valued more because it signifies robust solidarity and community mobilization. In the following sections, two place-based community enterprise cases are discussed to help conceptualize the notion of CBEs and explore the roles of CBEs in community capacity building.

Aboriginal Renaissance through CBE Eco-Tourism Innovation

Bulaubulau, in the language of aboriginal tribe Atayal, refers to wandering. Located in the remote mountain area of the east coast of Taiwan, the establishment of Bulaubulau village started with a social movement, "Returning My Land," to reclaim the ownership of aboriginal lands in the 1980s and 1990s. The development-induced displacement in Taiwan traces back to the Japanese colonial era after 1895. Taiwan was ceded to Japan under the Treaty of Shimonoseki in Qing dynasty. Under the Japanese colonial rule, the forced migration of indigenous people was associated mainly with the construction of dams, agricultural irrigation, mining, and exploitation of forest resources.

After the nationalist government's relocation to the island of Taiwan in 1949, the indigenous people's social issues associated with displacement were still not solved under the Republic of China regime. For decades, indigenous people suffered from cultural disruption due to the disconnection with their traditional lands and the deprivation of their livelihood that was tied to the forest and Mother Nature. Not until the indigenous rights legislation implementation in 1994 did the indigenous people's resettlement and tribal culture re-establishment become a political agenda and garner public attention. Nevertheless, being the disinvested population and the least powerful sectors of society, the struggle of tribal cultural restoration and displacement mitigation continues.

During this lengthy movement, 10 hectares of land were granted to a group of Atayal tribe members with seven households along the Loudong River in Yilan County. This has become the tribal education base for the Root Vocational School Program. Named as the Bulaubulau tribe, a village with approximately 85 residents has built a reputation for the scenic view, tranquility, and exquisite tribal eco-tourism experience.

Benefited by the geographic location with suitable temperature and moisture, the mountainous region of Yilan County yields the best quality and most sought-after gourmet mushrooms. Seeking organic mushroom cultivation as a main revenue for the village, residents managed to grow mushrooms in a traditional way, planting mushroom spawn in the punched holes of segmented native wood along the river. To have a better harvest, residents designed ways to prevent the squirrels and lizards from eating the precious crops. However, due to the lack of lizard predators and squirrel's intervention, termites came to chew off the logs on which mushrooms were planted. Learning from these experiences, Bulaubulau residents decided to follow their ancestors' wisdom and let Mother

Nature take care of the rest and allowed wild animals to have their shares – approximately 30% of the entire production.

Nevertheless, preserving the tribal wisdom and tradition is about more than cultivating mushrooms. Tribal culture is on the brink of extinction without succeeding generations, so it is critical to retain young people in the village in a way that balances conservation and livelihoods as well as tribal culture preservation and local economic development. Instead of delivering organic mushrooms and vegetables to the market, Bulaubulau residents began to ask whether it would be possible to generate public interest in coming to the village to experience the traditional tribal cuisine. An organic feast in a natural setting quickly attracted public attention, and more visitors came to the village to taste the tribal cuisine. In addition to the authentic and delicious meals, an educational and cultural tour to the village is also arranged so participants could learn more about tribal culture and traditions.

Successes with the gourmet meals and culture tours helped the village to immediately build a great reputation for its unique tribal eco-tourism. Access to the area without the tribal tour guide is restricted, and only 30 visitors per day are allowed with reservations. The extraordinary experience of Bulaubulau eco-tourism has made this one-day tour so popular that it requires a reservation waiting time of three months (Yang, 2016).

Nonetheless, the tribal culture is not solely about local cuisine, music, and dance. There is a unique philosophy that guides tribal social structure and way of living. The wisdom rooted in the nature and harmony value in tribal belief relies on a sustainable structure to pass on the ancestors' bequests. The solution involved more tribal education and Kwali, a young man in Bulaubulau village, is the key person in this innovation. Receiving a scholarship to join an educational program hosted by Brigham Young University (BYU) in Hawaii, Kwali was the first Taiwanese tribal youth to participate in this unique training program in 2013 (Tribal Youth Overseas Training, 2015).

Partnering with the Polynesian Cultural Center (PCC), the BYU–Hawaii learning program highlights an unusual educational and business symbiotic relationship to help students supplement their educational expenses by working at the PCC. Inspired by the collaborative model of BYU and PCC, Kwali actively participated in a variety of management meetings and cultural activities during his internship with PCC. The collaboration between BYU and PCC motivated him to rethink possible models that the Bulaubulau village could adopt to build a sustainable system that integrated tribal culture and economic development. The aspiration generated from the exposure to PCC prompted Kwali to design an educational innovation intended to integrate tribal tradition into the school curriculum. The intention is to pass on the tribal heritage to the next generation as a philosophy and way of living.

An unconventional self-learning curriculum that allows tribal teenagers in the village to learn vocational skills related to tribal tradition was proposed to the Ministry of Education in Taiwan. After years of coordinating and negotiating with the public sectors and local high school, the Root Vocational Study program was officially launched in 2015. In order to garner an equivalent high school diploma, students must attend additional general courses on subjects such as literature, mathematics, English, writing and reading, computer, art, and marketing (Ma et al., 2015). Based on individual interests, students can choose to study architecture, art craft, agriculture, tribal cuisine and restaurant management, or language for their vocational skills.

Adopting the educational and business model used by BYU and PCC, the Root Vocational Study program also provides students with opportunities to work at a tribal restaurant, coordinate the tribal culture tour, or be tribal tour interpreters with stable incomes while practicing learned skills (Yang, 2016). Through a collaboration with the tribal restaurant, sculpture and weaving art craft department, farming sector, and cultural tour coordinating center, the revenues generated from Bulaubulau eco-tourism can support the livelihood of more than 40 tribal members (Yang, 2016). The revenue surplus, after staff salaries and operation costs for the tribal kitchen are paid, goes to the village construction and infrastructure improvements.

The Bulaubulau economic mechanism is heavily embedded in a social relationship rooted in tribal tradition, values, and wisdom. Individual work performed by each member plays a critical part in the tribe and constitutes the whole system that makes the tribal community function well. It emphasizes the value of self-development and collaboration among tribal members.

Seeking a balance between human intrusion and wildlife habitat conservation is rooted in aboriginal culture and manifested through their ways of living and using the land. The semi-wild mushroom cultivation method launched from tribal tradition is preserved by the Bulaubulau community. Crop rotation with a fallow ground practice is the way to regenerate the soil and produce the highest quality crops. In preparing meals for visitors, nearly 80% of the food ingredients on the table are from the Bulaubulau tribe and local village farmers. Utensils serving the meals are made of natural materials to reduce waste and pollution. Cups, chopsticks, and spoons are made of bamboo; plates are carved from wood; and banana leaves are used to line a platter. Most village architectures and furniture materials are from locals to reduce the footprint and carbon emission.

A similar philosophy applies to the visiting tourists. By limiting their numbers, the hosting capacity remains balanced among workload, food production, and environmental protection. These measures and endeavors are testimonies to practicing tribal tradition, and a symbiotic economic system inherited from the tribal ancestors now passes to the younger generation and becomes a manifesto of coexistence of human and nature.

Community Co-Op Initiative: The Power of One Pack of Rice

Located in the southern agrarian plantation of Taiwan, the Shih-An community was a typical, small rural village facing challenges of aging population, loss of youth, and deteriorated buildings and vacant spaces. As young people leave for cities for jobs, the Shih-An community faces depopulation and becoming one of the low-income communities with less than 600 population. Among the permanent residents, more than 20% are older than 65 years, so geriatric care became a major concern in this remote rural area with lack of public transit and clinic service. The local leaders foresaw the pressing problem and initiated a free shuttle service for elderly who need transportation to nearby health centers or hospitals. In 2011, local community leaders, together with other sponsors, donated a van to the community for elderly transportation. However, providing this shuttle service did not solve community geriatric issues for long. Operating a senior care shuttle service entails the vehicle maintenances, driver, gasoline, and volunteer management. Making the service sustainable requires a long-term financial support plan.

Proposed by a small group of local farmers, the idea of non-chemical rice growing and selling has become real and possible through discussion and collective actions. It is designed to generate extra revenue to support the local senior care shuttle service and improve the environment by promoting the use of non-chemical pesticides. Although expectations for higher demand of organic or non-chemical food are promising, the uncertainty of crop yields due to the change in methods of growing rice and market price fluctuations made local farmers hesitate to join the non-chemical rice contract.

Shih-An has nearly 480 acres of paddy fields. However, only about 9 acres were contracted for non-chemical rice planting in the first year. To ease local farmers' concerns and anxiety, the Shih-An community started a production-wholesale club and managed to cover the production differences in crop yields. After agreeing to guarantee an extra 30% of the market price, the local farmers began using environmental-friendly pest control measures and biological fertilizers. By the second year, the Shih-An Production-Wholesale Club had a surplus and more local farmers joined the non-chemical rice contract. In the third year, the club registered as the Shi-An Co-op and was able to share profits with members as well as to support local welfare programs. The Co-op profits generated through non-chemical rice sales will be distributed proportionately to the management of the Shih-An Co-op (10%) and a local community welfare program (20%). Remaining profits are shared among members depending on the amounts they invest.

According to 2016 data, the Shih-An Co-op members can receive an average of 10% cash-back per year based on their equity contributions. Although the business may seem lucrative, it actually relies on immense volunteer efforts to make it happen. For instance, the people in charge of the Co-op management are mainly volunteers with some compensation by the end of the fiscal year. Qualified as social entrepreneur dedicated to local welfare, the Shih-An Co-op has tax exempt status from the government.

A majority of Shih-An community residents are engaged more or less in local community service in some form and contribute to the Co-op. Healthy elderly residents arrive in the morning to do mild cleaning work, while some residents spend some of their leisure time to help rice packing in the community center. The community solidarity cultivated through the collaboration initiated by the Shih-An Co-op provides a solid foundation for the operation of community-based economic practice.

An incident that happened in the neighborhood consolidated the trustful relationship between the community and Shih-An Co-op. In March 2016, a mentally-ill resident in the neighborhood began attacking people randomly. It was a chronic problem for a while until it became a safety issue in the community. Seeking a long-term solution, a special care facility took the case and placed the person in a life-long care system with subsidies from the government if the family could cover the rest of the expense, but the family still could not afford the remaining cost.

In response to the community's request, the Shih-An Co-op stepped in to negotiate with the facility with a workable solution. The Shih-An Co-op pays 50% of the remaining expense; another 25% is donated from the charity, while 25% is covered by the facility. The process of this problem solving advanced the reciprocity and bonding among the Shih-An Co-op, victim residents, and the community. It also emphasized the value of the Shih-An Co-op in the local social infrastructure. With the continued financial support from the Shih-An Co-op, the community plans to expand the welfare program by providing meal plans for elderly, scholarships and after-school tutoring for local kids, neighborhood safety environment maintenance, and other charity activities.

To advance the rice production, the Shih-An Co-op also planned to establish a local mill plant to make by-products from the rice-grinding process and generate more revenues. In a small plantation like Shih-An, the crop yield is not sufficient to support a local mill plant. After harvesting, Shin-An farmers had to send their grains to the nearby mill plant for rice processing. Consequently, the rice husk and bran layers from the first step of the grain-grinding process are not available for additional products. In addition to the loss of these side-products, Shin-An farmers had to harvest their crops earlier to have their grain-grinding orders accepted, which leads to less crops yield. In the harvest season, rice-producing mill plant would normally prioritize larger orders over smaller ones. Consequently, small farmers like Shih-An local farmers are easily marginalized and become less competitive in the capitalist market. In 2017, the Shih-An Co-op had its proposal approved and successfully received a government grant to start the mill plant construction.

As the reputation of the Shih-An community attracted more young people to join the community, the Shih-An Co-op manages to retain the young generation by creating job opportunities. In one collaborative project, the Co-op plans to provide the machine and materials to the young entrepreneurs to start a business. The Co-op will receive a certain percentage of the revenue, with the rest going to the producers or business operators. This model could be a good start for future collaboration since it lowers the threshold for young people to start businesses. In addition to entrepreneurship incubation, the Shih-An Co-op also induced several vacant space renovation projects through facilitating collaboration between property owners and college students.

The Tainan Corner Building program was launched in 2011 and is funded by the City of Tainan. The program encourages college students with architecture or related college majors to work with communities to renovate deteriorated spaces to improve environmental issues in rural areas. Through the Co-op's facilitation, students arrived with innovative ideas and renovated the abandoned spaces agreeing to have free space under a ten-year contract with the property owners. The Co-op also tries to advance the collaboration by introducing business opportunities to the students and incubating young entrepreneurs in the community. Through social media and news reports, the Shih-An community Co-op has garnered much public attention and earned a reputation for social innovation and community collaboration (Hsu, 2017).

Challenges and Discussion

The Buloubulou eco-tourism innovation and Shih-An community Co-op initiative have generated promising local economic development strategies through CBE practices. The successful start-up and development of successful cases may inspire the creation of CBEs in different regions and help to foster individual entrepreneurs.

Nevertheless, challenges of maintaining the collaboration momentum within communities and coping with service/product market share due to external competition and globalization have tested the community's resilience and adaptability in a variety of capacities, such as management practices, leadership development, learning technical skills, acquiring legal profession, and advancing financing ability. Although serving on the consulting committee of Taichung Coordinating Center for Community Enterprise Development, Huang[1] pointed out that the survival or success of CBEs, in the long run, relies on whether a community is capable of creating a supportive entrepreneurial ecosystem to retain the internal collaboration momentum and facilitate external network bridging.

The very features of flexibility and social bonding within a community may become paradoxical management problems when expediency outweighs legal protocol or local bonding becomes a driving force to exclusiveness. Based on Huang's observation, the political climate, governmental grant and funding, organizational proliferation, and leadership team changes also play imperative roles in the developmental stage of CBE establishment. In Taiwan, the political realignment provides alternative funding opportunities for community development projects when politicians aim to secure their political capitals through a grassroots approach.

A variety of community development funding and grants have given newly formed community-based organizations resources to incubate their entrepreneurship and launch a start-up business. Nevertheless, communities should examine their assets and core values to define their CBEs rather than changing their development trajectory based on government policy, grant opportunities, or a particular political agenda. Successful CBE cases often create a trend and generate popularity through social media dissemination or public promotion, which may lead to a swirl of local organizations or communities jumping on the bandwagon under the influence of government policy or marketing.

Management challenges generated through organizational proliferation also affect CBEs development. A successful start-up may build the confidence of communities in expanding their business. As the scope and scale of community business develops, the management hierarchy embedded in the growing administration and power structure involved in executive work may expand the divergence between the member's expectation and organization decision-making. Leadership team changes could introduce new momentum and bring in innovative ideas to the organization. However, retaining the consistency and transmissibility of CBE's core values may become organization's concerns and challenges when a new leadership team shifts the management focus from its core social values to business expansion or profit-making.

For the CBEs that are conceived through the regeneration of local cultural, natural, or ethnic endowments, maintaining the innovation momentum without compromising the authenticity and originality of local heritages has become major concerns in some organizations. Meanwhile, the land-based resources may also limit the ability of communities to diversify their economic activities (Peredo & Chrisman, 2006). In most disadvantaged communities or rural villages, the amount of resources available for entrepreneurship development is typically low in both environmental facilities and social infrastructure. Therefore, helping intentional communities acquire sufficient resources and needed skillsets to launch an enterprise becomes critical for developing CBEs.

Modified Community-Based Enterprise Model

Apart from these site-specific CBEs, one particular CBE model is interesting because it breaks geographical boundaries in its e-commerce platform and provides a variety of collaboration opportunities among communities. The conventional CBE model draws on a relatively linear economic activity that is based on the relationship of providers/suppliers and consumers. According to Huang's observation, the land-basis CBEs (mostly located in rural areas) that use environmental resources to provide products or services often encounter the challenges of effective marketing or lack of access to sales channels.

In the case of Shih-An Co-operative, farmers acquiring knowledge and skills of non-chemical farming, rice processing, and product packaging extended their capacity from rice farming to manufacturing. The sale part relies on another consumer co-operative to manage the marketing and product distribution efforts. Rarely is a single CBE capable of integrating product producing, manufacturing, marketing, distributing, and selling in one entity. Smaller communities with fewer human resources and insufficient social infrastructure are often limited in their entrepreneurial capacity.

On the other hand, cities and metropolitan areas possess abundant human resources and networks that can provide complementary services in marketing, distribution, and sales. Therefore, creating a vehicle to facilitate entrepreneurial collaboration among communities who share the same values may reduce the threshold for business start-ups and help newly formed CBEs find their niches in the market. Negotiating collaboration among communities with different specialties creates a supportive ecosystem that fosters multiple entrepreneurships with diverse partnerships. A reciprocal network generated through this platform not only provides resources to incubate entrepreneurship development, but it also is a catalyst for potential community development partnership. Under this approach, community-based entrepreneurship becomes an alternative development strategy to advance community capacity and may provide solutions for a variety of community issues.

A typical CBE model draws on linear economic activities and involves a one-way network relationship (Figure 8.1). A CBE playing roles either as producer/manufacturer or service provider in this linear economic system will rely heavily on the consumer's preferences or market needs to sell their products. Products manufactured by, for instance, an environment-friendly focused CBE may be branded by a reseller and could become not so environment-friendly by over packaging.

The social value embedded in the CBE dwindles when the products or services are channeled into a capitalist market or is compromised when the enterprise encounters competition and has to adjust their production approach. Although making a profit may not be CBE's priority as discussed earlier, a profitable CBE can help local organizations continue their community development work or support their local social welfare program.

Therefore, creating an entrepreneurial support ecosystem to establish an alternative social-value base economic network may provide solutions for the struggles that CBEs encounter in the capitalist economic system. The modified CBE model (Figure 8.2) illustrates a supportive economic network that revolves around shared social values among participating communities. Within

FIGURE 8.1 Conventional CBEs: linear economic activities.

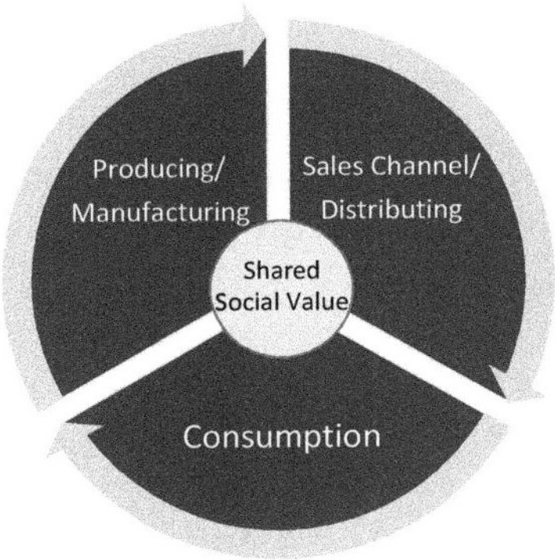

FIGURE 8.2 Modified CBEs: supportive economic activities.
Source: Compiled by the author.

this system, each segment either in the form of CBEs, COBs, CSEs, social enterprises, local economic entities, consumer co-operatives, or responsible consumer society, interactively creates a reciprocal and collaborative network to practice a variety of social-value base economic activities. Instead of seeking economic growth through increasing competition and economic efficiency, the modified CBEs model looks for an innovative collaboration mechanism to generate an alternative social-value base economic system. The ultimate goal of the modified CBE model not only solely seeks economic growth but also aims to amplify the essence and core value of a CBE, which integrates a wider spectrum of social factors, community issues, and local concerns into the equation of economy development.

Practice of the Modified CBE Model

To generate a social-value base economic ecosystem that includes partnerships or collaborations among a variety of CBEs, COBs, CSEs, local economic entities, social entrepreneurs, community co-op, and consumers, it is crucial to identify key ingredients or catalysts to facilitate a mechanism to launch the initiative. Since the modified CBE ecosystem concept is still evolving, a modified CBE framework through the fair trade e-commerce platform proposed by a local team provides a proper analytical departure point to conceptualize this modified CBE model.

Based on practical experience and field observation, community entrepreneur Ya-Sheng Huang noticed that smaller CEBs, especially the agriculture-based CEBs, rarely have the capacity to implement effective sales strategies or can afford extra expenditures for professional marketing services. The alternative e-commerce sale approach provides opportunities for the CBEs. However, not every CBE can afford a professional e-commerce platform but may join existing digital sale platforms, which results in price competition or unclear CBE branding.

The struggles and challenges that most small business entities encounter also resonate with some CEBs, COBs, or CSEs. The idea of fair trade e-commerce emerges when Huang experienced local struggles as he served as a CBE consultant. The framework of this community-based fair trade e-commerce aims to integrate a variety of suppliers in the forms of CBEs, COBs, local economic entities, CSEs, social entrepreneurs, and community co-op to create a robust and diverse supply chain.

In addition to providing consumers with quality products from diverse community suppliers, the fair trade platform also invites investors, donators, nonprofits, and charities that share core values of community development and social responsibility to join the system. Revenue generated from the e-commerce platform will be redistributed proportionally to the consumers as incentive measures or be channeled to nonprofits and charities to promote related community development programs. Investors or donators who seeks corporate social responsibility (CSR) or a social purpose will receive incentive rewards in the forms of various community projects or consultant services. Projects implemented by nonprofits or services provided by charities may be integrated with investors' or donors' activities and events to disseminate the CBE brand, advance the core value of CBE, and promote the community development agenda. Figure 8.3 illustrates a succinct fair trade e-commerce operation plan.

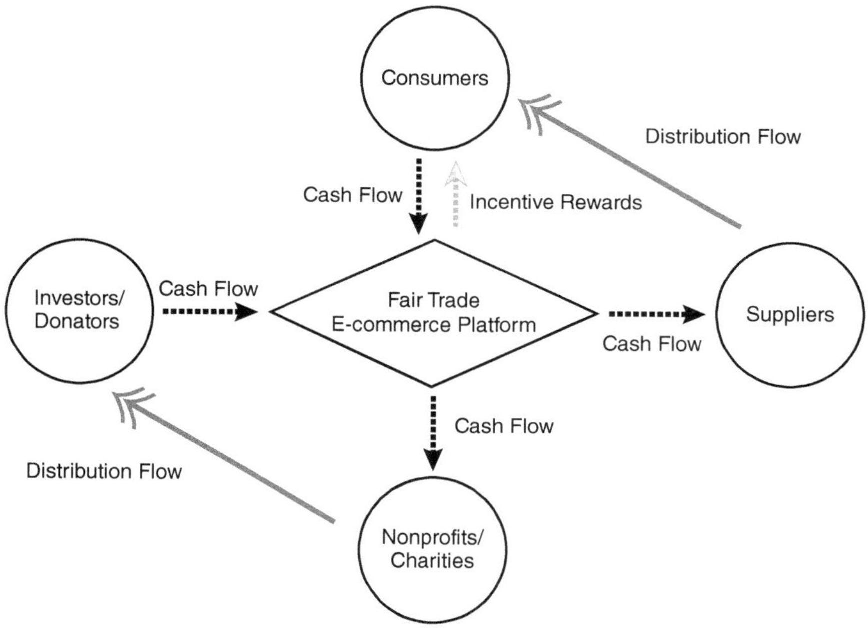

FIGURE 8.3 Fair trade e-commerce operation.

Source: Diagram revised from the original framework provided by fair trade e-commerce advocate Ya-Sheng Huang.

TABLE 8.1 Fair trade e-commerce stakeholder description

	Consumers	*Suppliers*	*Investors/Donators*	*Nonprofits/Charities*
Types of stakeholders	Individuals, groups, organizations, or party that has an interest in supporting social-value-based economic practices.	A variety of CBEs, COBs, CSEs, social entrepreneurs, local economic entities, community organizations, community co-operatives.	Individuals, entrepreneurs, or business entities that seeks for CSR, social purpose, or marketing.	Community-based entities, local community organizations, community development practitioners, or designated nonprofits charity, or individuals.
Way of participation	Purchasing goods, products, services through the Fair Trade Ecommerce Platform.	Joining the Fair Trade E-commerce Platform upon agreement of transaction fee generating through trading and deal-making.	Through investment in the Fair Trade Ecommerce Platform or purchasing the virtual currency.	Participating activities or event hosted by the Fair Trade E-commerce; providing designated services upon request by the donators or investors.
Incentive measures	Through cash rewards or special service to assist local community development work.	Special marketing and branding services based on product features and community story.	Providing marketing services and mediating collaboration upon request to expand the business opportunities.	Branding and dissemination of the nonprofits organizations and charity. Providing exposure and fundraising opportunities for the organizations/ charity.

Source: Table contents retrieved from original framework provided by fair trade e-commerce advocate Ya-Sheng Huang.

Social Purposes of Community-Based Enterprise

The Taiwan CBE case study illustrates the context that triggered local responses to take action, discerned the factors that contributed to its success, and analyzed its impact on the society. In the Shih-An community, the disadvantaged elderly and low-income situation motivated local community leaders to take action and initiate the Co-op. Seeking a sustainable and self-sustaining social welfare program provided a method to operate the Co-op actively. In the Bulaubulau village, diminishing tribal heritage and youth education challenges prompted local young leaders to respond to the crisis. Targeting tribal culture preservation and education, the Bulaubulau tribe initiated the co-operative education program to retain tribal youth and provide them with job opportunities after completing the courses.

Through the community-based eco-tourism operation, traditional tribal hunting and weaving skills are redefined as practical professional rather than cultural performance. Indeed, economic activities and local businesses play pivotal roles in community self-help development; however, it is the social value embedded in the economic practices that starts the engine and steers the direction. These social-value-based economic practices serve as vehicles to promote social inclusion and advance the foundation for a diverse economic system.

Sharing the same values with CBEs, the Bulaubulau tribe and Shih-An community both create a reciprocal and supportive network and further develop a self-determined economic system. Without confining themselves as isolated economic entities, the Bulaubulau tribe and Shih-An community established a self-sustaining community by leveraging what they have and advancing their resources to build a self-managed and communal economic system. Relatively small in scale and with limited market share in the economic pool, these two cases, nevertheless, have significant niches in the CBEs. They provide alternative economic perspectives regarding how these grassroots economic practices foster community solidarity, improve local quality of life, and leverage volunteering toward effective co-operation.

In Shih-An village, farmers and residents collaborated to advance their agricultural resources to grow non-chemical rice through the community-based co-operative (asset perspective). The local social welfare program supported by the Shih-An Co-op creates a reciprocal relationship and volunteering network in the community (reciprocity). The informal volunteer work provided by the retired, elderly, and unemployed found its niche in the community and contribute their services to enhance Co-op operation and local social welfare (social purpose). It incubates the community solidarity and facilitates the collaboration momentum (social capital) to advance the community Co-op practice (i.e., expanding from the rice growing to by-product manufacturing).

Furthermore, it also provides opportunities for individual self-efficacy development. Participation in the Shih-An Co-op or local social welfare program boosts individual self-esteem and confidence. Participants feel a sense of purpose and are motivated to engage in more community works (self-development). In addition to the internal community capacity building, the Shih-An Co-op develops a strong horizontal network by connecting to consumer organizations to consolidate its economic niche (creative bridging activity). To build a robust social-value-based economy, it also relies on consumer population who are willing to consider the social value within products rather than just low prices.

For Shih-An Co-op, 70% of their products sell to a consumer co-operative, a well-known Taiwanese nonprofit – Homemakers Union Consumers Co-operative (HUCC) that focuses on food safety and supports environment-friendly agricultural products. Initiated in 1993, the foundation of HUCC advocates non-chemical and organic food safety and creates a mutual-benefit relationship with producers and consumers to support the livelihoods of local farmers, producers, organizations, and companies that share the same values. Built on the diverse networks of producers, educators, consumers, activists, and COBs, the HUCC has created an enormous social impact in terms of consumers' rights, food safety education, and social entrepreneurship (Huang et al., 2015).

Ripple effects include not only advancing collaboration networks for local business and the community economy but also encouraging civic engagement in economic empowerment and social justice. This social embeddedness in the economic practices emphasizes the social consciousness in the exchange value, social responsibility in the production part, and social consensus in the consumption side. It requires individual behavior changes to support responsible businesses, social infrastructure to incubate social entrepreneurship, government intervention to enhance economic equality, and social movement to mobilize civic engagement. Every social actor in each section interweaves a meaningful and purposeful community and contributes to this social-value-based economy. It helps to alleviate social exclusion and creates a more sustainable society. Through the mechanism of social-value-based economic practices, communities develop the resilience and capacity to counteract a variety of social challenges and global crises. Either through agriculture-based co-operative or tribal eco-tourism, economic practices serve as a way or provide tools to facilitate the community engagement and advance community capacity.

Social-Value-Based Economic Practices

Studies of CBEs have shown that the emergence of CBEs was often triggered by social and economic stress (Peredo &Chrisman, 2006). This resonates with the causes of solidarity economy in Latin America (Miller, 2006) and advocacy of alternative economic practices in Europe (Castells et al., 2017). Emerged in Latin America in the mid-1980s and blossomed in the late 1990s, the practice of solidarity economy was a response to economic exclusion, dissatisfaction with the culture of dominant market economy, and counteraction of the neoliberal and neocolonial globalization. The social and economic stress forced local communities seeking a more creative, autonomous, and grassroots approach to improve their livelihoods. Initiatives such as worker co-operatives, neighborhood and community associations, collective kitchens, and mutual-aid organizations of unemployed or landless workers blossomed at this time (Miller, 2006).

In 1998, at the conference of the First Latin Encuentro of Solidarity Culture and Socio-economy in Porto Alegre, Brazil, participants from Brazil, Mexico, Argentina, Peru, Nicaragua, Bolivia, Colombia, and Spain created the Latin American Solidarity Economy Network to strengthen the mutual support and global partnership. Since then, the solidarity economy approach has become a global movement. The first World Social Forum (WSF) in 2001 in Brazil marked a significant year for the creation of the Global Network of the Solidarity Socio-economy. By 2004, up to 47 national and regional solidarity economy networks or entities had joined this global network alliance.

In the following two years, solidarity economy topics became the major event theme in the WSF. Seeking a self-determined, dynamic, and grassroots-approach economic practices, Miller (2006) emphasized that solidarity economy is not a sector of the economy. Rather, it is counterhegemonic project that aims to initiate a movement "linking together multiple actors across a diverse economic landscape to create synergies and collective power." It is "a view of the economy as a complex space of social relationship in which individuals, communities, and organizations generate livelihoods through many different means and with many different motivations and aspirations" (Miller, 2006).

In Spain, significant new economic practices were emerging at an individual level and have made a substantial impact on the society in response to the financial crisis in the European Union and United States from 2008 to 2011 (Castells et al., 2017). During the economic crisis, Barcelona reached unemployment of 20%, with youth unemployment at 45% (Castells et al., 2017). The austerity policies imposed by the government amplified the situation and created a series of social issues.

Suffering the consequences of financial crisis in their everyday lives, a growing number of Barcelona residents engaged in alternative economic practices to maintain their livelihoods. Up to 26 alternative economic practices in Barcelona were identified in a research project conducted in 2010–2011 (Castells & Hlebik, 2017). In the Barcelona case, residents managed to sustain their livelihood through service exchanges such as car and motorcycle repairing, housing repairing, children and elderly caring as well as clothing, home appliance, and exchanging other goods.

Other than self-sufficiency activities, these solidarity-based economic practices rely on a variety of exchange networks. An analysis of structures of the most active organizations and networks involved in these alternative economic practices in Catalonia identified networks including, but not limited to, Agroecological production networks, consumer co-operatives, social currency networks, shared parenting co-operatives, seed bank networks, ethical banks, and free universities (Castells & Hlebik, 2017).

The economic practices identified in Barcelona demonstrate a new economic culture that provides alternative economic practices for sustaining local livelihood during the economic crisis. It characterizes a solidarity economy based on non-capitalist activities that are built among individual networks and local connections. In an economic crisis like the 2008 financial collapse, the vulnerability of mainstream economic practice in the capitalist market highlights the necessity of a more resilient economic system and leads to the recognition of alternative economic practices. It highlights what a resilient economic system might entail and the apparatus that could be used in the current system to cultivate it.

Conclusion

In addition to creating sustainable local economic development, the CBE model also has the potential of building community capacity through engaging in entrepreneur-focused economic development. Critic of the problem of local entrepreneurship development has argued that the current approach has focused on the agency (individual entrepreneur) with less attention paid to the context (place) (Lichtenstein & Lyons, 2001). The success of entrepreneurship development relies on more system approaches than fragmented ones.

Therefore, it is important to provide an integrative strategy that connects community development practice with entrepreneur development practices to foster entrepreneurship across the community (Markley et al., 2015). Taking the entire community into account and adopting a suitable community development practice can establish a community-based entrepreneurial development system that constitutes an ecosystem for incubating entrepreneurship by leveraging entrepreneurship as a development strategy.

By taking similar approaches in valuing both community development and entrepreneurship incubation, the CBE model emphasizes the importance of community capacity building and sees community development practice as a prerequisite to establishing a successful CBE. Social infrastructures may provide pertinent sources for fostering robust collaboration or serve as an aid to facilitate the connection needed to create such an ecosystem that integrates community development and entrepreneurship incubation. Supportive public policy, public agency project specific grants, tax incentive measures, flexible administration process, and transparency of local decision-making all contribute to the successful integration of community development and CBE formation.

In the Shih-An Co-op case, a government-funded project caused Shih-An community to establish the community-owned mill plant. In order to sell rice to customers legally, the Agricultural & Food Agency officials helped the Shih-An Co-op acquire a rice-selling certificate. Meanwhile, the Internal Revenue Service officials helped the Shih-An Co-op obtain a tax exemption. In the Bulaubulau case, social innovation and flexible curriculum supported by the local Education Bureau made tribal co-operative education possible. To assist tribal teenagers in acquiring high-school equivalency diploma, the Nan-Oau Senior High School administration adjusted course schedules and class requirements to allow teachers and instructors to teach once a week with an intensive curriculum in tribal villages. Every year, the students' final evaluation conducted in the Bulaubulau village is a tribal signature event. The popularity of tribal eco-tourism allows Bulaubulau tribe to generate sufficient revenue to provide financial support to the students and village infrastructure improvements.

To construct a social-value-based production, exchange, and consumption system requires a supportive social infrastructure to facilitate the network and shared ideology to motivate social actors changing their behaviors. The cases of Shih-An Co-op and Bulaubulau eco-tourism demonstrate how community-based economic practices with social intention and shared value generated a self-help and sustainable social entity on a local scale. At the micro-level, each individual plays a meaningful part and contributes to the community in this self-help system. Collaboration among different sectors, leveraging a variety of resources, and social network bridging at a meso-level help communities advance capacity building and facilitate the community momentum to confront the challenges and counteract difficulties. Furthermore, the public policies, government intervention, democracy progress, civic culture, and grassroots public administrations all contribute to creating a dynamic supportive social infrastructure to incubate such social-value-based economic practices for social inclusion and equality.

In response to the limitation of the conventional CBE model due to its land-based feature, the modified CBE model amplifies the horizontal network bridging in order to counteract the globalization challenge and capitalist market competition. It is built on community-owned cultural, social, and environmental endowments (asset perspective), the solidarity embedded in its trust network and reciprocal relationship (social capital), and adaptive learning ability grounded in collective experience in response to the crisis and challenge (resilience). It is driven by a belief in a social-value-based economic system (social purpose), emphasizes the self-determined process and active participation (empowerment and ownership), and aims to break through the land-based limit to create an innovative network (creative bridging activity).

Likewise, the key elements of CBEs conform to the main ingredients of community capacity building in the field of community development practices. According to Bhattacharyya (1995, 2004), solidarity and agency seeking are fundamental constructs in conceptualizing community development. The essence of community development is the capacity to build agency. Expanding the notion of human development and appropriating the concept of agency from Giddens (1984), Bhattacharyya (1995) construes agency as "the capacity to create, reproduce, change and live according to their own meaning systems, the powers to effectively define themselves as opposed to being defined by others" (p. 61). This agency seeking relied on the community capacity of emancipating from the suppressed, being able to act otherwise from the mainstream, and cultivating self-determined mechanism to counteract the patriarchal social structure and institutional mentality in the field of capitalist politics and economy.

It also relates to the advocacy of feminist perspective's *diverse economy*, a notion aiming to widen the conceptualization of economy that can "include all of those practices excluded or marginalized by the theory and presumption of capitalist hegemony" (Gibson-Graham, 2006, p. xii). Echoing this alternative economic practice, the CBE provides the vehicle to fulfill the mission of social-value-based economic practices. By amplifying the community-oriented and heterogeneous collectivity cultivated through the grassroots approach, the CBE is a development strategy toward community capacity building that aims at making diverse economic practices available and transmissible to establish a resilient economy.

Note

1 Co-founder of Taiwan Pure Culture and Education Development Association, Ya-Sheng Huang devotes himself to the entrepreneurship incubation through community development approaches and serves as community enterprise consultant in a variety of organizations and government sector.

References

Banet-Weiser, S., & Castells, M. (2016). Economy is culture. In M. Castells (Ed.), *Another economy is possible* (pp. 4–33). Cambridge: Polity Press.

Begum, A. (2007). *Village women and Grameen Bank in Bangladesh*. New Delhi: Gyan Publishing House.

Bhattacharyya, J. (1995). Solidarity and agency: Rethinking community development. *Human Organization*, *54*(1), 60–69.

Bhattacharyya, J. (2004). Theorizing community development. *Journal of the Community Development Society*, *34*(2), 5–34.

Cahn, E., & Rowe, J. (1992). *Time dollars: The new currency that enables americans to turn their hidden resource-time-into personal security & community renewal*. Emmaus, PA: Rodale Press.

Castells, M. et al., (2017). *Another economy is possible*. Cambridge: Polity Press.

Castells, M., & Hlebik, S. (2017). Alternative economic practices in Barcelona: Surviving the crisis, reinventing life. In M. Castells (Ed.), *Another economy is possible* (pp. 160–186). Cambridge: Polity Press.

Chen, S. Y. (2019). The comparison on economic development model among three communities of Liugu, Dongying, and Shih-An: Perspective of collaborative governance (Master Thesis). National Chung Hsing University, Taichung, Taiwan.

Gibson-Graham, J. (2006). *The end of capitalism (as we knew it): A feminist critique of political economy*. Minneapolis: University of Minnesota Press.

Giddens, A. (1984). *The constitution of society*. Berkeley: University of California Press.

Hsu, C. (2017, January 2). 小農體驗故事行銷-學子行銷仕安米 [Participatory agriculture tourism- College students promote Shih-An rice]. *Central News Agency*. Retrieved from https://www.chinatimes.com/realtimenews/20170102002406-260405?chdtv

Huang, S., Pan, G., & Huang, J. (2015). Exploring a social enterprise business model – A case study of the Taiwanese homemaker's union consumers cooperatives. [社會企業的經營模式探討ー以臺灣主婦聯盟生活消費合作社為例]. *Management information Computing*, *4*(2), 221–234. doi: 10.6285/MIC.4(2).17

Lichtenstein, G. A., & Lyons, T. S. (2001). The entrepreneurial development system: Transforming business talent and community economies. *Economic Development Quarterly*, *15*, 3–20.

Ma, Y., Tong, Y., Wang, H., Kuang, K., Wei, C., Wang, S., … & Zhao, J. (2015). The echo of mountain and cloud-Bulaubulau tribe. [Study Report]. Taipei, Taiwan: Kang Chiao International School. Retrieved from http://librarywork.taiwanschoolnet.org/cyberfair2016/KangchiaoJunior/a1.htm

Markley, D. M., Lyons, T. S., & Macke, D. W. (2015). Creating entrepreneurial communities: Building community capacity for ecosystem development. *Community Development*, *46*(5), 580–598.

Miller, E. (2006). Other economies are possible! *Dollars & Sense*, (266), 11–15. Retrieved from http://search.proquest.com/docview/220964512/

Perodo, A. M., & Chrisman, J. J. (2006). Toward a theory of community-based enterprise. *Academy of Management Review, 31*(2), 309–328.

Seyfang, G. (2002). Time on our side: Time banks and active citizenship. *New Economy, 9*(4), 242–247. doi: 10.1111/1468-0041.00278

Seyfang, G. (2004). Working outside the box: Community currencies, time banks and social inclusion. *Journal of Social Policy, 33*(1), 49–71.

Tribal Youth Overseas Training. (2015, January 1). Retrieved from http://www.thealliance.org.tw/cover_show.php?cover_id=64

Walzer, N., & Sandoval, J. (2016). *Emergence and growth of community supported enterprises.* (Research Report). East Lansing, MI: North Central Regional Center for Rural Development.

Yang, C. (2016, July). 不老部落的原根自學團.向部落長老學習生活智慧 [The root vocational study in Bulaubulau tribe – Learning wisdom from tribal chiefs.]. *Parenting,* 80. Retrieved from https://www.parenting.com.tw/magazine/1349%E7%8E%A9%E4%B8%AD%E5%AD%B8%E7%9A%84%E5%A5%BD%E7%8E%A9%E5%85%B7100%E9%81%B8/

9

COMMUNITY-LED CROWDFUNDING FOSTERS RURAL PROSPERITY AND RESILIENCY

Jessica Brauer

Introduction

Community-supported fundraising for small businesses and organizations through crowdfunding has served as an innovative resource for building and growing rural economies by pairing online payment platforms with social networks since the early 2000s. Results from The Local Crowd's (TLC) 4SE platform, a tool developed to provide access to capital and markets for mission-driven entities, show impact catalyzed by mentorship, education, and focused local leadership. The TLC platform, piloted in rural communities across the United States, demonstrates an economy bolstering model that supports entrepreneurial success.

This chapter examines the impact of crowdfunding on growth opportunities through financing and the cultivation of social capital. New Hampshire's Monadnock and Upper Valley regions along with many other funded campaigns that met and exceeded goals from $1,000 to $15,000 are examined through data gathered via surveys and interviews with community leadership and campaign hosts.

Looking Local in Economic Crisis

In 2015, the Vermont Yankee Nuclear Powerplant, a 605-megawatt reactor and anchor employer for the town of Vernon, Vermont, and surrounding communities closed after 43 years of operation. The abolition of this nuclear facility was met with celebration among many locals; however, environmental impact aside, the negative influence on the economy was profound and widespread. In 2014, the facility employed an estimated 550 people and contributed nearly $500 million to the regional economy (Bidgood, 2015). In reaction to the shutdown, the town of approximately 2,200 was quickly forced to reduce municipal budgets by 20%, which affected the local library, recreation center programming, and eliminated the police and maintenance departments altogether (Gellerman, 2019).

Across the Connecticut River, 40 rural towns comprising New Hampshire's Monadnock Region also saw the impact of the economic downturn. The closure led to an estimated loss of 176 high paying regional jobs and reduced economic activity totaling $30 million (Risley, 2017). In the subsequent years, these towns have looked for alternatives to bolster the vitality of their communities.

Regional economic development organizations reached for non-traditional tools after participating in training from community economist and author Michael Shuman. Shuman's work details the environmental parallels between pollinating species such as bees, bats, and butterflies and the businesses, organizations, and individuals in local economies. "[These species] instinctively know that the intermixing of these pollens nourishes the entire ecosystem. Pollinator businesses similarly carry the best elements of one business to another, thereby fertilizing all local businesses and creating a healthy entrepreneurial ecosystem" (Shuman, 2015, p. 16).

Faced with the economic turmoil from the plant's shutdown, the "pollinators" of Monadnock recognized the need for a strategic venture to build capital collectively. Partners from New Hampshire Small Business Development Center, Greater Keene and Peterborough Chambers of Commerce, Monadnock Economic Development Corporation, an independent business alliance, and volunteer business advisors turned to crowdfunding, an innovative model for fundraising with growing popularity since the 2008 financial crisis. TLC crowdfunding platform provided the solution they were seeking.

Located in Laramie, Wyoming, TLC is a rewards-based crowdfunding platform that specializes in funding for local small businesses, especially in rural areas. It is also a resource for building social capital within communities. TLC accomplishes these objectives by utilizing a coordinated suite of services, including assessment, education, coaching, and networking – along with an online crowdfunding platform. The combination of education and crowdfunding creates an experiential learning environment that increases retention of learned concepts and results in positive action and crowdfunding success by users of the platform.

TLC takes crowdfunding to the local level and energizes each rural community around its own crowdfunding platform. The platform was developed with local needs in mind and includes locally focused features unavailable elsewhere. Community and economic development groups subscribe to the platform to provide a capital raising tool for businesses and organizations. Platform subscribers can brand the platform for their community and personalize it to meet their local needs (Wolverton & Vincent, 2020).

In 2017, Monadnock's economic development partners piloted the TLC platform and launched The Local Crowd Monadnock, which had raised $139,647 from 1,138 supporters for 20 crowdfunding campaigns as of May 2020. Speaking to Monadnock's efforts to bolster the post-shutdown economy, The Local Crowd Monadnock webpage states:

> We wanted to demonstrate that instead of recruiting businesses from outside the region to make up for [the loss]; we could empower community members to support values-aligned businesses based here. We gave preference to campaigns aligned with our regional master plan and contributed to a healthy, just, safe, and environmentally sustainable community. We supported efforts to build more resilient communities, including campaigns that focused on sustainable agriculture, local art, renewable energy, and alternative transportation.
>
> *(Risley, 2017)*

In addition to the financial effects, a community's investment in local businesses through CSE efforts like crowdfunding creates a rich foundation for social capital relationships among people and their place that allow for economic prosperity as well as quality of life. For example, when residents contribute to their local grocery store's crowdfunding campaign, their action provides the business with funding while rewarding the contributor with a service or good. In addition, an interpersonal connection between the grocery store owner and the contributor has been fostered based on a shared sense of identity and values.

Strengthened relationships create a foundation for further financial contributions, the potential for the reciprocation of support, and they build community resiliency. Communication, engagement, contribution to the common good, and collaboration are essential to successful, sustainable communities. These attributes lead to more effective decision-making, development of beneficial relationships, cooperation, enhanced creativity, and advanced trust among leaders and communities (Ricketts & Place, 2009). A community's ability to respond and withstand and recover from economic adversity is invaluable, especially in the face of unforeseen downturns such as 2020's COVID-19 pandemic.

According to the World Health Organization's "WHO Timeline – COVID-19," on March 11, 2020, the rapid spread of COVID-19 was classified as a pandemic, resulting in an international response of social distancing and stay at home orders. This resulted in an economic crisis that has hit small businesses especially hard. Data from credit card processors suggest that roughly 30% of small businesses shut down during the pandemic (*CardFlight Small Business Impact Report: April 15, 2020*, 2020). Lowrey in *The Atlantic* reported that millions of US small businesses are struggling and failing. "The great small business die-off is here, and it will change the landscape of American commerce, auguring slower growth and less innovation in the future" (Lowrey, 2020).

Research from the Federal Reserve Bank of New York shows that during the Great Recession of 2007–2009, small businesses suffered disproportionate declines when compared with their larger counterparts (Şahin et al., 2011). During this time, there were fewer start-ups, small businesses laid off employees in dramatic numbers, and nearly 2 million small businesses closed. Small business lending came to a halt and never recovered their pre-crisis levels (Weltman, 2020). The Harvard Business School reported that small firms are always hit harder during financial crises because they depend more on bank capital to fund their growth (Mills, 2014).

To compound that problem, small businesses in rural America find bank capital especially hard to acquire. More than half of all banks in America closed during the past three decades. In rural areas, these figures are even greater. Of all the banks that have been closed, nearly 96% of them were community banks – the primary source of lending in rural communities (Covington & Courtney, 2014). Without banks, rural small businesses have few resources to turn to, and according to Khanna of the Institute for Corporate Governance and Finance at NYU's School of Law, the government has not yet figured out a good way to intervene. "We know how to support the financial system. There's a playbook to follow," he said. "What we don't know how to do, or had no idea how to do, is provide direct support to your local coffee shop at scale" (Lowrey, 2020).

These are some of the reasons that recessions hit rural communities harder and longer than urban areas. In general, cities recovered much better than rural areas following the Great Recession. Only 40% of urban counties had fewer jobs in 2017 than in 2007; however, in rural areas, two-thirds of the counties had fewer jobs in October 2017 than in 2007. A decade after the start of the Great Recession, rural counties remained well below their pre-recession employment levels (Henderson, 2017).

Economists have warned that the impact of the virus is projected to be the steepest decline since the 1930s Great Depression, with an estimated 43% of American households hit by coronavirus-related job loss or pay cuts (Sherman, 2020). The US government has responded with relief funding and expansion of unemployment eligibility, while states have begun to reopen. In New Hampshire's South West Planning Region, home to TLC Monadnock's served communities, unemployment rates peaked at 12.2%, with 7,290 unemployed in April 2020, a jump from March's 2.7% unemployment rate, with 1,490 unemployed (State of New Hampshire, 2020).

Because the pandemic crisis is as much social and cultural as economic, it requires recovery strategies that address the social aspects and encourage the growth of social capital in rural communities. Social capital is broadly defined as the relationships and resulting networks among people in society who work and live with the intent to function effectively. It is recognized as a critical component in community resilience because communities with higher levels of social capital recover faster and more completely from adversity (Kerr, 2018, p. 268).

Much like the Monadnock region's response to the Vermont Yankee's abrupt closure, their leaders responded to the COVID-19 crisis by once again looking to the community for support and created a crowdfunding initiative specifically designed to help local businesses affected by the pandemic.

The Power of the Crowd

Rural crowdfunding is a financial strategy in an evolving field of Community Supported Enterprises (CSEs). CSEs, similar to Community Supported Agriculture (CSA) initiatives that support the production and distribution of food and goods, support community-specific needs and allow for the connection between consumer and producer (Walzer & Sandoval, 2016; Walzer, 2019).

Online crowdfunding emerged as an alternative way to raise capital for individuals with business ideas and gained popularity in the 2008 financial crisis, a time where access to traditional funding from banks or angel investors was less accessible. Unlike traditional financing, crowdfunding campaign hosts can garner benefits extending beyond the capital. Successful campaigns serve as a tool to test markets, engage audiences, and build relationships between contributors and campaign hosts (Calic, 2018).

Online platforms such as Indiegogo and Kickstarter have cultivated international recognition with high-publicity successes for campaigns in travel, technology, comic and graphic novels, gaming, and film. From January 2014 until July 2020, Kickstarter has had more than 350,000 projects with an average of 129 backers on each, and Indiegogo has raised an average of $59,125 (The Crowd-Funding Center, 2020).

Industry-specific platforms offering tailored interfaces and support for their community of patrons have emerged to support niches in the arts, agriculture, and entertainment as well. For example, Patronicity, a place-based crowdfunding platform created to partner with local agencies to raise capital for community projects and public spaces has funded over $18 million in 867 campaigns from over 100,000 contributors (Patronicity: Growing Communities Together, 2020).

Although today's crowdfunding has gained popularity since the early 2000s, the process of sourcing support from the community has been a successful means of capital building with an extended history. In 1885, New York publisher Joseph Pulitzer used the widespread reach of his newspaper, *The New York World*, to crowdfund the construction of the Statue of Liberty's stone base and installation on Liberty Island. When the statue's funding was not supported by New York Governor Grover Cleveland, Pulitzer turned to the public for financial support. Contributions were made in exchange for miniature models of the statue and a printed name in the newspaper's list of contributors – an early example of contributors receiving "rewards" for their contributions.

Platforms for today's crowdfunders benefit from the technology of social media, video hosting, and the modern perks of digital marketing. However, Pulitzer's success can be attributed to practices that are still used today, including a streamlined solicitation platform, small contributions made by a larger volume of individuals, and recognition or rewards for contributing. His initiative raised more than $100,000, and the national monument was able to stay in New York City. The iconic statue was in negotiations to be erected in Baltimore, Boston,

San Francisco, and Philadelphia and landed in its famed locale as a direct result of the power of community (Calic, 2018).

In 2012, The Local Crowd's first version of the rural crowdfunding platform was launched with the support of a USDA Small Business Innovation Research (SBIR) grant, which set out to prove the feasibility of using TLC's localized crowdfunding platform as a rural economic development tool. The concept was tested in pilot communities in Georgia, Idaho, Illinois, Indiana, Iowa, Montana, New Hampshire, North Carolina, Texas, Wisconsin, and Wyoming. During the research period, TLC honed its rural-focused crowdfunding offerings to include custom technology such as third-party rewards (the capacity for local merchants and organizations to support crowdfunding projects by offering products and services as rewards), local matching, in-kind contributions (the ability for contributors to offer non-cash services and goods in lieu of cash), and offline fundraising (the capacity to add dollars raised in local fundraisers to the online tally of funds raised).

The USDA research proved acceptance of the model by community hosts, project creators, and contributors. It also helped TLC understand the socio-economic dynamics within rural communities and the characteristics of the communities that were most successful using the tool. The most successful were predisposed toward localism and economic practices that support community well-being and social capital development. Leaders in those communities recognized the systemic nature of community ecosystems and saw crowdfunding as part of an ecosystem rather than a stand-alone tool (Sontum & Vincent, 2020).

Collaboration among community partners was critical to TLC Monadnock's success, TLC Monadnock's Jen Risley explained in a personal interview. Initial campaigns were launched with support from local newspapers, service providers, such as a videographer providing free campaign video support as an incentive to participate and community members willing to support and co-host collaborative events to launch the new platforms for local businesses. As the community gained traction and campaigns met their goals, local crowdfunding became a tool for regional conversation about what locals wanted to see succeed. Individual campaigns acted as tools for raising capital and cultivating relationships for a community-supported economy driven by the community itself (Risley, personal communication, March 2020).

The Emerging Fourth Sector of the Economy

Understanding the characteristics that made the original communities succeed led TLC cofounders Diane Sontum and Kim Vincent to develop a new innovation called TLC 4SE – a crowdfunding/education platform that stimulates caring economy activities in communities. 4SE (pronounced force) stands for fourth-sector ecosystem because it was designed to stimulate the development of fourth-sector ecosystems at the community level. The fourth sector is defined as an emerging economic sector that brings together the functions of the three traditional sectors – public (government), private (business), and nonprofit. For-benefit businesses, social enterprises, and hybrid nonprofits make up the fourth sector – and they work for solutions to everything from poverty, homelessness, and economic justice to domestic violence and environmental issues. Unfortunately, growth of the fourth sector is hampered by lack of a functioning ecosystem. The three traditional sectors all have their own ecosystems, including legal structures, tax laws, governance forms, regulations, measurement protocols, and support personnel – ecosystem components that are unavailable or undeveloped in the fourth sector.

The fourth sector accounts for 10% of GDP as well as nearly twice the job growth rate as traditional for-profit businesses in the US and Europe. Numerous studies suggest that there is significant demand for fourth-sector approaches among consumers, investors, and other stakeholders. According to a Global Entrepreneurship Monitor report, millions of fourth-sector start-ups are being launched around the world, and they need community leadership that can respond to their specific needs.

Recognizing the potential for fourth-sector organizations to address and solve many of the world's problems, international development groups such as the World Economic Forum have created initiatives to support fourth-sector growth and advance ecosystem development. In 2018, the National Science Foundation issued a Request for Proposal (RFP) for projects designed to support fourth-sector ecosystem development through its SBIR program. The Local Crowd responded and was awarded a Phase I SBIR grant to research the feasibility of using the TLC 4SE platform to stimulate fourth-sector ecosystem development within communities.

The TLC 4SE innovation includes the TLC crowdfunding platform combined with fourth-sector education and practices. TLC's 4SE platform was built with integrations for peer-to-peer support and ongoing education on best practices aligned with industry trends, allowing entrepreneurs to build skills to access the social and financial capital they needed to support their mission.

Testing in multiple communities proved this fourth-sector ecosystem concept. Four pilot studies were conducted. Three of them were conducted in physical communities, and one was conducted in a virtual community composed of Social Enterprise Alliance members. Physical communities included Monadnock Region, NH; Upper Valley VT/NH; and the OmniWorks business incubator in Los Angeles, CA. Each community participated in the following core activities: (1) identifying and selecting crowdfunding candidates, (2) training crowdfunding candidates, (3) supporting the candidates as they prepared and launched their campaigns, and (4) following up with candidates at the conclusion of the program to assess their experience.

Colorado State University's Institute for Research In the Social Sciences (IRISS) provided evaluation services for the NSF SBIR research project. The IRISS post-program survey showed the impact of TLC's dedication to education. Among 36 respondents, more than 80% said that their knowledge of crowdfunding campaigns, including information on weathering a campaign's lull phase, sharing their story, recruiting within their community, and developing a marketing campaign had increased (Stephens, Ratajczyk, & Cross, 2020). More than two-thirds of these respondents said that their knowledge of the fourth sector had increased. One small business participant commented about how knowledge about the fourth sector helped her understand her own business and its place in the economic ecosystem:

> A lightbulb went off when they started talking about the fourth sector because I'd never heard of it in that way. What we do on this farm is completely different from other entities, so I never could put my finger on it…but it was really an eye-opener, that we are definitely a fourth sector business.
>
> *(Sontum & Vincent, 2020)*

IRISS concluded that TLC 4SE succeeded in helping businesses raise funds, while participants became more knowledgeable about the fourth sector. Eighty percent of the fundraising campaigns launched during the research period met their goals, bringing in approximately $88,000 to local businesses and nonprofits.

In addition, participant commitment to the fourth sector increased. Post-surveys showed that 83% of respondents were extremely likely to purchase goods or services from fourth-sector enterprises in the future, and more than 50% said that they would be willing to pay more for those goods or services than they would pay at a traditional enterprise. Nearly 70% said that they would be extremely likely to donate to a crowdfunding campaign for a fourth-sector enterprise, and 45% said that they would be extremely likely to invest in a fourth-sector enterprise. Approximately two-thirds said that they would be extremely likely to work for a fourth-sector enterprise in the future (Stephens et al., 2020). Together, these results demonstrate increased local support for the fourth sector and the potential for behavioral change following the intervention of TLC 4SE.

Monadnock's participation in the 4SE pilot study fit well with the community's strategic plan. At the beginning of the study, Monadnock's partners generated community interest and identified potential fundraisers by issuing a RFP. The RFP invited local entrepreneurs and organizations to apply to participate in the pilot project, which included training programs and coaching on the practices of successful crowdfunding. This process permitted partners to vet campaigns and select those most equipped to move through TLC's crowdfunding best practices and ultimately meet their fundraising goals.

TLC Monadnock received 18 proposals (via two rounds of proposals) and selected 13 to participate in the program. Among those participants, five launched campaigns during the pilot study, four of which met their fundraising goals. The total amount raised was $33,150, with 290 contributors.

As the program gained momentum, TLC Monadnock honed the RFP process to strategically call for proposals in alignment with the community's goals and master plan that had been developed with collaborative analysis and survey gathering from local entrepreneurs and leaders. Her project qualifications included: a fundraising limit, achievable goals with positive local effect, economic benefit to the campaign host and others, and commitment to working on fundraising efforts within a month of application.

The Village Roots Permaculture Farm in Alstead, NH, used The Local Crowd to collect $11,229 from 104 supporters and raise a barn. Use of affinity groups significantly contributed to the success of the campaign. Reaching out to the college alumni association and permaculture networks enhanced the spread of the campaign, inspiring people to support the campaign.

In 2019, the second community in New England joined the TLC pilot study – Vital Communities – a nonprofit organization serving 69 towns in the Upper Valley region of Vermont and New Hampshire. Since launching TLC 4SE in December of 2019, Upper Valley has hosted six campaigns, raising nearly $200,000 from more than 1,700 contributions. The most successful of those projects is a response to COVID-19 from *Valley News*, a local daily newspaper in West Lebanon, New Hampshire. The *Valley News* COVID-19 Support Fund project raised $155,839 from 1,536 backers. Contributions of $25, $50, and $100 were solicited in exchange for a tiered donor recognition in a newspaper advertisement, harkening Pulitzer's *New York World* contributor listing in exchange for the five- and one-dollar donations that kept the Statue of Liberty in New York City (Calic, 2018; Vital Communities, 2020).

The third pilot community for the NSF research was OmniWorks Business Incubator at East Los Angeles College in California. OmniWorks offered researchers an opportunity to evaluate a non-rural community brought together by an academic institution rather than geography. OmniWorks integrated the TLC program into an existing incubator training curriculum, which prepares entrepreneurs for successful business operations. OmniWorks combined the TLC 4SE crowdfunding training with its entrepreneurial "boot camp" training and then selected four boot camp entrepreneurs for 4SE. Three of the four were at the initial stages of forming their companies and one was an existing home-based business. Each was selected based upon the abilities of the entrepreneur, the suitability of the products to utilizing crowdfunding, and interest in developing a campaign. OmniWorks director Brent Imai explained how the crowdfunding participants were selected for the pilot study.

> The OmniWorks curriculum takes the budding entrepreneurs through a process that begins with a bootcamp of about 80 participants, progresses to workshop series and college classes, and concludes with a two-week period of high-intensity mentorship for the 15 participants that showed the highest potential for business success. Of the 15 companies in the final cohort, OmniWorks selected four entrepreneurs for the crowdfunding training. Three of the four were at the initial stages of forming their companies and one was an existing home-based business. Each was

> selected based upon the abilities of the entrepreneur, the suitability of their products to utilizing crowdfunding, and interest in developing a campaign.
>
> *(Sontum & Vincent, 2020)*

According to the IRISS final report, "Incubating a Fourth-Sector Ecosystem with a Scalable Educational Crowdfunding Platform," raised more than $80,000 from hundreds of contributors during the NSF research period through campaigns hosted on the TLC platform in Upper Valley, the Monadnock Region, and the OmniWorks Incubator. Campaigns across Upper Valley and Monadnock lasted 55 days and averaged $8,000 per campaign (excluding Monadnock's Reality Check campaign, which did not complete the educational program). Monadnock received an average donation of $65, while Upper Valley received higher contributions exceeding $100. Both organization's averages were higher than those of an average Kickstarter campaign (Stephens et al., 2020).

As part of its research plan, IRISS conducted a Social Network Analysis (SNA) to analyze the number of connections between participants and to determine network density, which is an indicator of social capital. Baseline network density data will be used in future studies to measure change and provide a more complete analysis of TLC 4SE's impact on each community over time.

Data in Figures 9.1–9.3 represent the campaign contributors by the community, demonstrating a development of localized networks from donor contributions to multiple campaigns. The Reality Check campaign's isolation from the Monadnock network is seen clearly in Figure 9.2 as an example of what happens when a campaign does not follow best practices.

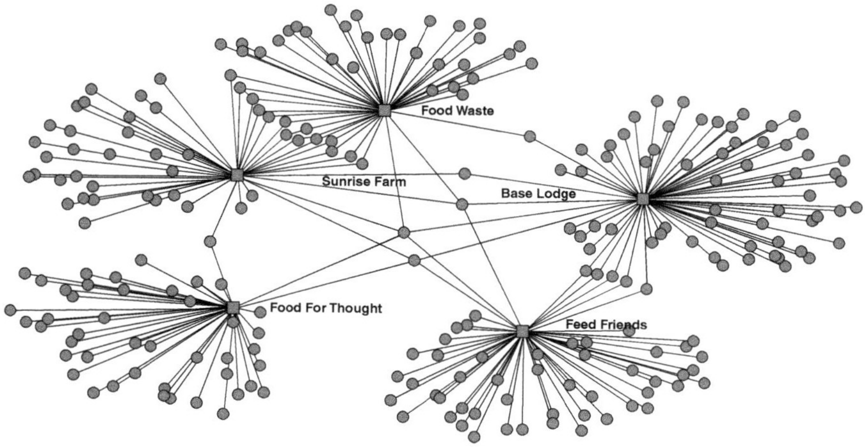

FIGURE 9.1 Upper Valley network shows 258 donors contributed a total of 289 times for resulting a network density score of 0.224.

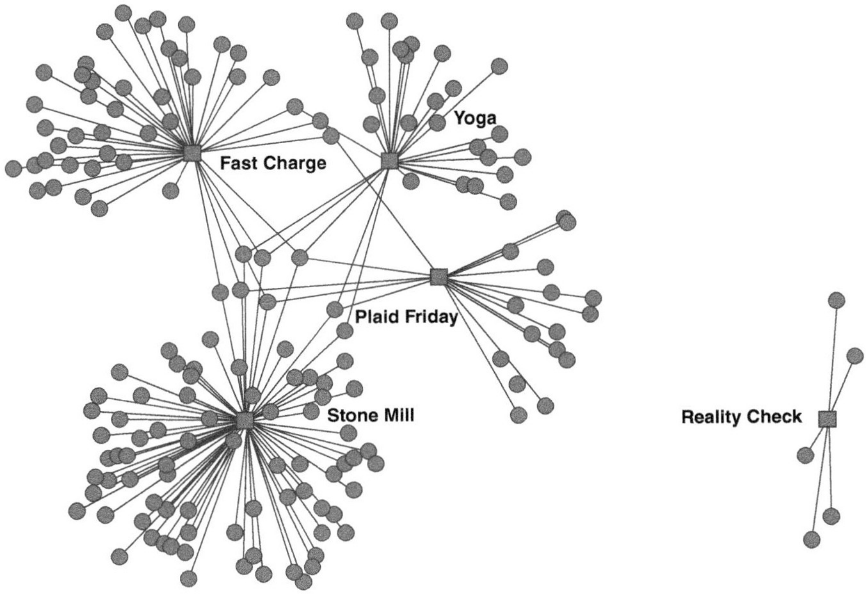

FIGURE 9.2 Monadnock network shows 212 donors contributed a total of 233 times for resulting a network density score of 0.220.

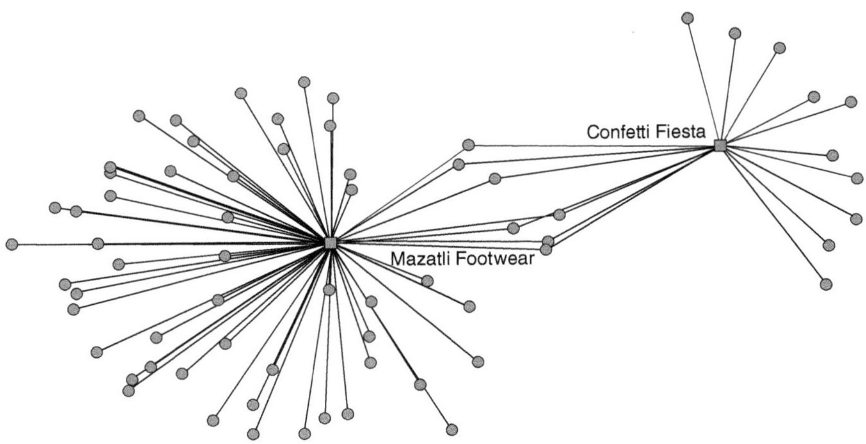

FIGURE 9.3 OmniWorks network shows 68 donors contributed a total of 82 times for a resulting networking density score of 0.618.

A 2019 article in the *Journal of Rural Studies* reported an analysis of social networks in Greece and Ireland. The study identified three types of social capital: *bonding* through common interest, *bridging* different networks within a community, and *linking* the resources between the bonded and bridged connections. These three ties are responsible for building community resiliency within and between entrepreneurial networks and supporters (Land & Fink, 2019).

SNA graphs from the TLC research period collectively demonstrate the bonding, bridging, and linking of social capital within the networks, pointing to evidence that the local-focused crowdfunding platform not only served as a tool for raising capital but also created cohesion and allowed donors to view and support multiple campaigns in their community. In addition, the data suggest that the bonding and bridging that occurs from the exchange of social capital strengthen these networks. The IRISS report asserts that strong networks are making an impact on the fourth economic sector with targeted community development efforts, the TLC 4SE platform, as well as strong local leadership in each of the three communities.

According to IRISS, a notable accomplishment from TLC's 4SE platform was the aid to participants in building support networks in addition to creating access to capital. Of the 24 program participants completing the post-survey, 71% said that the educational modules helped them connect with other local entrepreneurs. These ties were critical for supporting peer mentoring and allowing entrepreneurs to discuss concerns and share ideas. As one participant shared:

> [Contributors] will become part of our family...and by obtaining feedback from customers, that's how we design products that resonate with what people will want. So, it's a huge relationship building effort for the long term." Participants reported increased social media and newsletter audiences, deeper familiarity among customers and organization missions, and strengthened local entrepreneurial networks for brainstorming and collaboration.
>
> *(Stephens et al., 2020)*

In the Monadnock Region, past campaign leaders donated sponsored rewards to help support new campaign teams. For example, Cheshire Garden, a local preserve maker and past campaign leader, donated gift cards to help another business' campaign raise funds for COVID-19 safety equipment for the catering arm of their business. The donation was given without a request, just one business showing support for another business.

Research participants were also able to share resources with other members of their TLC training cohort. This worked especially well for participants working in similar topic areas. One participant commented:

> I didn't have the connection with [organization], officially, until we started the campaign. That kind of strengthened that connection that we worked together on the campaign. . .as we worked together, we figured out it was a cool partnership, so that helped. And then meeting the other people working in the industry, they reached out when they heard about our campaign, so I think [the biggest benefit was] just making connections with other people doing the same thing.
>
> *(Stephens et al., 2020)*

The TLC program encouraged entrepreneurs to tap into local business connections to generate connections and support campaign rewards. 4SE participants reported receiving email lists from partner businesses and/or nonprofits as well as connecting to local media sources. In addition, program participants recruited 89 local businesses to offer in-kind donations to reward campaign supporters. In addition, both Monadnock and Upper Valley businesses reported new and lasting connections.

The OmniWorks network hosted two campaigns with 68 total donors and 82 donations. Though their network was smaller than the other two pilot sites, data from their region show the highest number of donors contributing to multiple campaigns, thus creating a higher network density than the other communities (Figures 9.1–9.3).

The network density in the Upper Valley is represented in dyads A and B in Figure 9.4. The Sunrise Farm and Food Waste campaigns (Dyad A) were linked together as being the Base Lodge and Feed Friends (Dyad B) campaigns in the Upper Valley because each of these pairs shared many donors that contributed to both the campaigns. Thus, there are higher network densities between these campaign dyads than in the rest of the Upper Valley network.

Dyad A includes all donors who donated to either Sunrise Farm or the Food Waste campaigns or both including 87 total donors and 103 donations. The network density for Dyad A equals 0.592. Local knowledge from within the Upper Valley network reported that these two campaigns worked with one another during the process of development after meeting through the program. This suggests that stronger bridging social capital could explain higher network densities during the development phases of a campaign.

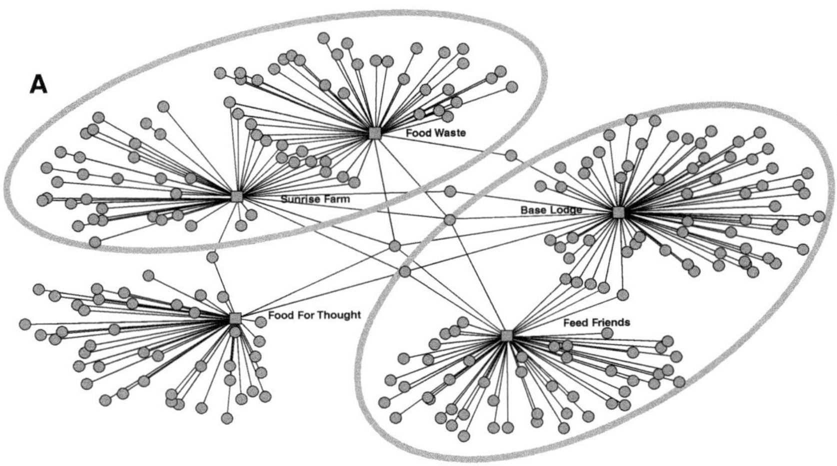

FIGURE 9.4 Campaign Dyads within the Upper Valley network.

Figures 9.1–4 from "Incubating a Fourth-Sector Ecosystem with a Scalable Educational Crowdfunding Platform," Stephens et al., 2020, with permission.

Dyad B was not quite as strong with 129 total donors and only 137 donations, resulting in a network density of 0.531, but still much higher than the overall Upper Valley network density. Local knowledge from within the network suggested that this may be because the owner of one campaign was also on the board of the other organization. This suggests that a donor with a high centrality within those two networks (bonding social capital) might have helped to generate higher network density within Dyad B as well.

During the research period, participants were trained using the TLC curriculum, which included how to use TLC crowdfunding software, fourth-sector basics, best practices for successful crowdfunding campaigns, and the importance of the fourth-sector ecosystem. Content was delivered using webinars, training templates, videos, downloadable workbooks, and online demonstrations and networking activities.

The TLC education program began with an assessment designed by the crowdfunding education specialty firm, Crowdfund Better. The assessment included questionnaires given to campaign creators before and after launching their campaigns. The Crowdfund Better report showed that of the campaigns launched, most reached or exceeded their financial goals.

A common pitfall in crowdfunding campaigns is setting goals too high for network size. TLC's training curriculum addressed this issue with financial analysis and realistic goal-setting tools and, in return, saw a success rate of 63% among participants, a rate higher than Kickstarter's 38%. Even those who did not reach their financial targets indicated entrepreneurial benefits and positive business impact from the crowdfunding process. The education program helps

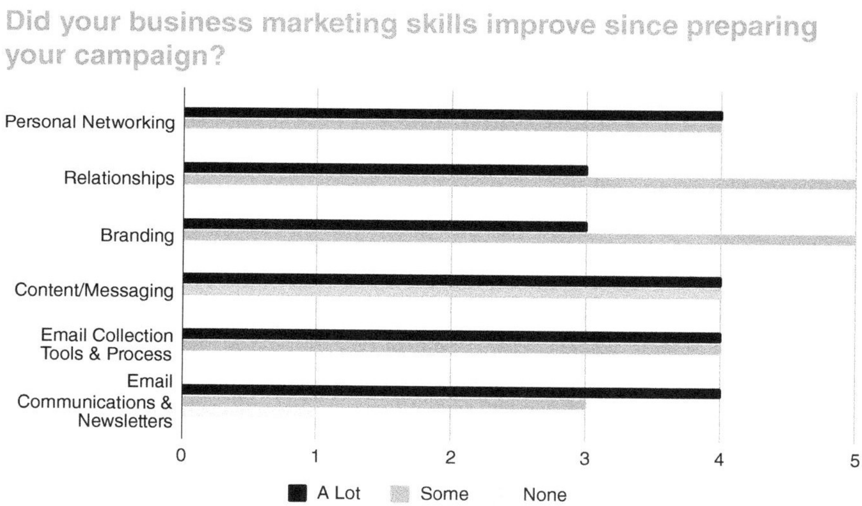

FIGURE 9.5 Participants expressed business improvements beyond capital gain after preparations for crowdfunding campaign.

Source: Crowdfund Better, 2020.

businesses become stronger by learning how to grow and use their networks, build confidence in their ability to raise capital, test market their innovations, and learn how they can support other businesses in their communities, as shown in Figure 9.5. In exit interviews with Crowdfund Better, campaign hosts commented that the crowdfunding process allowed them to purchase new equipment, actively network within their community, and gain confidence in working with marketing and social media tools (Crowdfund Better, 2020).

People Pollinators

In *The Local Economy Solution*, Michael Shuman asks, "How can a new generation of entrepreneurs and employees be trained for these new local business opportunities?" He explores the impact of leaders doing work to incubate and accelerate successful business across the globe and how "pollinator" businesses, financial institutions, economic developers, and individuals can bolster their community's future.

"People pollinators focus exclusively on local businesses already woven into the fabric of their community" (Shuman, 2015, p. 104). Monadnock's people pollinators recognized the opportunity and brought TLC to their economy in the face of the downturn from the Vermont Yankee's shutdown. The community partners spearheaded the program's efforts for the past three years, honing their process for supporting campaign creators looking to use TLC's crowdfunding tools.

Before launching TLC Monadnock, crowdfunding was unfamiliar to the economic development partners and volunteers as an economic driver. The program was launched with targeted outreach events throughout five of the communities in the Monadnock region, some of which were co-hosted with local organizations, allowing for shared audiences and the cultivation of social identity. These events were a platform to create familiarity with the TLC Monadnock brand and a conversation starter between local businesses and the new capital building tool.

As the partners planned and launched campaigns, they gained familiarity via word of mouth throughout the region, eventually reaching their neighbors in the Upper Valley of New Hampshire and Vermont region. Vital Communities, a regional organization for uniting local citizens, organizations, and municipalities in support of local vitality, launched Upper Valley's TLC campaigns in 2019 (Upper Valley, 2019).

In addition to issuing an RFP to bring in potential crowdfunders, TLC Monadnock personally approached potential campaigns, recognizing that the program's continued progress hinged on public success stories. Professionals from various sectors in the community were quick to demonstrate collaboration and connectivity. A local newspaper provided space to publish campaign announcements and articles from the program at no cost; a volunteer videographer provided free campaign videos as an incentive for businesses to participate; and the region laid the groundwork for TLC Monadnock's continued success.

Archway Farm, a small family farm raising sustainable pork, and Stonewall Farm, an educational farm and visitor center, both in Keene, New Hampshire, successfully launched fundraising campaigns in 2017. Archway Farm met its $5,000 goal by raising $5,191 from 59 supporters to develop a local sausage cart. Stonewall Farm more than doubled its $10,000 goal with $22,465 raised from 75 supporters to build an updated barn for their animals as well as community educational events. Monadnock has since funded 20 crowdfunding campaigns with goals from $1,000 to $30,000.

When the COVID-19 crisis shut down hometown businesses, those businesses stopped advertising and put independently owned rural newspapers at risk. Two newspapers in the Monadnock and Upper Valley regions of New Hampshire decided to ask their communities for help. They posted fundraisers on the TLC 4SE platform and raised tens of thousands of dollars – exceeding their goals and demonstrating the power of online community-supported fundraising. The Keene Sentinel raised nearly $47,000 with 414 contributors, and the Valley News raised more than $155,000 with 1,538 contributors.

Once the crowdfunding platform was recognizable among the public and economic development partners, TLC Monadnock began referencing surveys and city plans to create a "wish-list" for campaigns. Based on these data, campaigns with tangible impact toward health, safety, and environmental sustainability for the region were prioritized. This focus allowed TLC Monadnock's partners and campaign creators to raise capital, while also cultivating social capital with a collective mission to bolster the holistic wellness of the region.

TLC Monadnock's partners have identified themselves as "community supported activists;" working toward bonding, bridging, and linking the individual entrepreneurs in the community with the tools, partners, and education necessary for the benefit of the whole. Similarly, Vital Communities in Upper Valley used Monadnock's guidance to create a network of campaign hosts, supporters, and partners dedicated to bolstering the businesses and organizations in their communities. The aggregate of these efforts spread out to the local TLC marketing channels and invite locals to "pollinate" the campaigns surrounding them, creating a cyclical exchange of financial and social wealth. Just as Pulitzer spearheaded the erection of the Statue of Liberty and rallied the people around a cause, local leaders are raising barns and supporting local economies, one crowdsourced contribution at a time.

Conclusion

As crowdfunding gained popularity in the digital marketplace, an "if you build it, they will come" falsity has spread among entrepreneurs looking to cashflow large-scale projects. Although select ventures have benefited from viral campaigns, TLC's research has shown that a community focus, whether that community is defined by county lines or lifestyle elements, and an education-based approach to crowdfunding is necessary for success. In the conclusion of TLC's 2014 SBIR study, Wyoming Agriculture Economist Roger Coupal wrote:

> Among all the deciding factors that might drive donors, investors or potential entrepreneurs (social and private) to use a crowdfunding platform, familiarity with their community seems to elevate to an important level. The literature in economics and sociology confirm this result from the survey. The notion that entrepreneurs and investors are separate from the social structure of their communities has been a myth and continues to be. Risks associated with investing in local enterprises as well as risks incurred by social or private entrepreneurs are minimized by the familiarity of the community they are living in. Success in entrepreneurship requires community support.
>
> *(Wolverton & Vincent, 2014)*

Participation in the TLC 4SE platform from diverse regions has shown that mentorship and network support – often facilitated by a community leader coordinating communication within local networks of entrepreneurs, economic support systems, and regional customers – is decisive. Campaign development requires strategic planning, often more than expected from first-time campaign creators; however, the benefits from moving through the crowdfunding process not only connect businesses with capital but also foster relationships, support ongoing success, and make a tangible impact on the financial and social wellness of the participating community at large.

Connecting community with crowdfunding supports a thriving fourth sector, establishes resiliency, and creates opportunity for community-led restoration in the face of economic crisis. Moving forward, long-term effects on the prosperity of community networks and the impact of social capital from crowdfunding will be determined with ongoing research. Assuming the bonding, bridging, and linking activity supported by a community-focused approach to capital raising continues exponentially, and the potential for economic and social prosperity is plausible in rural communities worldwide.

References

Bidgood, J. (2015, January 4). Vermont Yankee Nuclear Plant Begins Slow Process of Closing. *The New York Times*. Retrieved from https://www.nytimes.com/2015/01/05/us/vermont-yankee-nuclear-plant-begins-slow-process-of-closing.html

Calic, G. (2018). Crowdfunding. In *The SAGE Encyclopedia of the Internet* (pp. 112–114). Retrieved from https://doi.org/10.4135/9781473960367.n40

CardFlight Small Business Impact Report: April 15, 2020. (2020). CardFlight. https://www.cardflight.com/small-business-impact/report-5

Covington, M., & Courtney, J. (2014). *Banking in Rural America: Insight from a Community Development Financial Institution (CDFI)*. Southern Bancorp. http://southernpartners.org/assets/SBCP_CDFIPaper_20141219.pdf

Crowdfund Better. (2020). *Crowdfund Better Rapid Assessment (RAP) and Exit Survey Analysis for 4SE Incubator* (pp. 1–12, Rep.). Crowdfund Better.

The CrowdFunding Center. (2020, July 20). *Platform Stats & Analysis*. The Crowd Data Center. https://www.thecrowdfundingcenter.com/data/projects

Gellerman, B. (2019, April 24). This Vermont Town Took a Big Hit When Its Nuclear Plant Closed. Retrieved March 5, 2020, from https://www.wbur.org/earthwhile/2019/04/23/vermont-yankee-vernon-lessons

Henderson, G. (2017, December 6). *Recession Lingers in Rural America*. Drovers. https://www.drovers.com/article/recession-lingers-rural-america

Kerr, S. E. (2018). Social Capital as a Determinant of Resilience: Implications for Adaptation Policy. In *Resilience: The Science of Adaptation to Climate Change* (pp. 267–275). https://www.sciencedirect.com/science/article/pii/B9780128118917000220

Land, R., & Fink, M. (2019). Rural Social Entrepreneurship. The Role of Social Capital within and across Institutional Levels. *Journal of Rural Studies*, 70, 155–168.

Lowrey, A. (2020, May 4). *The Bridge to the Post-pandemic World Is Collapsing*. The Atlantic. https://www.theatlantic.com/ideas/archive/2020/05/bridge-post-pandemic-world-already-collapsing/611089/

Mills, K. G. (2014, July 22). *The State of Small Business Lending: Credit Access during the Recovery and How Technology May Change the Game – Working Paper – Harvard Business School*. Harvard Business School. https://www.hbs.edu/faculty/Pages/item.aspx?num=47695

Patronicity: Growing Communities Together. (2020). Patronicity. https://www.patronicity.com/about-us

Ricketts, K. G., & Place, N. T. (2009). Making Communities More Viable: Four Essential Factors for Successful Community Leadership. *Journal of Extension*, 47(2). https://joe.org/joe/2009april/iw2.php#:~:text=Making%20Communities%20More%20Viable%3A%20Four%20Essential%20Factors%20for,Communities.%20...%205%20Conclusion.%20...%206%20References.%20

Risley, J. (2017). About TLC Monadnock. Retrieved March 5, 2020, from https://monadnockbuylocal.wildapricot.org/about

Şahin, A., Kitao, S., Cororaton, A., & Laiu, S. (2011). Why Small Businesses Were Hit Harder by the Recent Recession. *Current Issues in Economics and Finance*, 17(42011). Federal Reserve Bank of New York. https://www.newyorkfed.org/research/current_issues/ci17-4.html

Sherman, N. (2020, April 23). Coronavirus: US Unemployment Claims Hit 26.4 million Amid Virus. *BBC News*. Retrieved from https://www.bbc.com/news/business-52398837

Shuman, M. (2015). *The Local Economy Solution: How Innovative, Self-Financing "Pollinator" Enterprises Can Grow Jobs and Prosperity* (pp. 1–16, 103–115). White River Junction, VT: Chelsea Green Publishing.

Sontum, D., & Vincent, K. (2020, April). *NSF Phase 1 Research Final Report* (Award Number 1842729). The Local Crowd.

State of New Hampshire. (2020, June 15). *New Hampshire Employment Security*. GraniteStats. https://www2.nhes.nh.gov/GraniteStats/SessionServlet?page=LAUS.jsp&SID=12&planning=000004&planningName=Southwest%20Region%20Planning

Stephens, A., Ratajczyk, E., & Cross, J. (2020). *Incubating a Fourth-Sector Ecosystem with a Scalable Educational Crowdfunding Platform* (Rep.). Fort Collins, CO: Institute for Research in the Social Sciences (IRISS) at Colorado State University.

Upper Valley. (2019, November 12). Vital Communities. https://vitalcommunities.org/uppervalley/

Vital Communities. (2020). Valley News COVID-19 Support Fund. Retrieved May 5, 2020, from https://vitalcommunities.org/uppervalley/?cfpage=project&project_id=35658

Walzer, N. (2019). *Guidebook and Resources for Starting Community Supported Enterprises*. Retrieved from https:// https://www.cgs.niu.edu/Reports/cse-guidebook-final-2-8-19.pdf

Walzer, N., & Sandoval, J. (2016). *Emergence and Growth of Community Supported Enterprises*. Retrieved from https://www.ruralgrocery.org/resources/EmergenceandGrowth.pdf

Weltman, B. (2020, March 24). *10 Years after the Financial Crisis: The Impact on Small Business*. Investopedia. https://www.investopedia.com/small-business/10-years-after-financial-crisis-impact-small-business/

Wolverton, D., & Vincent, K. (2014). *Enhancing Rural Access to Capital through Development of a Local Crowdfunding Incubator*, The Local Crowd, Phase I Final Report.

Wolverton, D., & Vincent, K. (2020). *The Local Crowd Commercialization Plan*. Laramie, WY: The Local Crowd, Inc.

World Health Organization. (2020, April 27). WHO Timeline – COVID-19. Retrieved from https://www.who.int/news-room/detail/27-04-2020-who-timeline---covid-19

10

SOCIAL ENTERPRISE, IDD, AND COMMUNITY-SUPPORTED ENTERPRISES IN ONTARIO, CANADA

Ushnish Sengupta

The Cultural context of SE and IDD

The formation and continuity of Social Enterprises (SEs) employing individuals with Intellectual and Developmental Disabilities (IDD) depend mainly on the contexts of national culture and sub-national culture (Mazzei, 2017). In Canada, the cultural context for individuals with IDD frames the opportunities, quality of life, and organizations serving this group, including SEs. The cultural views of disabled versus non-disabled also shape opportunities and barriers for individuals with IDD. Cultural views on disability are not static and change over time – for example, opinion polls indicating increased support for physical accessibility in Canada (Angus Reid, 2015) – but these views of disability vary across provinces in Canada.

Views regarding roles of the government, private sector, and the social economy, on the other hand, determine the types of organizations in each province in Canada. An important outcome of the intersection of national cultural views of disability and IDD and sub national or provincial views of the role of the social economy is that SEs that employ individuals with IDD are non-profit organizations that depend on government funding. In the province of Ontario, in the current context and year 2020, no economically self-sufficient private-sector SEs that employ individuals with IDD were found in the literature. Private-sector organizations employ individuals with IDD, but they are not considered as SEs.

Thus, in this chapter, only non-profit SEs employing individuals with IDD are described as community-supported enterprises (CSEs). This distinction between non-profit government-funded SEs and private-sector organizations differs from other cultural contexts such as the United States (where there is a much higher level of private donor and private foundation support for non-profits) and will be expanded further later in this chapter. Community financial support for non-profit SEs in Ontario is in three different forms. First direct support in terms of purchasing goods and services; second through donations to the non-profit (if it is a charity); and third through redistribution of taxes through government payments to non-profit SEs – as described, all non-profit SEs employing individuals with IDD in Ontario are supported by government finances. Therefore, all non-profit SEs in Ontario that employ individuals with IDD are *partially* independent of governments through income generation, but none are completely independent of government. It is these non-profit SEs that are described as CSEs in this chapter.

Another important distinction in the social economy between the United States and Canada is that non-profits in the United States are charities and can accept charitable donations unlike in Canada where not all non-profits are charities. Charities in Canada are a specific legal organizational designation that can accept, for example, financial donations and issue charitable tax receipts. Non-profits in Canada have a broader legal designation that cannot for example issue charitable tax receipts. Therefore, in Canada, all charities are non-profits, but all non-profits are not charities.

Since the current discussions focus on Ontario, social enterprises in Ontario will be the center of attention while drawing on cultural frameworks for disability from the broader Canadian context. For example, the current lack of legislation in Ontario allows a broad range of organizations to label themselves as SE. At a national level, the Canadian Charter of Rights and Freedoms explicitly identifies physical and mental disabilities as a parameter of discrimination, requiring equal protection and equal benefit of the law (Government of Canada, 1982).

Even though some of the organizations employing individuals with IDD vary by provinces, there are uniform protections against discrimination based on disability across Canada, at least in principle. Government policy generally reflects prevalent cultural views of the electorate. In the current discussions, government policy on IDD and SE reflects the prevalent cultural views of individuals with IDD and SE. The types of SEs supported by the government, and therefore funded, are circumscribed by government policy, and government policy in turn is circumscribed by culture.

This section builds on two news articles that reflect the cultural views of SE and IDD. These articles serve as a starting point since, as artifacts, they more closely reflect cultural views than peer-reviewed journal articles. The first article describes a business case for hiring individuals with disabilities (Wafer, 2017), written by a franchise owner with experience hiring them. The second article is a *Toronto Star* report on the closing of sheltered workshops in Ontario (Welsh, 2015). It is useful to note that a business, especially a franchise business employing individuals with IDD, does not consider itself a SE, is not supported financially by the community any differently than any other private-sector franchise and therefore is not considered to be a CSE.

The first article reflects the prevalent cultural view that private-sector organizations should hire more individuals with disabilities. The second reflects the culturally prevalent view that sheltered workshops are not an appropriate employment solution for individuals with IDD and therefore should not be allowed to operate as CSEs. The underlying fundamental view is that private-sector employment is of greater value and more appropriate for individuals with IDD than employment in social economy organizations. Long-term employment in private-sector organizations is seen as a success for individuals with IDD, whereas long-term employment in social economy organizations is viewed as a failure of the system.

An underlying principle for valuing private-sector employment over social economy employment is the reduction in long-term costs for government (Graefe, 2006). Private-sector employment is viewed as reducing long-term social support costs for government and potentially generating additional tax revenues. Social economy employment, on the other hand, is seen as an ongoing cost for government and a drain on potential tax revenues. This trend toward the preference of private-sector employment of individuals is in part a Neoliberal trend, a move away from tax-based redistributive financial support of social economy organizations to an onus of individual responsibility on the individuals with IDD to find private-sector employment.

The role of the social economy, especially SE employing individuals with IDD, is therefore reduced to being trainers and supporters of private-sector employment rather than as long-term employers. As a result of changing government policies, most SEs employing individuals with IDD in Ontario in 2020 are organizations that prepare these individuals for private-sector employment. *Enterprising Non-Profits* (2014) reports that 40% of all SEs in Canada are Employment Social Enterprises, organizations that support transitioning to mainstream employment or directly employ individuals with multiple barriers to employment.

These SEs are referred to in the literature as Work Integration Social Enterprises (WISE), affirmative or alternative businesses and supported social enterprises (Chan, Ryan & Quarter, 2017) depending on local geographical context. WISE are a subset of CSE since they are again supported by local communities. They are supported by local community members since they have an explicit mission of hiring and employing individuals with multiple barriers to employment. Local community members fundraise for and donate to WISE, purchase goods and services directly from WISE, with a majority of WISE being non-profit organizations are indirectly supported by local taxes.

In contrast to the United States, Chan et al., (2017) show that many WISE organizations in Canada obtain most of their revenues from public rather than market sources. This fact highlights one of the reasons government views the long-term employment of individuals in social economy organizations as an ongoing cost with a long-term financial liability.

The definition of SE by the Government of Ontario is: "A social enterprise is an organization that uses business strategies to maximize its social or environmental impact" (Government of Ontario, 2016b). WISE and many sheltered workshops where most employees are individuals with IDD, generating some market revenues, would be considered as SEs under this definition. A private for-profit franchise that hires individuals with IDD would not be considered a SE, since the primary goal is not social impact.

A non-profit organization employing a minority of employees with IDD, and generating some market revenues, such as some Groupe Convex (GC) businesses, is considered a SE, due to its explicit social impact mission. Simultaneously, an organization like GC is a CSE since it is financially supported by the local community, directly and indirectly. The most direct form of community support for GC includes purchases of goods and services not only at an individual level but also by businesses, towns, municipalities, and the administrative region.

An indirect form of community support is through local organizations that have purchased and leased facilities to GC at preferential rates. At the same time, social economy organizations such as GC are under financial pressure from government to close down operations that provide long-term employment for individuals with IDD and change to providing support for private-sector employment of individuals with IDD (Sengupta & Quarter, 2017).

Krupa, Lagarde, & Carmichael (2003) describe the transformation of sheltered workshops employing individuals with psychiatric disabilities changing to affirmative businesses when organizational survival becomes an issue. Some authors argue that the long-term reduction in funding for social economy organizations employing individuals with disabilities is a part of the Neoliberal agenda (Bates, Goodley & Runswick-Cole, 2017). This chapter argues that the trend is not completely explained by Neoliberalism and is more holistically explained by longer-term Canadian cultural views on disability.

SEs as Solutions for Market, Societal, and Institutional Failures

SEs that serve individuals with IDD mitigate different types of societal and institutional deficiencies (Santos, 2012). The first is a market failure of employers who do not hire these individuals in proportion to the population. *Statistics Canada* (2015) reports that 78% of individuals with developmental disabilities, age 15–64, are not in the labor force or unemployed.

A second failure is the limited employee training and development plus an expectation of just-in-time, job ready employees, especially in the private sector. The Institute for Research and Development on Inclusion and Society (2011) reports that inadequate training is a common barrier (after accessible transportation and discrimination) for employment for individuals with intellectual disabilities.

The third failure is in the educational system that does not adequately prepare individuals with IDD for employment (Reid et al., 2018) and, in Ontario, does not provide support past the age of 21 (Ontario Ombudsman, 2016). The final failure involves inadequate support from families to provide home-to-work transition skills for these individuals (Carter, Austin & Trainor, 2012).

These societal and institutional failures rest with Canadian socio-cultural views of individuals with IDD. A majority of employers do not view them as valuable and possessing the required skills for employment (Zwicker, Zaresani & Emery, 2017). The K-12 educational system streams students, therefore limiting career choices; segregates those with IDD limiting social skill development; and leaves them at age 21 without sufficient transition to adult services (Ontario Ombudsman, 2016). In other cases, families internalize prevalent cultural views of individuals with disabilities and set low expectations for these children (Broberg, 2011). Combined, the societal and institutional limitations result in high unemployment of these individuals, a gap which SEs try to address at different points in the system.

Therefore, the literature on SE and disabilities is examined through a socio-cultural lens. Specifically, the cultural context, or cultural view of disability, provides a basis for government policy (Ingstad & Whyte, 1995), including those with IDD as a subset of individuals with disabilities. Government policies, in turn, determine the types of organizations, including SEs interacting with individuals with disabilities, the services provided by these organizations, and individuals eligible for these services. Therefore, cultural and policy differences, where relevant, are highlighted in reviewing the international literature on SE and disability.

Published Research on SEs Employing People with Disabilities

The previous section described how the prevalent model for CSEs in Ontario employing individuals with IDD are non-profit SEs, with a gradual shift toward private-sector employment in organizations not considered CSEs. This section reviews the evidence in literature on what works and what does not work in terms of employment of individuals with disabilities.

Significantly, the term "Community Supported Enterprise" is not a term found in the literature describing organizations with explicit missions of employing individuals with disabilities. The argument made here is that instead of focusing on the label CSE, policies should consider the function of organizations. In Ontario, non-profit SEs employing individuals with IDD are functionally similar to CSEs elsewhere with parallel missions. This section, therefore, focuses on SEs employing individuals with disabilities as a functional subset of CSEs, and there are several identifiable trends from the published research on SEs and disability.

The first is a "publication bias" toward projects that have delivered successful outcomes. Many articles try to identify best practices within SEs employing individuals with disabilities. The identification of best practices would ideally be useful for the sector in learning from the experience of different successful organizations. Articles often include case studies of an organization, or a few organizations, making it difficult to generalize the best practices identified or to identify issues or successes and best practices that can be translated to different contexts.

A second trend is that few of the articles describe comparative evaluation methods such as a Randomized Controlled Trial making it difficult to determine the quality of the conclusions and best practices identified. Without a comparative evaluation, it is not clear that the benefits described are solely attributable to the program or organization described. In a designed experiment, the positive and negative effects of the program would be separated from other effects that would be present without the program. Experiments of this type are difficult and therefore expensive to setup in the delivery of social services, and therefore inferences must be made from more natural experiments. In summary, few articles describe the comparative evaluation of different programs within an organization or across organizations. The term "programs" here is prevalent in the non-profit literature and means the main operational activities of an organization.

A third trend is some articles tackle the difficult task of a more refined definition of SE and related organizations employing individuals with disabilities. Presumably, the sub-classification of different types of SEs employing individuals with disabilities would enable more refined research and identification of more specific success factors that can be replicated.

Corbiere & Lecomte (2009) attempt a distinction between sheltered workshop, transitional employment, SEs, and supported employment, ultimately favoring supported employment as the most advantageous solution. The argument against favoring a specific organizational form is that there are individual differences in the support that people with disabilities need, not all of which are effectively provided by a single type of organization (Brennan-Krohn, 2016).

Agreeing with the philosophy of differential needs, Tan (2009) uses a case study of an organization in Taiwan to emphasize the bridging role the SE provided between a sheltered workplace and supported employment, therefore identifying the need for different types of organizations to meet changing needs over time for the same individuals. Notably, in the discussion of appropriate organizational form for employment of individuals with disabilities, the importance of community support is not highlighted. Although specific case studies make clear that community support, financial and nonfinancial, or direct and indirect is essential in the success of SEs employing individuals with disabilities.

An additional notable thread is the prevalence of SEs where the managers and workers are usually individuals without identified disabilities employing clients who are individuals with disabilities. Caldwell, Parker Harris, & Renko (2012) make the case that SEs have potential for expanding the citizenship rights for individuals with IDD by providing individuals with IDD the supports required to develop their own SEs.

One constraint in this approach is the severity of the disability, with it likely being limited to those whose disabilities are less severe. The authors also describe a simultaneous risk of SEs reinforcing existing negative socio-cultural biases for individuals with IDD. Subsequent articles (Parker Harris, Caldwell & Renko, 2014; Renko, Parker Harris & Caldwell, 2016) show that organizations developed by individuals with disabilities are the most appropriate for services not provided by other organizations since they are based on lived experience. Finally, Caldwell, Harris, & Renko (2016) claim that individuals with disabilities forming organizations for self-employment are de facto social entrepreneurs whether they use the SE label or not.

The socio-cultural process of creating binaries of disabled and non-disabled in Canadian society has implicitly assigned associated roles for individuals with IDD. They are not viewed as social entrepreneurs capable of developing their own organizations. Critical Disability Theory, as described in the subsequent section, can be used to show that individuals with IDD should lead organizations employing individuals with IDD, first due to lived experience and second to be equal citizens with equivalent opportunities to lead organizations, in addition to being employees.

As described at the beginning of this chapter, those with IDD are viewed as capable of being employees preferably in the private sector. Wolfensberger (2000) claims that employment is an essential element in changing cultural views of those with disabilities. He describes this cultural change process as "Social Role Valorization," where the social roles of individuals with disabilities are viewed as hard-working employees in local organizations.

In terms of organizational implications, organizations that employ individuals with disabilities as part of their explicit mission, Affirmative Enterprises as Wolfensberger (2000) describes them, in Ontario, are mostly a subset of non-profit SEs. Therefore, they are also seen as valuable entities in the community worthy of local support. This view strengthens the argument made earlier that non-profit SEs employing individuals with disabilities function as CSEs, but without the label. It is not sufficient that primarily non-profit SEs employing individuals with IDD are considered CSEs. The extended argument is that self-employment, and organizations led by individuals with IDD, should also be considered SEs and CSEs so should benefit from the same level of direct and indirect community support.

The difference in both formally and informally designating organizations as deserving of additional community support is a social and cultural issue. Changing this social and cultural view requires a shift in imagination of the roles of those with IDD. One such approach of viewing them as capable individuals rather than with deficits is to identify examples demonstrating their capabilities. An examination of the peer-reviewed literature revealed only one example of an organization started by an individual with IDD for the purpose of employment in Ontario. The early development of Common Ground Cooperative was described by Lemon & Lemon (2003). However, there are examples of SEs formed by mental health service consumers/survivors in Ontario, including some businesses managed under the umbrella Working for Change, previously known as Ontario Council for Alternative Businesses (Warner & Mandiberg, 2006).

Geographical Commonalities and Differences

The difference in both formally and informally designating organizations as deserving of additional community support is a social and cultural issue, and culture is often nationally and geographically defined. Although there are cultural differences on how organizations that employ individuals with IDD are supported by local communities across different national and subnational cultures, a survey of the international literature is useful for comparative purposes.

Many similarities exist among SEs employing individuals with disabilities in the Anglophone countries, Canada, the United States, the United Kingdom, and Australia. Williams, Fossey, & Harvey (2012) identify guiding principles for sustainable employment for mental health service users, using a case study of an Australian social firm similar to a Canadian SE. Secker, Dass, & Grove (2003) identify effective practices in developing social firms employing individuals with disabilities through interviews with 20 social firms in the United Kingdom.

Several commonalities exist among early SEs employing individuals with disabilities in Canada. First is the importance of parent organizations for SEs that provide essential social supports, as described for SEs in Canada by Chan (2015). Second is the importance of decision-making capabilities by employees with disabilities through the organizational form such as co-operatives, as described for Canadian SEs by Owen, Readhead, Bishop, Hope, & Campbell (2015b). In a Canadian example, Owen et al., (2015a) use the case study of Common Ground Co-operative (CGC) to calculate a positive Social Return on Investment (SROI) from employing individuals with IDD. The Owen et al., (2015a) article does make definitional distinctions between a sheltered workshop, SE, and supported employment, with Common Ground as the SE.

In significant contrast with articles favoring a particular type of organizational solution, Schroeder & Schroeder (1990) advocate for a brokerage model, where individuals are directed to appropriate services to provide the best outcomes for children with IDD, based on a case study of Anne Sullivan Enterprises in North Carolina. Although the case study focuses on children with disabilities rather than adults, there are useful parallels to the policy implementation enabling Independent Facilitators in Ontario (Ontario Independent Facilitation Network, 2017), recognizing the dichotomy between client needs and agency needs.

Articles from other countries also provide insights into alternative cultural views of disability and how the cultural views affect government policy and SEs. Huang, Guo, & Bricout (2009) identify a substantial policy shift for individuals with disabilities in China from government employment to private-sector employment. Significantly, Huang et al., (2009) identify employment quotas (1.5% of employees) for people with disabilities as an important policy tool in maintaining accountability of the private sector to government targets.

In a study of SEs in Uganda, Daniels & Jeans (2009) describe the importance of entrepreneurship for individuals with disabilities, reflecting the entrepreneurial nature of the Ugandan economy. Daniels & Jeans (2009) also describe a community-based program that involves families, including training of "shadow workers" who are family members and who can therefore temporarily run the enterprise during time periods when the person with a disability is unable to do so.

Definitions of Intellectual and Developmental Disability (IDD)

The preceding discussion defines and discusses organizational structure and form but equally important is to understand the populations served. Persons with IDD must be considered as a unique population in terms of interaction with organization form. As previously discussed, nonprofit SEs that employ individuals with IDD are considered CSEs, while self-employed individuals with IDD do not have the same level of formal or informal community support. In Ontario, services for individuals with IDD are governed by the Services and Supports to Promote the Social Inclusion of Persons with Developmental Disabilities Act (Government of Ontario, 2019). The Act defines Development Disability as follows:

> Developmental Disability
>
> 1 A person has a developmental disability for the purposes of this Act if the person has the prescribed significant limitations in cognitive functioning and adaptive functioning and those limitations
>
> a originated before the person reached 18 years of age;
> b are likely to be life-long in nature; and
> c affect areas of major life activity, such as personal care, language skills, learning abilities, the capacity to live independently as an adult, or any other prescribed activity. 2008, c. 14, s. 3 (1).

Government-funded services require that individuals with IDD complete tests and be diagnosed as having IDD by the medical profession. The Ontario government's definition of disability is therefore based on a medical model of disability. The main critique of the medical model is that it individualizes disability rather than identifying broader social barriers faced by individuals (Mckenzie, 2013).

In this paradigm, the group of individuals classified through medical criteria, therefore, form a community of people. A community of individuals with IDD as described here does not have to be geographically bounded, such as a city or a town, but possesses several common characteristics, the most common being that individuals have a medical designation plus government classification that broadly represents cultural stereotypes.

People with IDD are treated by other individuals, the government, and society at large in the same way. In a binary classification of disabled and normal, individuals with IDD are classified as 'disabled.' So, we need an established body of knowledge that counters this classification of individuals with IDD to challenge the dominant cultural view that limits the possibilities for individuals with IDD. Critical Disability Studies argues against binary classifications of disabled and 'normal' individuals, where the social constructs for 'normal' foster discrimination against disabled individuals (Goodley, 2017).

To make the case further, individuals with Intellectual Disability (ID) and individuals with Developmental Disability are not separated in North American culture but grouped as a community. In practice, they are served by the same government departments and social economy organizations such as the American Association on Intellectual and Developmental Disabilities (2010). In the case of social economy organizations employing individuals with IDD, for example, the not-for-profit organization GC, located in Eastern Ontario, employs individuals with intellectual disabilities, but some of these employees would also have developmental disabilities.

Similarly, Common Ground Co-operative focuses on individuals with developmental disabilities, but some of their clients have intellectual disabilities. The inclusive term Intellectual and Developmental Disability (IDD) is used here to describe this community. In this section, the group of individuals classified by society as having an IDD is considered as one group, while the following section discusses CSEs working with individuals with IDD.

Definitions of Social Enterprise

Preceding discussions involved organizational forms of CSEs employing individuals with IDD as well as government-based definitions of IDD and how both are culturally mediated. The next section includes official definitions of SE since it is also culturally mediated but is specific to a sub-national culture. In other words, the definition of SE is specific to sub-national provinces in Canada and differs by province within the same country.

There has been a long-term policy emphasis on SE as a solution for some employment issues involving individuals with IDD, and the discussion here is on not-for-profit SEs for individuals with IDD. Not-for-profit SEs are supported by the communities they represent or where they operate so are CSEs (Walzer & Sandoval, 2016). The term social enterprise does not have a broadly accepted or commonly used definition because new organizations are created that do not fit into previous definitions. Significantly, policymakers have kept the definition of SE as wide as possible to include the broadest range of organizations and support the claim that SEs are used as a policy tool in solving a broad range of social issues. A similar definition issue exists in classifying different types of organizations that support individuals with IDD.

Since this discussion centers on CSEs in Ontario, the definition of SE used by the Government of Ontario has applied: "A social enterprise is an organization that uses business strategies to maximize its social or environmental impact" (Government of Ontario, 2016a). Note that by not specifying a form of incorporation, SEs can be either market-based or not-for-profit or even unincorporated entities. Most SEs employing people with IDD in Ontario operate as not-for-profit organizations. In this discussion, not-for-profit SEs are considered CSEs. They are collectively owned by the community in legal terms and generate revenues through sales of goods and services from the SE.

A SE employing people with IDD earns revenues as a business selling products or services and pays employees with IDD an income for working. GC, an organization in the Prescott Russell region of Eastern Ontario that manages nine enterprises, is an example of a SE where every individual with IDD employed by GC is engaged in income generating activities (Sengupta & Quarter, 2017). Common Ground Co-operative, on the other hand, engages individuals with IDD as associates who can earn an hourly wage as well as a portion of distribution of profits for the enterprise. Both examples are CSEs.

Importance of Government Policy for CSEs

Policies involving IDD clients in Canada are in a state of flux, and any change in policy has a magnified effect on these individuals, their families, and communities as well as the necessary organizational support system. Government policy changes affect individuals through the services and funding available affecting equity of opportunity and quality of life. For families, the changes affect funding provided to them as caregivers and services. For parents, choices are between employment and being a home caregiver for disabled children.

For service organizations, changes in government policy affect the ecosystem of services and funding, enabling formation of new organizations, closures of existing organizations, and adjustments to services offered by each organization. In Canada, federal and provincial government policy determines possible legal organizational structures and government funding, which often represents major sources of revenues for not-for-profits. Ontario has no separate legal designation for community-supported organizations. For current discussions, not-for-profit SEs are supported by the communities they represent or communities where they are located (Walzer & Sandoval, 2016).

SEs employing people with IDD depend on government programs and funding, so are vulnerable to policy changes. For example, through the Passport program, the Government of Ontario provides funding to people with IDD who can then select the organizations and services they want to patronize (Ontario Ministry of Community and Social Services, 2017). In an environment where funding is provided per client, social economy organizations are incentivized to maximize the number of clients (Pedlar & Hutchison, 2000).

In a context of funding based on achievement of goals such as employment for clients with IDD, social economy organizations are incentivized to "cherry pick" or "cream skim" higher functioning clients more likely to achieve goals with less support rather than those requiring higher levels of support (Koning & Heinrich, 2010). SEs tend to act in self-interest (Koning & Heinrich, 2010), signing up clients for services to achieve headcount objectives due to the financial incentives previously outlined.

Consequently, policy analysis and implications for SEs employing individuals with IDD are important areas of research. Due to the practices of "cherry picking" or "cream skimming" by SEs, disability advocates do not see SEs as a universal solution in employing people with IDD. Returning to the argument that those individuals form a community with common characteristics, they do not feel holistically supported by SEs who focus on employing high functioning individuals. In current discussions, this is the primary distinction between a community of individuals with IDD and a local geographical community that may support a SE. The interests of these often overlapping communities are not always positively aligned.

Need for Evidence-Based Government Policy Analysis

One reason why governments encourage more use of SEs to provide social services is that SEs generate revenues that can reduce government social program spending (Fairbairn, 2009). According to Albrecht (1992), products and services for individuals with disabilities also provide substantial business opportunities. As such, during funding cutbacks to organizations in the broader social economy, the government of Ontario has periodically provided small increases in SE funding (Government of Ontario, 2016b).

Lobby groups, including disability rights advocates, parent groups, and other organized citizens groups, have succeeded in obtaining legislative and funding changes to improve quality of life with better equity for individuals with disabilities. Thus, new policy implementation must be examined in the context of dynamic and, sometimes opposing, competing interests rather than a linear process. Government policy regarding disabilities is not a linear progression and often vacillates between progressive and regressive policies based on support from the electorate.

Employment of individuals with IDD is considered the primary policy outcome since most SEs employing individuals with IDD focus on employment. The education system is also geared to employment outcomes and often limits career options for individuals with IDD. Students with IDD graduating from high school are placed in programs with limited pathways to post-secondary education at an earlier age. The result of streaming in the education system and subsequently fewer employment options ultimately results in a high employment rate. *Statistics Canada* (2014) reports that the unemployment rate for individuals with (all) disabilities was substantially higher at 11% compared with 6% for the total population. Consequently, the social economy and especially non-profit SEs or CSEs often are the employer of last resort for this group.

The same report shows an overrepresentation of individuals with disabilities in sales and customer-service-related professions, indicating limited employment opportunity in other professions. It also reports an unemployment rate (19.8%) for individuals with developmental disabilities higher than the average unemployment rate for all individuals with disabilities. Some forms of IDD are more limiting in employment opportunities than others. Individuals with IDD are often classified as high- or low-functioning on a battery of intellectual and psychological tests. Different criteria are used by organizations to qualify individuals for support services: for example, Common Ground Co-operative requires participants to have an IQ below 70.

Organizations employing people with IDD include the public sector, private sector, and a broad array of organizations in the social economy. Using the definition of the social economy from Quarter, Mook, & Armstrong (2017,

p. 4), "social economy bridges the many different types of self-governing organizations that are guided by their social objectives in the goods and services that they offer," this study includes social purpose businesses, not for profits, and co-operatives, but focuses mainly on not-for-profit SEs.

The social economy, broadly speaking, plays a major role in improving the quality of life for individuals with IDD. Not-for-profit organizations, including healthcare services, are the largest group of social economy organizations serving individuals with IDD. Social economy organizations also include consumer survivor associations such as organizations supporting individuals with mental health-related issues, often in opposition to institutionalized forms of care (Canadian Mental Health Association, 2005).

Co-operatives such as Common Ground Co-operative are multi-stakeholder, non-share capital, or not-for-profit co-operatives that include a variety of stakeholders with a common goal to improve quality of life for individuals with IDD. The coalition of stakeholders with a formal role in the multi-stakeholder Common Ground cooperative can be considered a community of support. There are a small but growing number of private organizations that employ individuals with IDD, and an even smaller number of organizations are started by entrepreneurs with disabilities (Parker Harris et al., 2014; Renko et al., 2016).

Theoretical Basis: Critical Disability Studies

Critical Disability Studies can be used to question how North American cultural norms interact with IDD. The framework of these studies extends to employment for individuals with IDD, whereas, for example, anti-subordination theory explains that current structures are intended to develop individuals with IDD as subordinate employees, rather than independent citizens (Colker, 2006). Caldwell et al., (2016) use a CDS approach to argue that individuals with disabilities forming their own organizations are social entrepreneurs, but they are not given the supports as other social entrepreneurs.

In CSE terms, non-profit SEs employing individuals with IDD are explicitly supported by the community due to their explicit social mission, yet simultaneously entrepreneurs with IDD who are self-employed or run their own business do not have the same explicit recognition. Therefore, community support is often *mediated* through organizational form and by organizational leadership. Geographically defined communities are much more apt to financially and otherwise support not-for-profit organizations that employ individuals with IDD than to financially support organizations led by individuals with IDD.

The Role of Culture in Interactions with Individuals with IDD

Previous sections made the argument on why organizational forms such as non-profit SE employing individuals with IDD are formally supported by communities and are CSEs, whereas self-employed individuals with IDD or entrepreneurs with IDD do not receive the same formal community support. This section provides additional background for this phenomenon, which applies to individuals with IDD, but does not necessarily apply to all individuals with disabilities. Essentially, the primary issue of binary separation of disabled and non-disabled individuals critiqued by Critical Disability theory is deeply rooted in North American culture.

In the case of IDD, the dominant North American culture draws a sharp culturally mediated dividing line between disabled and non-disabled. One aspect of dominant North American culture is a deep level of trust in medical professionals such as physicians. Therefore, the dividing line between individuals with IDD and without IDD is defined by the medical profession: "Intellectual disability is a disability characterized by significant limitations both in intellectual functioning (reasoning, learning, problem solving) and in adaptive behavior, which covers a range of everyday social and practical skills" (American Association on Intellectual and Developmental Disabilities, 2010). "Developmental Disabilities" is an umbrella term that not only includes ID but also includes other disabilities that are apparent during childhood (American Association on Intellectual and Developmental Disabilities, 2010).

The institutions that separated individuals with IDD from the general population through a form of incarceration were supported by local communities at the time and represented cultural views of IDD. Disability advocates point to this history of institutionalization of individuals with IDD to counter the benefits purported by organizations that formerly operated sheltered workshops employing those with IDD at below minimum wage. Some advocates view the employment of individuals with IDD in non-profit SE and CSEs being a continuity of historic institutionalization, especially when simultaneously self-employed individuals with IDD are not provided similar community supports (Brennan-Krohn, 2016; Renko et al., 2016).

The institutionalization of individuals also continues in different forms, for example, individuals with IDD are overrepresented in Canadian prisons (Crocker, Côté, Toupin, & St. Onge, 2007). In the United States, these individuals are more likely to be arrested than those without disabilities (McCauley, 2017). A study of adults in Ontario with ID revealed that police respond more often to these individuals with ID facing a crisis than for individuals without ID facing a crisis (Lunsky, Raina, & Jones, 2012).

Culture and Employment of individuals with IDD

In North America, a high level of value is placed on employment and work. Monetary salaries are the material proxy for the value of labor, and an individual with IDD who is unemployed is seen as less valuable than one who is employed. IDD individuals with IDD employed part time (and earn less than) full-time employees are seen, in this system, as less productive and perhaps less valuable to the economy.

The rate of production by individuals is an additional part of the Neoliberal economic value hierarchy. For example, those who take longer than the norm to do the same work may be seen as less valuable when some individuals with IDD require modifications to the rate of task completion as a work accommodation.

The focus in the current discussion is on the need for employment for individuals with IDD, examined through the lens of Critical Disability Studies. Thus, the need for employment of individuals with IDD can be approached from three somewhat different culturally mediated directions. Organizations that have historically used individuals with IDD as their primary workforce, but did not pay them a market wage, have been described as sheltered workshops (Krupa et al., 2003).

Individuals and businesses purchasing goods or services from sheltered workshops perceived their efforts as charitable acts beneficial to the employees with IDD. Some of these organizations are not-for-profit SEs and, therefore, CSEs. Community support in the form of purchases of goods and services from organizations that employ individuals with IDD is an organization *mediated* form of community support. The sheltered workshop model has generally fallen out of favor as an employment solution for individuals with IDD in Ontario (Welsh, 2015).

A second model recognizes fairly paid employment in workplaces that integrate individuals with IDD with other individuals as a central mechanism for reducing the stigma of individuals with IDD (Wolfensberger, 2000). The model considers individuals with IDD as full- fledged employees recognized as valuable and contributing members of society. This approach is exemplified by organizations such as GC (Sengupta & Quarter, 2017) and Common Ground Co-operative (Owen et al., 2015b). It accepts the importance of market-based sales of goods and services, while simultaneously recognizing a need for workplace accommodations and support for individuals with IDD and typically are financially supported by government subsidies. This model is prevalent across Canada but is increasingly being contested by more Neoliberal models less dependent on government support.

The third approach views individuals with IDD simply as units of labor in a Neoliberal framework (Bates et al., 2017). Private-sector employment is valued over not-for-profit organization employment. Since most not-for-profit organizations employing individuals with IDD depend to some extent on government funding subsidies, they are seen as less desirable employers by those advocating for smaller governments, less government spending, and more individual responsibility.

Therefore, more Neoliberal governments place more emphasis on, and greater support for, employment of individuals with IDD in private-sector organizations than not-for-profit organizations. One outcome of this approach is that the community support element becomes more diluted and less direct since the employment of individuals with IDD is typically within larger corporations with the capacity to accommodate differing workplace needs.

In the case of not-for-profit organizations with explicit social missions, and often a majority of employees being individuals with IDD, community support from purchases of goods and services can be directed toward them. Where the organization is a large corporation employing only a few individuals with IDD within a large workforce, the ability of local communities to obtain direct support is diluted.

An emerging employment model is employment based on the ability to execute a specialized skill such as the not-for-profit Specialisterne, which specializes in finding employment for individuals on the Autism spectrum (Austin & Sonne, 2014). Since this is an emerging model, it is difficult to classify within other models described. It combines a mission and vision-driven social economy organization to find employment for individuals with IDD with employment primarily in large private-sector employers seeking specialized skills such as software testing and fraud detection. The jobs held in this model are limited to certain types of tasks, less strategic or creation-oriented, and more typically back-office administrative tasks.

But if the goal is fulfilling the potential of all individuals with IDD, further research and development is required. In all models, an unemployed IDD individual receiving social assistance and not being gainfully employed is viewed as an unproductive drain on government resources, whereas those performing paid work are considered productive and contributing citizens.

Critical Disability theory can be used to question the concept of employment itself as a barrier for individuals with IDD. Containing underlying Neoliberal theories of employment, Workfare was introduced in the Ontario Works Act of 1997 by a Conservative government that made employment a requirement to continue receiving social assistance. Recognizing the differential needs for employment, the Liberal government in Ontario operating under a more Socialist ideology, introduced Basic Income pilots in April 2017 (Government of Ontario, 2017). For IDD individuals who are unable to be employed under current economic conditions for a variety of reasons, a basic income unrelated to employment allows them a greater ability to participate as a citizen.

At least one largely successful experiment on basic income in Canada has been conducted in Manitoba, and this program was discontinued after a few years with a change of government (Simpson, Mason, & Godwin, 2017). The Conservative government elected in 2018 canceled the Basic Income Pilots in Ontario before long-term conclusive data could be drawn. From a Critical Disabilities framework, the basic income pilot demonstrates at least one approach that partially questioned the value of government assistance for individuals with disabilities, being tied to employment. In the context of the COVID-19 pandemic, a Guaranteed Basic Income at the national level in Canada is being considered as a solution to living with the long-term economic effects of the pandemic (Bryden, 2020).

Conclusion

A positive trend regarding people with IDD is the gradual changing of cultural attitudes toward accepting IDD as a form of diversity, specifically neurodiversity. At the same time, statistics show failing outcomes for these individuals in terms of education, employment, and healthcare. SEs employing this group are often a response to institutional failures in education systems, private-sector employment, or the implementation of government policy. Government policy in Canada involving this group has shifted away from CSEs toward private-sector employment, specifically employment in large private-sector companies not typically considered community-supported organizations.

In the province of Ontario, this shift includes closing sheltered workshops because government funding was eliminated. Institutions failing to meet their needs in the education sector where they can learn employment and citizenship skills, in the private sector with a majority of employment opportunities, and in the provision of social services funded by the government have left CSEs, especially not-for-profit SEs, as organizations of last resort.

SEs employing IDD individuals are often in the difficult position of developing employment skills not obtained through educational institutions, providing employment supports not typically provided by private-sector employers, and delivering other services that are not available from government agencies.

Last, but not least, SEs receive public funding and support for their social mission, while simultaneously the self-employed or those who run their own business are not provided similar support. In other words, community support for individuals with IDD is mediated through both organizational form and leadership. Critical Disability Studies, which document the cultural roots of the binary classifications of disabled and non-disabled individuals, provide a lens to question interactions between the community of individuals with IDD and the local geographical communities that support community enterprises. This lens questions many assumptions and beliefs, especially long-term cultural beliefs that need to change to recognize or view individuals with IDD as leaders, as employers, as self-employed entrepreneurs who deserve additional support from local communities. Fortunately, culture is not static, and changes over time, and cultural views have been changing over time.

Financial Impact of COVID-19 on Non-Profit SEs Employing Individuals with IDD

This chapter was mostly researched and written before COVID-19 became a global pandemic. The COVID-19 pandemic has two different types of impacts on the operation of non-profit SEs employing individuals with IDD. The first is that the commercial revenue generating activities ceased when the economy was shut down. Although this did mean that many individuals with IDD became unemployed, the government of Canada had implemented a fiscal policy that provided all individuals unemployed due to COVID-19 with a Canada Emergency Response Benefit along with other temporary measures that protected individuals from consequences such as bankruptcy or evictions.

This was important since a vast majority of non-profit SEs that employed individuals with IDD are physical workplaces where the work activities completed do not allow for social distancing and other practices to minimize COVID-19 outbreaks. GC, for example, an organization in the Prescott Russell region of Eastern Ontario that manages nine enterprises, operates a recycling facility where recyclable items are manually sorted by hand (Sengupta & Quarter, 2017). Common Ground Co-operative, on the other hand, engages individuals with IDD as associates who make and deliver food services, again requiring working in close quarters.

Second, with the commercial revenue generating activities of these organizations coming to a standstill, the organizations themselves were kept afloat by continuing government financial transfers from different levels of government. Remembering that all non-profit SEs that employ individuals with IDD in Ontario are dependent on government funding at some level, this was a continuation of government policy rather than a change of government policy.

At the same time, the temporary changes in government policy in financially supporting individuals have kept the communities of employees at these organizations cohesive, since they did not have to move out of their homes or change employers. In the case of GC and Common Ground Cooperative, both organizations remain affiliated with charitable organizations that incubated them and continue to be affiliated with them. The charitable organizations affiliated with the non-profit SEs continue to provide social services required by individuals with IDD that are outside the scope of employment.

Once again, in Canada, charities are supported more substantially by government than by private foundations. Therefore, in the context of the COVID-19 pandemic, the community of employees at each non-profit SE employing individuals with IDD has maintained some level of community cohesiveness through a combination of government funding at individual and organizational levels, and existing social economy organizational infrastructure.

Significantly, during the COVID-19 pandemic, there has been no identifiable trend in geographically local communities increasing support for non-profit SEs that employed individuals with IDD. In fact, individuals with disabilities have passionately argued that the experience has been the opposite of much required community support, resulting in higher case rates and deaths during the COVID-19 pandemic in facilities housing individuals with IDD (DeClerq, 2020). This indicates that the long-term cultural view of people with disabilities remains a strong determining factor not only in terms of possibilities for employment but also the right to life itself.

References

Albrecht, G. L. (1992). *The disability business: Rehabilitation in America*. Newbury Park, CA: Sage Publications.

American Association on Intellectual and Developmental Disabilities. (2010). *Intellectual disability: Definition, classification, and systems of supports*. Washington, DC: American Association on Intellectual and Developmental Disabilities.

Angus Reid. (2015). Disability and accessibility: Canadians see significant room for improvement in communities where they live. Retrieved from http://angusreid.org/rhf-accessibility/
Austin, R. D., & Sonne, T. (2014). The dandelion principle: Redesigning work for the innovation economy. *MIT Sloan Management Review*, 55(4), 67–72.
Bates, K., Goodley, D., & Runswick-Cole, K. (2017). Precarious lives and resistant possibilities: The labor of people with learning disabilities in times of austerity. *Disability & Society*, 32(2), 160–175.
Brennan-Krohn, Z. (2016). Employment for people with disabilities: A role for anti-subordination. *Harvard CR-CLL Review*, 51, 239.
Broberg, M. (2011). Expectations of and reactions to disability and normality experienced by parents of children with intellectual disability in Sweden. *Child: Care, Health and Development*, 37(3), 410–417. https://doi.org/10.1111/j.1365-2214.2010.01198.x
Bryden, J. (2020). Guaranteed basic income tops policy priorities for Liberal caucus at upcoming convention. CBC. Retrieved from https://www.cbc.ca/news/politics/guaranteed-basic-income-priorities-liberals-1.5721943
Caldwell, K., Harris, S. P., & Renko, M. (2012). The potential of social entrepreneurship: Conceptual tools for applying citizenship theory to policy and practice. *Intellectual and Developmental Disabilities*, 50(6), 505–518.
Caldwell, K., Harris, S. P., & Renko, M. (2016). Social entrepreneurs with disabilities: Exploring motivational and attitudinal factors. *Canadian Journal of Disability Studies*, 5(1), 211–244.
Canadian Mental Health Association. (2005). *Consumer/survivor initiatives: Impact, outcomes & effectiveness*. Retrieved from https://ontario.cmha.ca/documents/consumer survivor-initiatives-impact-outcomes-and-effectiveness/
Carter, E. W., Austin, D., & Trainor, A. A. (2012). Predictors of post-school employment outcomes for young adults with severe disabilities. *Journal of Disability Policy Studies*, 23(1), 50–63.
Chan, A. N. W. (2015). Social support for improved work integration: Perspectives from Canadian social purpose enterprises. *Social Enterprise Journal*, 11(1), 47–68.
Chan, A., Ryan, S., & Quarter, J. (2017). Supported social enterprise: A modified social welfare organization. *Nonprofit and Voluntary Sector Quarterly*, 46(2), 261–279.
Colker, R. (2006). Anti-subordination above all: A disability perspective. *Notre Dame Law Review*, 82, 1415.
Corbiere, M., & Lecomte, T. (2009). Vocational services offered to people with severe mental illness. *Journal of Mental Health*, 18(1), 38–50.
Crocker, A. G., Côté, G., Toupin, J., & St. Onge, B. (2007). Rate and characteristics of men with an intellectual disability in pre-trial detention. *Journal of Intellectual and Developmental Disability*, 32(2), 143–152.
Daniels, A., & Jeans, A. (2009). Integrated approaches to enabling the most vulnerable to participate in markets. *Enterprise Development and Microfinance*, 20(2), 139–157.
DeClerq, K. (2020). Sixth death reported at facility for vulnerable adults dealing with major COVID-19 outbreak. CTV News. Retrieved from https://toronto.ctvnews.ca/sixth-death-reported-at-facility-for-vulnerable-adults-dealing-with-major-covid-19-outbreak-1.4914834
Enterprising Non-Profits. (2014). *Success themes in supportive employment: How social enterprise connects people with jobs and jobs with people*. Vancouver, BC.
Fairbairn, B. (2009). *A rose by any name: The thorny question of social economy discourse in Canada*. Victoria: Canadian Social Economy Hub.
Goodley, D. (2017). *Disability studies: An interdisciplinary introduction*. Thousand Oaks, CA: Sage Publishing.

Government of Canada. (1982). Canadian charter of rights and freedoms. Retrieved from http://laws-lois.justice.gc.ca/eng/Const/page-15.html

Government of Ontario. (2016a). Impact: A social enterprise strategy for Ontario. Retrieved from https://www.ontario.ca/page/impact-social-enterprise-strategy-ontario

Government of Ontario. (2016b). Ontario's social enterprise strategy 2016–2021. Retrieved from https://www.ontario.ca/page/ontarios-social-enterprise-strategy-2016-2021

Government of Ontario. (2017). *Ontario's basic income pilot: Studying the impact of basic income*. Retrieved from https://www.ontario.ca/page/ontario-basic-income-pilot

Government of Ontario. (2019). Services and supports to promote the social inclusion of persons with Developmental Disabilities Act. Retrieved from https://www.ontario.ca/laws/statute/08s14

Graefe, P. (2006). Social economy policies as flanking for neoliberalism: Transnational policy solutions, emergent contradictions, local alternatives. *Policy and Society*, 25(3), 69–86.

Huang, J., Guo, B., & Bricout, J. C. (2009). From concentration to dispersion: The shift in policy approach to disability employment in China. *Journal of Disability Policy Studies*, 20(1), 46–54.

Ingstad, B., & Whyte, S. R. (1995). *Disability and culture*. Berkeley: University of California Press.

Institute for Research and Development on Inclusion and Society. (2011). *The employment of people with intellectual disabilities in Canada: A statistical profile*. Toronto: Cameron Crawford.

Koning, P., & Heinrich, C. J. (2010). Cream-skimming, parking and other intended and unintended effects of performance-based contracting in social welfare services, IZA Discussion Papers, No. 4801. IZA Institute for Labor Economics. Retrieved from https://www.iza.org/de/publications/dp/4801/cream-skimming-parking-and-other-intended-and-unintended-effects-of-performance-based-contracting-in-social-welfare-services

Krupa, T., Lagarde, M., & Carmichael, K. (2003). Transforming sheltered workshops into affirmative businesses: An outcome evaluation. *Psychiatric Rehabilitation Journal*, 26(4), 359.

Lemon, C., & Lemon, J. (2003). Community-based cooperative ventures for adults with intellectual disabilities. *The Canadian Geographer/Le Géographe canadien*, 47(4), 414–428.

Lunsky, Y., Raina, P., & Jones, J. (2012). Relationship between prior legal involvement and current crisis for adults with intellectual disability. *Journal of Intellectual and Developmental Disability*, 37(2), 163–168.

Mazzei, M. (2017). Understanding difference: The importance of 'place' in the shaping of local social economies. *VOLUNTAS: International Journal of Voluntary and Nonprofit Organizations*, 28(6), 2763–2784.

McCauley, E. J. (2017). The cumulative probability of arrest by age 28 years in the United States by disability status, race/ethnicity, and gender. *American Journal of Public Health*, 107(12), 1977–1981.

Mckenzie, J. A. (2013). Models of intellectual disability: Towards a perspective of (poss)ability. *Journal of Intellectual Disability Research*, 57(4), 370–379. https://doi.org/10.1111/j.1365-2788.2012.01547.x

Ontario Independent Facilitation Network. (2017). Ontario Independent Facilitation Network Home Page. Retrieved from http://www.oifn.ca/

Ontario Ministry of Community and Social Services. (2017). Passport program. http://www.mcss.gov.on.ca/en/mcss/programs/developmental/servicesupport/passport.aspx. Retrieved November 15, 2017.

Ontario Ombudsman. (2016). Investigation onto the Ministry of Community and social services' response to situations of crisis involving adults with developmental disabilities. Retrieved from https://www.ombudsman.on.ca/resources/reports-and-case-summaries/reports-on-investigations/2016/nowhere-to-turn

Owen, F., Li, J., Whittingham, L., Hope, J., Bishop, C., Readhead, A., & Mook, L. (2015b). Social return on investment of an innovative employment option for persons with developmental disabilities. *Nonprofit Management and Leadership*, 26(2), 209–228.

Owen, F., Readhead, A., Bishop, C., Hope, J., & Campbell, J. (2015a). Common ground co-operative: Supporting employment options. In J. Quarter, S. Ryan & A. Chan (Eds.), *Social purpose enterprises: Case studies in doing business differently* (pp. 27–51). Toronto: University of Toronto Press.

Parker Harris, S., Caldwell, K., & Renko, M. (2014). Entrepreneurship by any other name: Self-sufficiency versus innovation. *Journal of Social Work in Disability & Rehabilitation*, 13(4), 317–349.

Pedlar, A., & Hutchison, P. (2000). Restructuring human services in Canada: Commodification of disability. *Disability & Society*, 15(4), 637–651.

Quarter, J., Mook, L., & Armstrong, A. (2017). *Understanding the social economy: A Canadian perspective*. 2nd Edition. Toronto: University of Toronto Press.

Reid, L, Bennett, S., Specht, J., White, R., Somma, M., Li, X., Lattanzio, R., Gavan, K., Kyle, G., Porter, G., & Patel, A. (2018). If inclusion means everyone, why not me? ARCH Disability Law Centre, Canadian Research Centre on Inclusive Education, Community Living Ontario, University of Western Ontario, Brock University, Brockville and District Association for Community Involvement and Inclusive Education Canada. Retrieved from https://communitylivingontario.ca/en/if-inclusion-means-everyone-why-not-me/

Renko, M., Parker Harris, S., & Caldwell, K. (2016). Entrepreneurial entry by people with disabilities. *International Small Business Journal*, 34(5), 555–578.

Santos, F. (2012). A positive theory of social entrepreneurship. *Journal of Business Ethics*, 111(3), 335–351.

Schroeder, C. S., & Schroeder, S. R. (1990). The future of children is now. *Journal of Autism and Developmental Disorders*, 20(3), 367–378.

Secker, J., Dass, S., & Grove, B. (2003). Developing social firms in the UK: A contribution to identifying good practice. *Disability & Society*, 18(5), 659–674.

Sengupta, U., & Quarter, J. (2017). Groupe convex: Social Enterprize case study. Retrieved from https://tricofoundation.ca/groupe-convex-social-enterprize-case-study/

Simpson, W., Mason, G., & Godwin, R. (2017). The Manitoba basic annual income experiment: Lessons learned 40 years later. *Canadian Public Policy*, 43(1), 85–104. University of Toronto Press. Retrieved from Project MUSE database.

Statistics Canada. (2014). *Insights on Canadian society: Persons with disabilities and employment*. (Catalogue no. 75–006-X, ISSN 2291–0859). Ministry of Industry, Author: Martin Turcotte.

Statistics Canada. (2015). Canadian survey on disability 2012: Developmental disabilities among Canadians age 15 years and older, 2012. (Catalogue No 89–654-X2015003). Ottawa: Minister of Industry.

Tan, B. L. (2009). Hybrid transitional-supported employment using social enterprise: A retrospective study. *Psychiatric Rehabilitation Journal*, 33(1), 53.

Wafer, M. (2017, March 25). Employees with disabilities can have a positive impact on profitability. Globe and Mail. Retrieved from https://www.theglobeandmail.com/report-on-business/rob-commentary/employees-with-disabilities-can-have-a-positive-impact-on-profitability/article28540451/

Walzer, N., & Sandoval, J. (2016). *Emergence and growth of community supported enterprises.* Retrieved from https://www.cgs.niu.edu/Reports/Emergence-and-Growth-of-Community-Supported-Enterprises.pdf

Warner, R., & Mandiberg, J. (2006). An update on affirmative businesses or social firms for people with mental illness. *Psychiatric Services*, 57(10), 1488–1492.

Welsh, M. (2015, November 29). Ontario's sheltered workshops to close forever. Toronto Star. Retrieved from https://www.thestar.com/news/canada/2015/11/29/ontarios-sheltered-workshops-to-close-forever.html

Williams, A., Fossey, E., & Harvey, C. (2012). Social firms: Sustainable employment for people with mental illness. *Work*, 43(1), 53–62.

Wolfensberger, W. (2000). A brief overview of social role valorization. *Mental Retardation*, 38(2), 105–123.

Zwicker, J., Zaresani, A., & Emery, J. H. (2017). Describing heterogeneity of unmet needs among adults with a developmental disability: An examination of the 2012 Canadian survey on disability. *Research in Developmental Disabilities*, 65, 1–11.

11

APPLICATIONS OF CSE PRINCIPLES

Norman Walzer and Sean Park

Introduction

Community Supported Enterprises (CSEs), in whatever form, can finance business and social venture in changing times. They operate on the premise that local investment in a community is essential to its future prosperity, as documented by Shuman (Chapter 2). The investments are more than financial and emphasize buying local and continued patronage of stores as well as committing time and other resources to a broad range of other local initiatives.

CSEs and other types of community-owned businesses involve residents and interested parties investing usually relatively small amounts of money and/or time in a venture addressing an important local issue. These investments are long term since many projects may take years to complete. CSEs have often been used to retain or reopen a local source of supplies including grocery stores or cafés as in England, Germany, and Wales described by McCusker (Chapter 4). In these initiatives, the businesses are organized and managed to keep them as nearly self-sustaining as possible. These operations often involve volunteer efforts to reduce the operating costs.

Uses of CSE financing approaches extend to many other types of services such as in Italy and Canada where they supplement public-sector financing lost for various reasons. These partnerships offer other attractions such as gaining acceptance for public programs in the community and providing opportunities to help targeted populations find employment in local businesses.

Perhaps, more important than differences among CSE applications are the recognized community development concepts used in new settings. Of special relevance in this regard is the work by Sohney and Hegemann (Chapter 5) with German villages. The analyses show that interactions among the Community Capitals are more important than one specific Capital, for example, Social Capital, an often discussed topic in community development.

Subsequent discussions also recognize other local considerations important in selecting specific projects and implementation approaches. The discussion then applies these principles in examining several projects in the Midwest, especially rural Illinois, where groups in small communities have rallied local resources and used some of the concepts described. Finally, several practical steps that interested readers can take to launch a CSE in their community are discussed based on materials in Walzer (2019; Walzer & Sandoval, 2016). The intent is to help readers incorporate the findings from the international comparisons into local initiatives and applications.

Common Principles

An element running through successful ventures described in this volume is a broad recognition within the community of a need for local action to address a concern. As noted previously, the issues can involve retaining a local source of supplies such as groceries, preserve local heritage, or deliver essential public services during times of eroding budgets. Rallying support for a project can be difficult, but once the need was recognized and accepted, residents organized around a specific approach(es) by investing time and money in the effort.

Local acceptance of a need to act can be stimulated in many ways depending on specific circumstances. In the case of private services such as retaining a grocery store, the recognition is almost immediate when residents realize that they must travel long distances to obtain basic supplies. This situation is a strong motivation to residents of all ages whether in England, Germany, Wales, Kansas, or Illinois. While these stores provide access to essential goods, they also are often a local gathering place that builds camaraderie within the community.

The need for local investment may be less obvious in the case of efforts to serve residents with learning disabilities (Canada) or other public services (Italy). Those instances may require dedicated and concerted efforts to gain local support for the approaches selected to address specific issues or concerns. The news media can be an important tool to inform residents about the concerns and rally support for this investment.

Perhaps equally important to successful outcomes are the organizations and tools available to address the issues. In Italy, cooperatives were used, while in Canada, nonprofit social enterprises provided the services with support from private businesses to employ populations that needed special services. While cooperatives may be the most often used legal form, other structures such as nonprofits, Limited Liability Corporations (LLCs), and cooperatives also have succeeded (Walzer, 2019).

Whichever legal options are available, the recognition of a pending issue or concern must translate into broad-based acceptance by residents that addressing it is a community-wide issue that can be remedied with selected approaches. In many ways, gaining this commitment is a communication issue that motivates various groups with both a vested interest and something worthwhile to contribute. Examples of ways in which small rural communities in Illinois managed this issue are discussed next.

Recognizing a Need to Act

Throughout the rural United States, small rural communities are facing a loss of traditional grocery stores with local markets, including departments dedicated to meat, produce, dairy, deli, frozen, and grocery being replaced by "dollar stores."[1] This shift in merchandising has to do with economics set in place decades ago. As food shopping patterns switched to both more processed food and eating produce available year-round, the production of food became centralized in distant locations with extended growing seasons. The ability to produce and ship in mass quantities to capture economies of scale had the effect of requiring food to be shipped hundreds of miles to reach communities that often pride themselves on their farming heritage.

A complex distribution system including production, packaging, trucking, and logistics caused companies involved in warehousing and retail sales to face a feasibility decision. Does it make sense to incur these costs to sell food in relatively small communities with limited markets? Typically, in the case of fresh food, the answer is no. Fresh food (i.e., produce, meat, delicatessen items, and some dairy) requires refrigerated shipping and storage. It has a limited lifespan during storage and often incurs labor costs to properly prepare and display at the retail level.

Dollar stores, on the other hand, rely on bulk storage and shipping of processed foods to sell products at a discounted price based on economies of scale beyond the financial capabilities of small local grocers. The pressure to compete drives out small grocers, leaving the dollar stores and the community losing its only retail outlet for fresh produce, meat, and deli items. This situation can place a small town or neighborhood in what is sometimes called a "Food Swamp," with access to heavily processed food but very limited access to healthy, whole foods. Residents can still buy snacks and soft drinks at a gas station convenience store or a dollar store but cannot buy fresh vegetables even in a farming community.

Rural communities that face this challenge typically are small with fewer than 3,000 residents, but specific community demographics do not seem to make a significant difference. What is demographically consistent is a small population with geographic isolation of at least 10–15 miles, and up to 100 miles, from the nearest food center. Demographic projections suggest that this pattern will be even more important in the future with expected population declines.

While the average household income in affected communities ranges from upper middle to very low income, rural food swamps have a unique income distribution that affects their ability to raise capital for community projects. Unlike urban food deserts or food swamps where household income levels are most often uniformly low, rural communities have a mix of household incomes, so that 20% or more may be below the poverty line while other residents are in the national upper-middle income levels. These residents share community services, healthcare, and shopping.

The demographics in small towns mean that community members with both the disposable income and a vested interest in the community's development can be tapped for CSE funding. In fact, the school system is often an area where community Social Capital is developed across income levels as students participate together in activities such as marching band, sports, and academic competitions. While the students build Bonding Social Capital from these activities, the parents build Bridging Social Capital as well.

When a vital community service is suddenly lost, such as access to healthy food, these community ties often come into play in discussions about how to address the situation. The higher the level of Social Capital, the more likely these conversations are to occur but as was pointed out in the analyses of German villages, the interaction among capitals is especially important. Some of these capitals may be eroding in small towns. This informal level of information sharing, which might be called a "Social Capital Communications Network," extends from school events to civic groups and religious organizations. Higher levels of Social Capital allow more residents to engage in discussions about ways to address a community need. This process is enhanced many times over by the use of Social Media into discussions in these community groups.

While these communities have residents with the financial wherewithal, there is a delicate balance between families with disposable income and those without which can pose issues in fundraising for CSEs. Those who can invest may wish to do it quietly and not flaunt their good fortune. To maintain the Social Capital needed for CSEs, organizers must exercise caution not to alienate those residents unable to invest since a successful CSE requires participation by as many residents as possible.

Winchester, Illinois (pop. 1,700) illustrates this Social Capital in action. In 2016, its only grocery store closed after a year-long competition with the local dollar store (https://www.facebook.com/great.scott.market/). Lack of food access, along with the loss of civic pride from the closing of the last grocer in the county, prompted the community to act. In the fall of 2017, a local group organized a community meeting with the Illinois Institute for Rural Affairs (IIRA) to discuss the idea of a CSE grocery store to replace the lost services. Eighty adults from a town of only 1,700 attended an initial meeting that as a percentage of population is remarkable. This level of commitment enabled the community to replace the original store with a smaller, fresh food-focused retail store that specialized in local products.

While the IIRA could provide the technical services in the form of enhanced business models, community organization strategies, and strategic planning, none of them would have been useful without such a strong sense of community to underpin the effort. Residents participated in rehabbing the building, provided materials and labor, and were active in many other ways to promote the project. Over time, the importance of this engagement was reinforced as other communities watched Winchester's success and tried to replicate it. The level of community involvement varies, but it is directly correlated with the success of the CSE.

Importance of a Local Champion

A second common ingredient is a local person(s) or group that serves as a "local champion" for the venture. These people are not necessarily elected officials but must be accepted by residents or be in a position to move the project ahead. Past experiences with similar ventures or long-standing successes in the community may have helped them gain the respect or reputational leadership needed to succeed in these endeavors. They sometimes surface because of interest in a specific project or a direct need for the service provided.

Alternatively, they may be residents with resources available including time to assist with the project or want to participate in a community-wide initiative. The projects may be also championed by an agency seeking to expand its local influence and/or supplement its operating budget by adding a financially sustainable venture to support a social mission in the area served. These agencies then provide the needed personnel or financial resources to move the project ahead.

The importance of Bonding and Bridging capitals in these efforts should be emphasized. Not all residents in a community have equal experiences with holding leadership positions. They may not have been engaged in traditional organizations that led these types of efforts in the past. Instead, it may be necessary to reach out to bring them into the process. Thus, it is important to build strong relationships with residents who have been active in past efforts (Bonding), but equally important is to attract new participants (Bridging). If, and when, they become involved, they must receive back-up support to minimize the chances of failure (Bonding). Sohney and Hegemann (Chapter 5) addressed these issues in more detail previously. The broader the base of local support and acceptance, the more likely the desired outcomes are to succeed as noted in Procter (Chapter 6).

Winchester, Illinois, described previously, had two such champions both of whom had grown up in the Winchester area. As often happens in small rural towns, high school graduates pursue college as an avenue to broaden their horizons. Many do not return to their communities after graduation because of limited professional job opportunities. Fortunately, this was not the case in Winchester, and the CSE project benefited from two locally grown champions bringing their education and skills back to the community. The first was a banker, specializing in agricultural lending since he was raised in a large farm family with strong ties to the community. The second was in a family with a legal background, and after completing law school, he returned to Winchester to follow in the family tradition and became the city attorney.

Both men with young families were deeply affected by the inability to buy healthy food for their children in the hometown where they had been raised.

They also brought substantial skills in financial and legal issues that they used to advance the CSE project. Their knowledge of community history, positions of respect, and the bonds built during their childhood allowed them to take leadership roles in guiding development of the CSE in its crucial formation stages.

A similar project in the town of Mt. Pulaski also benefited from two champions – one from the community and the other was a recent transplant (https://marketonthehill.com/contact). Both farmed in the area, were struck by the lack of a community grocery store, and felt that a community-led grocery store in Mt. Pulaski would be a source of civic pride.

This leadership coincided with a development windfall for the community. A wind energy company had recently constructed a wind farm in the county with opposition by many residents. In response, the energy company provided funds to be used for community improvements. It is important to note that the capital raised for the Mt. Pulaski grocery store did not come from the wind energy company itself. Rather, the funds provided for economic development started a cascade of improvements in the community including remodeling in the downtown square. The added tax base allowed construction of a new school and other improvements.

The local champions built on this newly generated momentum to expand the Social Capital and energize the community. The CSE planning group organized a local food dinner and fundraiser to be held the night before the annual fall festival began in the town. The outdoor dinner was attended by nearly 100 residents from throughout the county and raised more than $50,000 in pledges in one evening. While the IIRA was on hand to explain the details of the future grocery store's business plan, the entire event was organized and produced by community residents and was led by these two project champions.

Selecting an Organization Legal Structure

The appropriate business organizational format is important in most cases because each legal structure appeals to different groups of investors or may be more compatible with local customs, experiences, and regulations. Cooperatives have been used for long periods of time. If they currently exist, attaching a new venture or activity to an ongoing cooperative movement, such as in Italy (Bianchi, Chapter 7), may be most convenient and expeditious. This business format also makes members part-owners of the venture giving a vested interest and strong motivation to continue purchases.

At the same time, however, forming a CSE as a nonprofit may offer tax-savings and reduce operating costs if a lower cost of capital is obtained. It may also simplify management activities when fewer investors are involved in the process. There are a variety of other formats available for a nonprofit as noted in Phillips, Siefert, and Walzer (Chapter 3). Social Benefit Corporations, when feasible, are a way to link desired social purposes directly to the venture as is the case in Vermont (USA).

In other cases, a LLC or its comparable legal format in other countries may be beneficial when it reduces the number of investors and provides a more focused leadership for the venture. Variations of this business format are tied to size of business, social motives, or other characteristics. The main point is that groups have several choices in organizing and managing a CSE-financed venture.

Each type of legal business structure has strengths and weaknesses so it must be weighed carefully. Its suitability is usually specific to the situation and social reasons for choosing one governing structure over another are also important. As mentioned earlier, the Social Capital in a community is crucial to the success of a CSE, and organizational structure can reinforce it and vice versa.

The use of cooperatives in the U.S. Midwest offers an interesting perspective. The northern states of Minnesota and Wisconsin have a long history with cooperatives and thus have some of the most progressive laws for cooperative businesses. The idea of a CSE being a cooperative is not at all foreign in these states and others with previous experiences. The same is not true in all states, however.

Communities in states south of Minnesota and Wisconsin sometimes are less predisposed to the abstract concept of cooperatives. One could speculate that rural communities tend to lean conservative in the political sense anyway, and this tendency increases as one moves geographically south into Illinois, Iowa, Missouri, and Indiana. In these areas, cooperatives are sometimes associated with a liberal or even Socialist ideal that is ironic in that these communities are surrounded by cooperatives in the forms of agricultural co-ops, electric co-ops, educational co-ops, water district co-ops, and credit unions. However, the agencies are long-standing entities, and the community-controlled, cooperative aspect is sometimes forgotten.

The CSE projects in both Winchester and Mt. Pulaski, Illinois deliberately chose not to use the term "cooperative" in the business name but use the co-op model as a legal entity and management style. In both cases, project leaders felt that a "food cooperative" would not be well received by the community, or it might seem like a charity rather than a business.

Thus, a community developer must consider social and political norms when designing a potential CSE to maximize the use of available Social Capital. Communities with previous successes with nonprofits or investment companies will have that frame of reference and be more inclined to follow a specific model. And, provided that there are no overriding financial reasons to choose one structure over another, it makes sense to capitalize on the momentum and use a structure with which a community is comfortable.

Also worth noting is that although a CSE might choose a specific legal structure for business reasons, its management style is directed by the bylaws of a nonprofit, LLC, Corporation, or Cooperative. In other words, if a LLC legal structure makes financial sense, it may be possible to incorporate elements of cooperative governance within the bylaws of the LLC such as "one member one vote" or the distribution of profits based upon participation. Each situation is unique to the community at that point in time.

Financing the Venture

The ways in which the business or venture is financed are also important in launching a successful CSE. In the case of providing local supplies, such as a grocery or general store, the financing includes obtaining a building and inventory. Procter (Chapter 6) describes the process used in Kansas which, after trying several approaches, led to a municipal government owning and operating the grocery store. While this specific approach is relatively uncommon, it illustrates how both the public and private sectors can collaborate on a community project. In some ways, this is a direct application of the fourth-sector approach described by Brauer (Chapter 9).

Specific implementation approaches used are determined to a significant extent by resources available. McCusker (Chapter 4) noted the roles played by the financial support and programs available in England, Scotland, and Wales. One finding was that the broad-based local support and engagement are more important than external grants, which, nevertheless, were important local stimuli in some instances. The internal commitment to the project in many ways determines how it can and will be financed.

In assembling the financing scheme for al CSE, the importance of funding in grants and subsidized loans from central agencies varies, but certainly, they are important factors to consider. Perhaps, more important in many cases, though, is the ability to leverage the financial investments by residents against loans from a local financial institution. Likewise, at least in the US, local governments can use economic development tools to help support CSE types of ventures. This broad-based community support can be a deciding factor determining whether a local venture will succeed. However, as discussions throughout this volume make clear, the types of support vary by country and specific locations depending on local regulations and commitment to these types of initiatives.

The two grocery stores described above, Winchester and Mt. Pulaski, Illinois, respectively, were legally established as cooperatives. In the US, each state has a unique set of cooperative laws that differ substantially. In general, they have the benefit of being able to add an unlimited number of members, each of whom can pay membership fees. They also offer the benefit of being able to sell shares of the CSE without major oversight from local Securities and Exchange committees. While specific cooperative regulations and rules govern the sale of shares, the streamlined legal issues mean fewer resources expended in terms of legal fees, and other costs (Shuman, Chapter 2).

And, because of the unique way that profits are disbursed in cooperatives, each member has an incentive to participate financially. Unlike a corporation, profits in a cooperative are disbursed based on patronage or use of the cooperative by members. In the case of cooperative grocery stores, the more a member spends during the year, the more s/he receives of the profits made that year.

In contrast, the option to operate as a nonprofit can allow a CSE access to grant funds not available to other legal entities. Many grants are open only to nonprofit groups because of tax benefits that organizations receive. In a nonprofit structure, a CSE no longer has members, but now has donors. This difference can be important since the idea of a charity is different than a business to many people. As a donor, community members do not benefit directly from the financial success of the CSE as do member/owners of a for-profit CSE.

And, if a for-profit CSE should fail, an opportunity exists to sell assets and make local investors whole. Legally, if a nonprofit organization fails, the assets must be transferred to another nonprofit, and any local investment is lost. Some for-profit businesses work around the grant issue by working with local community foundations. The foundation applies for the grant in the name of the CSE and then receives and disburses the grant funds while taking a small percentage for administrative fees. The grantor receives the tax benefits, the foundation receives operating income from administrative services, and the CSE receives the bulk of the grant funds. Other traditional business models can be used as well.

The community of Toulon, Illinois used a combination of sole proprietorships and LLCs to fund a local grocery store (https://www.facebook.com/toulonmarket/). In the first iteration, the Toulon grocery store was funded by Stark County Ventures, LLC, a local investors group. This group regularly invests in the community through various projects agreed upon by the board of directors. In the case of the grocery store, they constructed and outfitted the entire store that was then run by outside contractors. However, in 2018, the last in a string of contractors found it unprofitable to operate the facility and closed leaving the town without a store.

At that point, Stark County Ventures LLC contacted the IIRA to explore alternatives. The IIRA presented a business concept that included a smaller facility, better product mix, and lower overhead. It then served as an "expert witness" at a local city council meeting in which Stark County Ventures requested Tax Incremental Financing funds to try the new business concept. The City of Toulon allocated $127,000 to remodel a downtown building, making the CSE grocery store a collaboration between local government, a community investment LLC, and a sole proprietor operating the business on a daily basis.

Whether the CSE is a grocery store, daycare, or another business, sound management practices will determine its success. Often, the question of how a business can be run with so many people providing input comes up during the planning stage. This might seem like a fair question, but almost all large companies rely on input from more than one source. Careful planning is key, especially during the initial development stages.

One often-used management structure in CSEs, regardless of legal designation, is a cooperative management approach. That choice is popular because it has checks and balances in the decision-making process so that no person interested in participating is left out, which also enhances Social Capital. In the cooperative management structure, a rotating board is elected by the entire group involved in the project. Board members volunteer to serve and are usually not compensated for their time. This board then hires a qualified manager who manages day-to-day issues and reports to the board monthly with larger issues handled by the board of directors. The board reports to the full membership on an annual basis, and on major issues such as a business expansion, are decided by group vote like in a stockholders meeting.

Finding a qualified manager for a CSE can be difficult partly due to the small size of operations. The skillset needed can be hard to find and may require more compensation than the CSE can afford. With the CSE grocery in Toulon, the management expertise was provided by the sole proprietor leasing the facility. In both the Winchester and Mt. Pulaski CSEs, management was locally sourced and trained specifically for that store. In the Winchester example, apparently, the manager was hired based mainly on personality and trustworthiness. The person then received training and technical assistance regarding business management.

Following the example in Winchester, the CSE in Mt. Pulaski contacted the IIRA for management training before hiring a general manager. Many other organizations provide suitable management training as well. The US Small Business Administration offers both a SCORE program in which retired business professionals provide free mentoring to businesses. The Small Business Development Centers (SBDCs) hire business professionals to consult with entrepreneurs and assist in business starts. Both can be valuable assets throughout the creation of a CSE including management training. Many local colleges and university agencies also have programs that can assist in area business development.

So, what are the results of these CSE grocery stores? In the cases of Winchester and Mt. Pulaski, both communities had lost a long-standing grocery store. And, because the economic conditions that closed those stores persist, attempts to encourage a developer to open a new store did not succeed. Adverse economic factors included decrease in rural populations, aging facilities of existing rural grocery stores, ease of travel that encourage community members to shop in larger cities, increasing age of existing store owners, and the changing shopping habits of consumers that existing store owners may not understand and/or lack the capital to make changes to meet those new shopping habits. And this same situation is happening in many small rural communities.

In some respect, it is fair to say that if there were significant profits to be made in the grocery market, entrepreneurs would move in on their own and a CSE would not be necessary. But that is exactly the point of the CSE – it fills a need that market actions do not. In the case of these two small communities, the CSE grocery is looking for a break-even level of sales, not a financial return to investors. The payoff is in the local access to healthy food.

Both communities were able to replace their access to fresh foods lost when their grocery stores had closed. But there are other quantifiable results from the CSEs. Eight jobs were created between the two towns as well as sales tax collected on nearly a half million dollars in retail sales. And, both communities remodeled historic buildings on their town squares. Many rural communities have crumbling 100+-year-old buildings that may become condemned properties or vacant lots in the future. However, they may lack funds to demolish derelict buildings on their own.

The initiatives discussed above were possible for approximately $100,000 investment in each of these two communities. In the world of community and economic development, that is considered a bargain plus this investment was by community members. It was not funded through government grants or even financed through commercial loans. What they did require was a significant level of community Social Capital and some technical assistance to channel and guide the effort.

Monitoring and Communicating Progress

Communications with investors and the public are important in building lasting support for the CSE. Key to its survival is continued patronage by residents confident that it will perform at a high level and will continue operating. All too often, initial enthusiasm for a novel idea diminishes over time and as other interesting projects surface. Maintaining continued support is necessary if the CSE is to prosper and grow.

Measuring and documenting progress vary with the type of activities being performed. Perhaps most common for a business venture such as a grocery store is whether it remains financially sustainable and meets sales, revenue, or profit targets. A challenge for the types of CSEs being discussed is that they also have a social purpose. Measuring the value of this contribution to the community and the local economy is difficult as noted by Hsia (Chapter 8). Nevertheless, the value must somehow be included in local decision-making calculations.

Both Winchester and Mt. Pulaski communicate with residents through monthly board meetings with the general manager and semi-annual meetings open to all members of the CSE. In cooperatives, this communication plan is almost always included in the bylaws, but in other legal forms of CSEs (LLC, nonprofits, etc.), it can be a useful addition to their management structures.

Another possibility is an "open books" policy in which the financials of the business are public knowledge. This reduces the privacy of the CSE and can be a business liability if things financially take a turn for the worst, and shoppers assume that it will close. On the other hand, having that knowledge in the hands of more people means greater insights into potential problems. One of the stores mentioned above had a very good first six months, followed by a large loss in profits over the next two months. Once the issue was recognized, the board of directors sought expert help, reviewed the operations, and made changes to put things back on track. In a sole proprietor/entrepreneurship situation, an owner may not be able to right the ship alone and does not want to include the community in the business decisions. This is one reason why cooperatives have a better three-year average success rate than entrepreneurs.

> Cooperative businesses have lower failure rates than traditional Corporations/small businesses: after the first year (10% failure versus 60–80%) and after 5 years in business (90% still operating versus 3–5% of traditional businesses).
>
> *(World Council of Credit Unions study in Williams 2007)*

Looking to the Future

Demographic trends in the next decade or longer plus changes in technology favoring the information economy and businesses more often located in large centers will likely challenge small rural communities to find ways to maintain access to local services needed to keep them viable for current and future populations (Henrikson, Muro, & Galston, 2018). Aging store owners will retire, often without someone willing to invest sufficient funds to operate the business. While some products will be available from internet businesses, loss of a local store can remove a place where residents regularly interact and build a sense of community. Many discussions in this book focused on rural areas, but a similar situation can occur in urban neighborhoods facing population and business declines.

These situations mean that community leaders and policymakers must find and adopt alternative strategies to make their communities continue and prosper. Conditions will be made even more difficult because of the COVID-19 economic downturn. While overall economic conditions will ultimately return to a new normal status, many small businesses that closed during the downturn will not return in the same way, if at all, without new financing approaches.

Discussions in this book illustrate several important factors. First, an effort is needed to cause residents to buy local and consider local businesses as worthwhile places to invest. This approach may take changes in regulations and local policies that foster and encourage these strategies. The aging Baby Boom population may be financially positioned to invest in these businesses under the right conditions and with local encouragement.

Second, CSEs are more of a method or approach to local financing than a specific development tool. The financing strategy can be implemented in many ways to meet local issues as is shown in the previous chapters. Whether the local group succeeds depends largely on the local situation and how the project was implemented. This means that residents must be well-informed and committed to using this method of financing.

Third, the benefits from using a CSE extend well beyond retaining access to a specific service or line of products. Even more important now and in the future as internet purchasing expands is the impact on the community capitals. Enhancing the ability of residents to interact, volunteer time, and participate in community efforts will remain a strong component of successful community development efforts. CSEs played a strong supportive role for local development in the past and will continue providing new opportunities for these interactions.

For sure, CSEs and other community-based enterprises are not the only approaches to consider in pursuing local development objectives. However, this financing approach can work in many settings and environments. The economic recovery will pose challenges for many areas that will require different financing approaches. The discussions in this book demonstrate that a community-based financing approach can continue as an effective alternative to more traditional strategies.

Note

1 These stores typically sell a broad variety of general merchandise but usually do not stock healthy fresh items such as meat and produce as would be the case in a full-service grocery store.

References

Henrikson, C., Muro, M., & Galston, W. (2018). Countering the geography of discontent: New Strategies for left behind places. Available at: https://www.brookings.edu/research/countering-the-geography-of-discontent-strategies-for-left-behind-places/

Walzer, N. (2019). *Guidebook and Resources for Starting Community Supported Enterprises.* East Lansing, MI: North Central Regional Center for Rural Development. Available at: https://www.cgs.niu.edu/Reports/cse-guidebook-final-2-8-19.pdf

Walzer, N. & Sandoval, J. (2016). *Emergence and Growth of Community Supported Enterprises.* East Lansing, MI: North Central Regional Center for Rural Development. Available at: https://www.cgs.niu.edu/Reports/Emergence-and-Growth-of-Community-Supported-Enterprises.pdf

INDEX

Note: **Bold** page numbers refer to tables; *italic* page numbers refer to figures and page numbers followed by "n" denote endnotes.

For Product Safety Concerns and Information please contact our EU
representative GPSR@taylorandfrancis.com
Taylor & Francis Verlag GmbH, Kaufingerstraße 24, 80331 München, Germany

www.ingramcontent.com/pod-product-compliance
Ingram Content Group UK Ltd.
Pitfield, Milton Keynes, MK11 3LW, UK
UKHW020009200926
475702UK00015B/2565
9780367485450